RODGERS & HART

BEWITCHED, BOTHERED, AND BEDEVILED

AN ANECDOTAL ACCOUNT

BY SAMUEL MARX
AND JAN CLAYTON

RODGERS & HART

BEWITCHED, BOTHERED, AND BEDEVILED

G. P. PUTNAM'S SONS
NEW YORK

SBN: 399-11786-5

Library of Congress Cataloging in Publication Data

Marx, Samuel, 1902–
    Rodgers and Hart: bewitched, bothered, and bedeviled!

    1. Rodgers, Richard, 1902–   2. Hart, Lorenz Milton,
1895–1943.   1.   Clayton, Jan, 1917, joint author.
II. Title.
ML410.R6315M4   782.8'1'0922[B]   76-12494

Acknowledgment and thanks are made by Samuel Marx, Jan Clayton, and G. P. Putnam's Sons
for permission to publish the following lyrics:

"Prayer"
Words by Lorenz Hart; music by Richard Rodgers Copyright © 1933, renewed 1960 by Metro-
Goldwyn-Mayer, Inc. Rights throughout the world controlled by Robbins Music Corporation.
Used by permission.

"The Pelican"
Copyright © 1919, 1922 by Edward B. Marks Music Corporation, Copyright Renewed 1947,
1950. Used by permission.

"The Lady Is a Tramp"
Copyright © 1937 by Chappell & Co., Inc. Copyright Renewed ALL RIGHTS RESERVED. International Copyright Secured. Used by permission of Chappell & Co., Inc.

"Bewitched"
Copyright © 1941 by Chappell & Co., Inc. Copyright Renewed ALL RIGHTS RESERVED. International Copyright Secured. Used by permission of Chappell & Co., Inc.

"Life with Father"
Copyright © 1967 (unpub.) by Chappell & Co., Inc. ALL RIGHTS RESERVED. International
Copyright Secured. Used by permission of Chappell & Co., Inc.

PRINTED IN THE UNITED STATES OF AMERICA

To my grandchildren
Peter and Francesca
Whose joy in Rodgers and Hart lies ahead
SAMUEL MARX

and that darling little lady who
loathes being called Vera Willie, but loves
being called my mother
JAN CLAYTON

Contents

Foreword

IT HAS been said—Richard Rodgers acted like a stockbroker who happened to be a composer and Lorenz Hart acted like a poet who happened to be a lyricist.

It has also been said—two heads are better than one.

Rodgers and Hart were perfectly matched collaborators.

So this book is a collaboration about a collaboration. Everything in it has gone in one head and in the other. We brought to the writing an intimate knowledge of both men, gleaned from personal association and sharpened by a year of research and exploration into aspects of their lives that others knew better than we. It is explicit, revelatory at times, and contradictory to what some believe. We stand by our beliefs.

It is anecdotal—we intended it to be. It is tragicomic—we had not expected that.

Rodgers is an exceptional man; he would have written beautiful music in any century; he is the indomitable man, he is a man for all reasons. His life makes up half of this

9

book, and he has given us halfhearted approval. Hart, too, is a most extraordinary subject. It is our conclusion that his life would have been happier and less guilt-ridden if he were alive today. We have attempted to show why.

Collaboration is no easy thing. The path is strewn with difficulties that range from arguments to battles. Then one forgets the aphorisms about dual-headed superiority or that animals achieve better balance by standing on four legs. No, that doesn't necessarily go for humans. Few collaborators consistently see eye to eye. Astigmatism is the occupational disease of collaborations.

But Rodgers and Hart survived twenty-four years, and together they wrote 496 songs. It may be symbolic that their first was "Any Old Place with You" and their last was "To Keep My Love Alive."

They created twenty-nine theatrical productions (one was unproduced), eight movies, a smatter of ballet, tone poems, nightclub ventures, and occasional stabs into a realm that show biz cloaks under an all-encompassing label of Special Material.

They met everyone worth meeting in the years between 1919 and 1943, in and around the theaters of New York and London and the studios of Hollywood: the great and not-so-great, the famous and not-so-famous, the brainy and beautiful, the rich and the poor. They heard all the jokes and contributed their own, for Larry liked to play them, even the impractical kind. Their days were a medley of fun and frolic, congenial words, and lilting melodies. This is our record of those times.

Until the music stopped, they blazed a trail of novelty and sophistication through the history of musical comedy. Words and Music by Rodgers and Hart—It had its own rhythms; it breathed of an intimate relationship, a professional love affair that would last their lifetimes. However,

10

it isn't true that harmony begets harmony and those that have music wherever they go must be harmonious.

The remarkable thing is not that they finally broke away from each other; the remarkable thing is that they ever stayed together at all.

—Samuel Marx and Jan Clayton

1

Not Swell but Witty

IN THE FIRST year of the twentieth century, Lorenz Milton Hart was five years old. Wound up like a fine-fashioned watchspring, he was alert, agile, and precocious. He also possessed something else—a fascination with language. His father, Max, made the happy discovery that the boy had a gift for rhyming, that he was already composing light verse. Thereupon the old man began to pull him out of bed late at night to recite to the guests who crowded their home at 59 West 119th Street, Manhattan.

As a result, Lorenz (who became Lori and then Larry to everyone but his mother) was asked to innumerable weddings, anniversaries, bar mitzvahs, and similar joyous occasions. He delivered his poems with boyish charm, was hailed as a prodigy, and became a child celebrity. He enjoyed his fame and the admiration that went with it, which later prompted his friend Henry Myers to observe, "He'd rather be an unsuccessful actor than a successful lyricist."

Father Max was pleased by the boy's acclaim and shared

13

the bows. He was coarse, bald, and fat and spoke with a heavy German accent. Mother Frieda had an accent, too, but hers was delicate and refined.

They lived in a three-story brownstone house in Harlem near Morningside Heights. It was bigger than they needed, but Max wanted everything around him to have *size*. Size was an obsession with him; he wanted to do everything in a big way although he and Frieda were barely over five feet tall.

O.M., as Larry called his old man, had an unfathomable personality. He screamed and yelled uncontrollably, not only when he was angry but also when he was happy. His coarseness was no secret to the neighbors; for example, he often found it more convenient to urinate out the window of the dining room than walk down the hall to the bathroom.

He was a compulsive rainbow chaser, in so many businesses simultaneously that nobody could truly fix his basic means of livelihood. Everyone who knew Max regarded him as a good provider, as well as a scoundrel and possibly even a crook.

He spent money with happy abandon. Often, when being expansive about his holdings to his guests, Frieda was out on one of her periodic visits to a Lenox Avenue hockshop, pawning her jewelry.

O.M. was an unregenerate gambler. He was a bookmaker who enjoyed playing the races, and he nearly wiped himself out on occasion.

He sold insurance and real estate; he also loitered in the wings of show business. Always the promoter, he partnered for a time with William Hammerstein, who owned an interest in a theater and had a son Larry's age named Oscar, II, grandson and namesake of a famous impresario. O.M. didn't linger long around William Hammerstein; he preferred his partnership (also temporary) with Polly Adler, New York's best-known madam.

The roly-poly figure of Max Hart was a familiar one to the middle-class Jewish families who lived, as he did, near Lenox Avenue, a wide, impressive thoroughfare. On a map of Manhattan it is seen as an extension of downtown's Sixth Avenue, which runs uptown until it hits Central Park. The Hart neighborhood, above the park, was fashionable; its private houses and six-story apartment buildings were mostly occupied by the older generation from Mittel-europa with American-born children. Max was popular with all ages.

O.M. wanted political muscle to help his multifarious activities. His popularity made him welcome at Tammany Hall, the Democratic Party's celebrated stronghold. It had just emerged from behind the cloud that enveloped it during the dark days of the Boss Tweed gang.

O.M. helped Tammany put over Richard Van Wyck as mayor and, in an intense display of fealty to the party, named his second-born son Theodore in honor of President Roosevelt, then in office, and gave the boy Van Wyck as a middle name. Somewhat typical of New York's prevailing mode of government, Van Wyck's administration disgraced itself almost immediately. This upset O.M., who felt it reflected on his own reputation. He retreated from politics quickly. Larry's younger brother was called Teddy, like the illustrious Roosevelt, but there were no further allusions to the elegant but tarnished Van Wyck.

Without question Larry was always the family pet. The Old Man's pride and indulgence in him were such that he was known to hand Larry a hundred-dollar bill in his very early "growing-up days," with just one admonition: "Have fun, kid!"

Max Hart loved to entertain. He and Frieda gave nonstop parties aided by a full complement of servants; O.M. be-

15

lieved it was important to have a butler and footman in residence.

Their parties often continued long after Larry and Teddy were upstairs asleep. Even after the servants had gone to bed, the Harts and guests would be spouting poetry, talking theater, philosophizing until morning. They would come in and out of the house, go to the kitchen, help themselves to food and drink, and leave as they pleased.

Among the drop-ins proudly welcomed by O.M. was the renowned stage beauty Lillian Russell. Neighbors peeked through windows to see this regal ample-breasted creature, beautifully attired, escorted by her husband, Alexander Moore, a millionaire newspaper publisher and onetime ambassador to Spain. Moore's large railroad holdings were sufficient to intrigue the social-climbing Max. But O.M. had a short-lived association with him, too, for Miss Russell found his manners less than amusing. Max proclaimed love for the arts, but his crudeness alienated the artists.

Frieda, in her gentle way, guided Larry toward the best in literature. O.M. approved, but had no time to assist in his son's education. Frieda taught him German; his childhood fascination with languages developed into an aptitude. In a few years his knowledge of the great poets surpassed that of older companions.

He would tote an armful of books into Central Park and devour Heinrich Heine in the original German, drawn to the poet over others because his father called him Uncle Heinrich. O.M. bragged that Heine was the original family name, but he couldn't prove the relationship. Later Larry claimed it too, but jocularly.

He was influenced by Heine's works; the poet has been described as "A wit with powers of the highest order . . . who struck a new lyric note with concrete expression to the

16

spiritual forces of heart and soul . . . his lyric method, his cynicism, introduced new and invigorating elements into poetry." Lovers of Larry Hart lyrics might easily see the resemblance.

The warmth of the Harts' open-house policy was irresistible to the young intellectuals in the neighborhood. Larry always attracted people, and when he was in his early teens, he and his friends often congregated around the large breakfast table in the basement on 119th Street. Loud, exuberant, and hungry, they exchanged their ideas, hopes, and theories, expanding their minds, while incidentally doing the same for their stomachs.

Frieda's cooking had not always qualified as the attraction. When Max first came wooing, Frieda was aware that he loved good food and that she couldn't cook. But her married sister was a queen in the kitchen, so for all of their dinner-at-home courting the sister prepared everything in her own kitchen and sneaked it onto their table. Max would put it away with fullest praise, at which the modest maiden Frieda demurely blushed her thanks.

When they married (more quickly than Frieda expected), she was hard pressed to achieve a crash course in cooking before the wedding. After they married, Max is said to have commented many times on the slump in the quality of her cooking, but attributed it loudly, to all within earshot, to the fact that he kept her so happily occupied elsewhere. Then her blushing embarrassment was real.

By the time Larry and his friends reached puberty the oldest form of education—"talking it over"—had taken place. Sex, its wonders and mystique, occupied center stage in the conversations. There were no girls in the group; it was all-male rhetoric and uncertain argument, heated and overheated. Sometimes, when their voices were raised in the

17

night, O.M. would rush downstairs, clad in an old-fashioned nightgown that emphasized his immense belly, screaming obscenities.

"How in Christ's name can anyone sleep with the noise you're making? Haven't you any goddamn homes of your own?"

The boys would have the presence of mind to invite him to join in their discussions. Instantly O.M. would become sociable, pour himself a glass of beer and say, "Gentlemen, I ask all of you to drink a toast to Larry's mother." The toast would be solemnly drunk; then O.M. would seat himself and preside. On the subject of show business, he told them that Larry knew all there was to know about the theater and was destined to be a great actor.

Sig Herzig, another of Larry's friends who would later gravitate toward playwriting, recalls a time Max caught them in an argument about sex. O.M. could be a smooth plagiarist, especially if his audience was unlikely to recognize a source, so he sagely summed up his view of sex with the borrowed observation "Do anything you like as long as you don't frighten the horses!" The boys were impressed, sensing interesting qualities about Larry's O.M. that they couldn't exactly define.

Morrie Ryskind said, "If Larry had written dirty lyrics, his old man would have sold them."

Larry was as amused as any by his father's ways but tried to keep his mother from hearing the obscenities that accompanied O.M.'s bursts of temper. She was the most important element in his life, concerned, consoling, and positive he would succeed in whatever he aimed to do. She kept him going; she was his anchor and his grip on life.

He needed her support because it was soon apparent he was going to be as short as O.M. He towered under the other boys, and it bothered him terribly.

18

A few years later Howard Dietz wrote this playful jingle which he called "A Tender Tribute":

> Larry Hart, the troubadour,
>   Seems to stand just four feet four—
> But measured by the human trait
>   Rises like the Empire State.

Larry had another cross to bear: his appearance. His head was of normal size, and some people admired his high brow, emblematic of intellect, and saw beauty in his dark eyes and power in their earnestness. But his body would never grow to normal height, and it made him seem grotesque.

He masked his feelings with wild displays of gaiety and in defense affectionately twitted those he liked with colorful descriptions. One of these was Sig Herzig, whose tendency to make the ashes from a single cigarette cover his pants, shirt, and jacket earned him Larry's sobriquet of the "tweed ashtray."

Brother Teddy was just as short as but more acceptably formed than Larry. Teddy didn't mix with Larry's friends; the three-year difference in their ages was a chasm that made him persona non grata in those basement bull sessions.

The younger Hart had a passionate disinterest in the advantages of higher education. Larry was concerned, and so was Frieda, but not Max. He said that any son of his could cope with the world by using the brains his father had endowed him with.

Teddy remained an easygoing, unobtrusive, and uneducated boy, leagues apart, intellectually, from Larry. It was unlucky for Teddy that Larry's intellect impressed the other kids, and because of that, Teddy suffered by comparison. But his greatest defender was always brother Larry.

19

Life in the Hart household tended to give an impression it was divided into two camps: Larry and his mother in one, Teddy and O.M. in the other.

Henry Myers noted, "This schism, if it really was one, seemed to be on the basis of vulgarity, a tendency to shrink from it or like it. Larry and Frieda were the more sensitive, more consciously in alliance."

O.M. never outgrew his tendencies to favor larcenous dealings. Arthur Schwartz, starting to practice law while trying to write songs on the side, remembers Larry offering to get him Max as his first client.

"Then," said Schwartz, "I found that his father had a new lawyer every month because he had a new business every month and the last lawyer wouldn't do the new job because he had learned Max was a crook. . . .

"At this point he was in the shipping business. I went up to Mystic, Connecticut, where there were a lot of ship-yards, to investigate something for him and, if necessary, sign some papers for him. I don't remember what it was he wanted me to sign, but had I done so it would have landed me in jail.

"I never got paid for my work. I probably did five hundred dollars' worth of business, and come to think of it, I never got a penny."

Meetings of the young literati were suspended when school closed for the summer. The boys needed vacations from the city, and their parents needed vactions from them. The neighborhood offspring dispersed to summer camps, selected in accord with special desires.

Larry's preference was a place where he could indulge his love of reading, writing, and acting. He attended Camp Paradox in New York's Adirondack Mountains. Counselor Mel Shauer was put in charge of Larry when he first appeared at the pier of the Hudson River night boat that was the beginning of their journey.

"I was told by the owner of the camp to look out for him," said Shauer. "And I found him to be the most polite kid I ever knew. We shared a stateroom on the steamer that took us up the Hudson. He declined the lower berth that I offered him, saying he knew I would sleep better in the lower. Then he proceeded to keep me awake all night, quoting Shakespeare."

It was compulsory for the boys to bring regulation attire. Outwardly, Larry's trunk looked like the others, but it was heavier and could hardly be lifted. Curiosity about it was keen. Finally, it was discovered that he had brought only books, the very thing most campers wanted to avoid.

He had none of the clothing stipulated that he must bring, but with total aplomb he asked one boy, "Can I use your shirt?" and told another, "I'll want a pair of your pants, and I'll need a pair of socks, too!" He wore a borrowed camp uniform all summer. It gave him a ragamuffin appearance that didn't bother him in the least.

The campers dubbed him "Shakespeare Hart," and the faculty placed him in charge of Sunday night entertainments. He loved this; it was his first brush with show business and also gave him an excuse to avoid the hikes, boating, and swimming events that held no attraction for him. The zeal he displayed for his camp shows earned him awesome attention; no talent among other campers remained hidden from him. His energy amazed everyone.

After five summers, Larry switched from Paradox to Brant Lake Camp; its owner had show business affiliations. Lyric writing had become the most natural thing in the world for him; he was constantly doodling with words that went well together and longed for music.

21

Arthur Schwartz was a junior counselor at Brant Lake; his talent for composing was emerging. He and Larry wrote a camp song that was a smash with the boys.

> I love to lie awake in bed,
>> Right after taps I pull the flaps above my head.
> I let the stars shine on my pillow,
>> Oh, what a light the moonbeams shed.
> I feel so happy I could cry
>> And tears are born within the corner of my eye.
>> To be home with ma was never like this,
>> I could live forever like this.
> I love to lie awake at night
>> And go to sleep with a smile.

Years later Howard Dietz was to write a new lyric to the melody and turn it into an international hit. He called it "I Guess I'll Have to Change My Plans"; it also became known as "The Blue Pyjama Song" and was sung on Broadway in *The Band Wagon*.

Just as soon as he was eligible, Larry joined an extension class in dramatic technique at Columbia College. The course was conducted by Hatcher Hughes, whose *Hell-Bent fer Heaven* created a Broadway sensation and won the Pulitzer Prize. Larry wasn't terribly impressed with the class. Dramatic technique was held to be a collection of formulas, patterns, and tricks. They were labeled "suspense," "comedy relief," and "conflict." "The well-made play" was a much-used phrase and a mystical goal. It was an affront to his instinctive feeling that play construction shouldn't always go by rules.

Nor did he share Professor Hughes' belief that Ibsen, rather than Shakespeare, was the ideal. However, playwriting wasn't his real target. Putting words to music was his driving demon. Meanwhile, Columbia offered opportunities to let one's creative impulses flow, and Larry wrote some sketches and acted in them for the 1915 Varsity Show, *On Your Way.*

Oscar Hammerstein II was playing a leading role, and he recalled: "Larry was skipping and bouncing around the stage like an electrified gnome. I think of him always, then, as skipping and dancing. I never saw him walk slowly. I never saw his face in repose. I never heard him chuckle quietly. He laughed loudly and easily at other people's jokes and at his own, too. His large eyes danced and his head would wag. He was alert and dynamic and fun to be with."*

Another Columbia student, Mortimer Rodgers, took his thirteen-year-old brother, Dick, to see that annual student caper. Larry was having a marvelous time onstage, and the audience loved him. The little balding fellow had stubby legs, a noble brow, and almost too-black eyes, but these were hidden because, as "America's Sweetheart," Mary Pickford, he cavorted in a skirt, long blond wig and heavy eye makeup.

After the show, Mortie Rodgers took Dick backstage, and they met some members of the cast; but Larry Hart was not one of them.

*From the foreword, *Rodgers and Hart Song Book.*

2

A Sail Without a Ship

DICK WAS born in the summer of 1902, when Larry was seven years old. His father was a highly respected doctor, William Abraham Rodgers; his mother was Mamie, née Levy. Their antecedents were Russian; Dick had some of the stolid, withdrawn character of the Slav.

Although they lived at 3 West 120th Street, only a block from the Harts, the families didn't know each other. This was not uncommon or unusual. New Yorkers allow years to pass without ever saying "Good morning" to next-door neighbors.

The climate of the Rodgers household was more serious and restrained, its atmosphere utterly different from that of the happy-go-lucky home of the Harts.

Dick's parents owned a Steinway grand, and he was still too small to climb on its stool unassisted when he first discovered how much he loved music. He had absolute pitch, his ear so perfectly attuned that he could capture any melody that he heard. The ability to "play by ear" is a gift of infinite value, but it depends on how the beneficiary makes use of it. In most cases, he takes the lazy way and bypasses the task of learning how to read notes or suffering through lessons in harmony and fingering.

Dick followed that route into his teens. He loved to play loudly, often to the point of being thunderous, and he could stretch the fingers on each hand across ten notes. By the time he was thirteen his mastery of the piano was impressive, far beyond his grasp of technique.

"After all," he said,* "my mother was a first-rate pianist, the best sight reader I ever knew. In the area of imitation I was imitating my mother before I was three years old. I would be lifted on a stool and reproduce what she had played a few minutes before. . . .

"In fact, one of my early basic problems was that my ear was too good. Anything I could hear I could play—almost. I took my first lessons from my Aunt Tillie—there is always an Aunt Tillie around a musical family, isn't there?—but I didn't really learn from what she taught me. I just recorded what she said in my mind and got by. With a little bluff and charm I could play the pieces she taught, so what was the point of learning to read music, which I found very dull?"

Recalling more of those early days, he said, "I had nothing but encouragement from my family. When Mother and Dad went to the theater, they brought the scores home and we absorbed them. As a child I knew *The Merry Widow* better than I do now. The first musical I ever saw was *The Pied Piper of Hamelin*, which I didn't really like very much. I don't remember why.

"Soon after that I saw Victor Herbert's *Little Nemo*, which was impressive to me, but when I saw Jerome Kern's

*In a radio interview.

26

Love o' Mike, I just sat there saying, 'I have to write like this!'

"It was important for me to be *in* the theater, not just be a songwriter."

He began to extemporize whenever he sat at the piano. "Extemporizing is really a form of composing, and I was doing it before I was in my teens."

When Dick was thirteen, the family moved to another part of the upper West Side of the city. They settled on Eighty-sixth Street, center of the area that mainly comprised wealthy Jewish families living in twelve-story apartment houses. West End Avenue and Riverside Drive, parallel to each other, were posh, desirable, and residential. Nearby Broadway was the shopping district, lined with small merchants and tradespeople; its delicatessen-restaurants were the Sunday night gathering places with droll names like Dew Drop or Tip Toe Inn. The neighborhood had movie theaters galore, on Broadway, rendezvous points for the younger set; after school their high brick walls supplied perfect backgrounds for the kids to bounce balls against or play games in front of, away from apartment house entrances.

Dick Rodgers never participated in these pastimes; he was home with his beloved piano.

Dick, at fourteen, went off to summer camp. Camp Wigwam, situated on a patch of land that remained quiescent in the winter, came to life on the Fourth of July. It fronted on Bear Lake, near Harrison, Maine. It was similar to the camps that Larry attended.

Like Larry, Dick spent minimal time at athletics; he knew where he wanted to be and where he was going. He never let himself stray from his target; he spent his days inside the lodge, playing the piano. It was almost impossible to drag him away from the keyboard; this explains why he is rarely found in official photographs of the assemblage.

Dick and Samuel Marx met at Wigwam. One day they escaped an afternoon's activity in one of the camp's Indian canoes. "We drifted onto a bed of lily pads," remembers Marx. The lake was a mirror that day; it cracked only when a small turtle poked its little head up and spread ripples away in wide circles.

The fragrance of the lilies was sweet and heady; to fight off a desire to sleep we fell into contemplation of our future. We knew each other's ambitions.

"If you're going to be a writer," he said, "you should read Dickens and Shakespeare instead of that Rover Boys trash."

"I *like* the Rover Boys," I said. "Who wants to write like Dickens or Shakespeare? Are you going to write like Bach or Beethoven?"

"I'll settle for Jerome Kern," he said—and meant it.

Bugles sounded from the camp, reminding us it was time for the afternoon swim. As we dipped our paddles into the water again, he said, "Another thing—if you're going to be a writer, you ought to stop biting your nails. You'll need your fingers, you know."

I grinned back at him. The only camper who bit his nails worse than I did was Dick Rodgers.

In his second year at Wigwam one of Dick's contributions was a song dedicated to a boy unfortunately saddled with the name of Ovid:

O is for Ovid, who svam to the raft.
V is for Vy did he svim to the raft?
I is for I saw him svim to the raft.
D is for Did you see him svim to the raft?

28

During his third year Dick worked as a counselor. He waited on tables and played piano accompaniment to the Sunday night entertainments. He wrote some words and music considered good enough to be in the camp's repertoire, sung with such inevitables as "She'll Be Comin' Round the Mountain" and "I've Been Workin' on the Railroad."

His songs were more noted for their sentimentality than originality. The following is one of his typical lyrics:

> Wigwam, your braves will love you
>> While the moon shines o'er Bear Lake.
> We'll keep your campfires burning
>> For each fleeting mem'ry's sake.
> Future years will bring us
> Happy days in glad review.
> Each passing year makes you more dear;
> O, Wigwam, we're true to you.

Abraham "Mandy" Mandelstam, one of the camp's owners, was a music buff, a foppish, effeminate little man who swooned over celebrities and maintained a bungalow at the campsite for those who accepted his invitations to visit him. He knew and frequently entertained important authors, athletes, and theatrical personalities. One of his guests was Leopold Godowsky, a concert pianist who listened to Dick play his tunes but was not impressed.*

In New York in winter, Dick spent his Saturdays at matinees. Times Square was a short subway ride away from his home; its theaters glittered with grandiose Ziegfeld revues,

---

*Mandy's pride in Dick grew noticeably *after* he became a success, and for that belated recognition the composer never took pleasure in a "glad review" of his days at Wigwam.

Dillingham's lavish musical comedies, and the Shuberts' ornate operettas, usually based haphazardly on the lives of celebrated composers. But it was the intimate show that attracted Dick's interest, one with a plot that omitted the usual chorus line. That seemed to him to be a great innovation, a forward step in play construction, as indeed it was.

The most popular of these were by Guy Bolton, P. G. Wodehouse, and Jerome Kern at the 250-seat Princess Theater. The little playhouse presented musical comedy repertoire; a new show opened as soon as the old one closed. Dick was fifteen when he saw *Oh, Boy!*; the score was one of Kern's best.

Although handicapped by his limited ability to read notes, Dick devised a musical shorthand which enabled him to jot onto the margin of his program the songs that were sung and the tunes the orchestra played. He used the alphabet and added a dot or two to indicate tempo. With this method he copied them all down, then went home and played the music from overture to final chorus on the piano, simply reading off the scratches he had scribbled that afternoon.

Marx was with him on many occasions. Years later he said, "I never knew anyone else able to do that. I am still amazed by it."

3

Any Old Place Without You

ALTHOUGH PAST his twentieth birthday, Larry continued spending summers at the camp as a counselor in charge of weekend entertainment. He wrote jingles for the boys to sing, and they marveled how easily he turned out rhymes.

When they returned to the city, the word spread and songwriters talked about him in Tin Pan Alley, where the professionals hung out. Geographically, that colorfully named locality was simply a street of mind, nonexistent on the maps but descriptive of any block in New York that housed two or more music publishers.

One of the sharpest professionals on that mythical street was Billy Rose, a superhustler among hustlers, credited with having created numerous hits, sharing honors with others as author and composer of words and music, some of which he had actually written. He was dynamic, grasping, and self-important. Unlike Larry, who flinched at any mention of his height, Rose wasn't the least bit inhibited by his.

Just as short as Larry, Rose entered his life at this time, a little Napoleon of Tin Pan Alley.

He went to see Larry at camp, staying at one of the nearby resort hotels. An immaculate dresser, he never took off his collar and tie and maintained an indoor look even outdoors. Larry's fellow campers, greatly impressed, labeled Rose "snappy," the accolade of sophistication. Rose had more than a social visit in mind.

Arthur Schwartz, who now lives in London, recalls Rose and Larry together:

"They would take a rowboat and some sandwiches and go out on the lake. I never heard any of the lyrics they wrote; they were kept secret because Larry, who hadn't made it yet, was not getting credit. But at the end of every day—I saw this—Billy gave Larry a hundred-dollar bill. I don't know which songs they wrote. It was the era of 'That Old Gang of Mine,' 'Barney Google,' songs like that—the period of 'Me and My Shadow.' I saw Billy and Larry together; I saw the hundred-dollar bills."

Alice Weaver, a delectable little specialty dancer, sang a song attributed to Billy Rose in the act she performed at the Healy Hotel, Boston. It was a time of many inane ditties like "Barney Google," and she remembers hearing that hers contained lyrical contributions by Larry Hart, although he received no credit for it. Most likely, he contributed the rhyming effect to Rose's conception. Called "If You Will Be My Lolly, I Will Be Your Pop," it gave no hint of Larry's erudition. It was corn without spice, barely a speck in a spectrum of musical foolishness, and as a song it lived an insignificant life and, except for Miss Weaver, died unsung.

If you will be my lolly, I will be your pop
And we'll stick around together all the time.

32

If you will be my lemon, I will be your drop,
   I'm daffy, I'm daffy, come on and feed me taffy.
If you will be my chocolate, I will be your cream,
   If you will be my jelly, I will be your bean.
You make me feel so Wrigley every time I chew your
   gum.
   If you will be my lolly, I will be your pop
   And we'll stick around together all the time.

In recalling the song, Miss Weaver said the most notable moment that comes to her mind in connection with it was when she sang it for the inmates of a Massachusetts prison: "There were a number of retarded men, segregated in one section of the audience, and when I sang, 'I'm daffy, I'm daffy,' they shouted back at me with great good humor, 'So are we!' "

Larry turned twenty-three less than a month after the United States entered the war against Kaiser Wilhelm of Germany in April, 1917.

He was a pacifist. Walking past a recruiting booth, he was asked by an army sergeant to enlist. There were height limitations in the military, of course, and Larry said he was tempted to take up the sergeant "just for the fun of it." Friends who were with him dissuaded him. He then told the sergeant that he would wait to be drafted, but they were certain that, had he been called up he would have refused to serve and taken the consequences.

Later he *was* rejected by his draft board because of his height. Although he was adamantly antiwar, this was an additional humiliation.

An extremely embarrassing occurrence added to his complex about his height. As customary in wartime, every theatrical performance began with "The Star-Spangled Ban-

33

ner." At one of these, an usher tapped Larry on the shoulder and ordered him to stand up, which, of course, he was doing.

He quit Columbia's class of '18, looking for a partner to write music for his words, feeling there was no way college would help him attain his goal as a lyricist. But he couldn't find a composer in tune with him, and on the day he would have graduated, he was still a stalled lyricist.

Gustave Amberg imported operettas from Europe to the Irving Place Theater. He needed a song translated and gave Larry a chance at it, having heard of his rhyming abilities and his fluent knowledge of German.

It was sung during a beach scene, with the chorus girls poking fun at the fat comic:

> Meyer, your tights are tight,
>   As tight as tights can be,
>   As tight as tights can be.
>   They don't fit properly.
> Meyer, those tights were never
>   Fashioned for the sea;
> If you should try
> To wink an eye
>   You'll lose your dignity.

Listeners laughed appreciatively, and it launched Larry into the work he loved. From Amberg's shows he moved uptown to Broadway, doing lyrics to Jacques Offenbach's *La Belle Hélène* and translating successful foreign operettas like *The Lady in Ermine* for Lee and J. J. Shubert, but his name never appeared in the programs. He was still engaged in a battle for recognition.

A Broadway *bon vivant*, Barney Glazer, who could do excellent translations himself, took the easy way and paid Larry $200 to ghost-write Ferenc Molnar's *Liliom* into English for him. The play was a hit. Glazer took all the credit and the royalties, too.

Only a few privileged friends know *Liliom* was Larry's work, and they were sworn to secrecy. But he was deeply anguished. He believed the cards were stacked against him. His usual good humor vanished, and he gave way to self-pity.

"Bad luck sticks to me like a disease," he told Henry Myers. "They won't let a new man in. But I'll show the bastards I can write lyrics!"

Phillip Leavitt was another youth in Larry's circle of friends who was seeking a place in the theater. He fixed his sights on writing, acting, and directing; he liked them all.

The youngest student in Columbia's class of '17, he left college to go to war. When he returned, his business-minded father influenced him to go into a commercial enterprise that delivered a weekly paycheck—his own paint business—"which, incidentally, I loved," says Leavitt—and then into a Wall Street brokerage firm, "which made me a lot of money."*

Leavitt vividly recalls the beginnings of the team of Rodgers and Hart, to which he made the greatest contribution:

"It all started with a small group called the Akron Club, a bunch of gregarious kids who banded together in order to have enough members to add up to five for basketball in the winter, nine for baseball in the spring, and eleven for football in the fall. To us, uniforms were the big thing, and the

---

*Now retired, living with his talented wife, Kim, in Scottsdale, Arizona, Leavitt is a very creditable painter, his landscapes sought by collectors.

more colorful they were, the better we played our games. They were the riding silks of our pride.

"We couldn't buy uniforms on the token allowance given us by our folks, so we covered their cost by throwing a dance or a raffle. In order to sell more tickets, we were resourceful enough to specify that a portion of the net profits would go to charity. Our raffles were never much of a success; it's pretty hard to trap grown-ups to take a chance on a baseball or a watch for a prize. It's even more difficult to entice them to a dance.

"Then some genius member suggested we put on a show. The Akron Club was perhaps more responsible than anyone else for the rash of amateur shows that spread like the measles in those days.

"We used everyone and everything that could be of assistance. Any gifted acquaintance or relative was in them. Girlfriends who could sing or dance were drafted; blackout sketches from Broadway revues and vaudeville were switched around or just pirated. For the music, there were topical songs or parodies. But our show had a chance to go a little original because one of the Akron members had a kid brother who could compose music. The member was Mortie Rodgers; his brother was Dick. That's how lightning struck. Richard Rodgers, composer, was born right then and there.

"His music had a lilt. The real difficulty was to find someone who could match words to it. A few club members took a crack at that, even Dr. Bill Rodgers, his father. Mortie wrote at least one. Dick and Ralph Engelsman, who put together the book of our first show, *One Minute, Please,* did the others.

"A book," Leavitt went on, "was a stealable item. They all looked alike; they had been done before and would be done again and again and again. Lyrics were something else.

36

While the spirit of our volunteer lyricists was willing, the results didn't measure up to the quality of the music. The members realized that they had an unusual find in Dick, a composer, but in order to round out his original score, it was necessary to find a suitable lyricist."

A year later, when the next show, *Up Stage and Down*, was ready, no satisfactory lyric writer had yet appeared. Dick put words to all but three of his songs; Oscar Hammerstein II, already graduated from Columbia, pitched in on two of them, "Weaknesses" and "Can It," and a club-member lawyer, Benjamin Kaye, wrote a comedy exercise for girls, "Prisms, Plums and Prunes." The idea behind it was that the words made the girls pucker their lips, making their lips more luscious and kissable.

"Dick's father financed publication of the songs that Dick wrote lyrics for; they went on sale after the show in the lobby of the Waldorf-Astoria Hotel the night of March 8, 1919. They were Dick's first published songs," says Leavitt.

With the Akron Club planning to put on more shows, the need for a regular lyricist became acute. But where to find someone with that talent? It was Phil Leavitt who remembered a boy named Larry Hart he had met when they were both at Columbia. Relaxing at Larry's home, they played recordings of Kern and Wodehouse while Larry had quoted some lines of his own, written to German melodies. Leavitt was impressed by them, and it all came back to him, and he suggested the Akron Club should bring Larry Hart and Richard Rodgers together. Here is his account of Dick and Larry's first meeting:

"It was easy for me to arrange an appointment; it was for a Sunday afternoon in spring, 1919. Larry was waiting for us on the stoop of the Hart home, and he was already talking as Dick and I climbed the stairs.

37

"Larry was several years older than Dick but ages older in sophistication. He was dedicated to perfection of meter and rhymes and, like Dick, enamored of the songs of Wodehouse and Kern. His shrine was a phonograph that continuously spilled out the music of the Princess Theater shows. He listened to them for hours in rapt, critical silence. He felt sure that, in certain respects, he could do better than Wodehouse.

"He was working on a lyric he called 'Venus.' The first line went something like 'Venus, there's no difference between us!' He was a pixie! An extrovert! Always rubbing his hands together, pistonlike. When he spoke of lyrics, he could be very convincing. He was sure 'Venus' would be a hit song.

"He led us back to a library stuffed—no, overstuffed—with Victorian furniture. There was a piano, and it wasn't long before Dick was fingering out some tunes. It was all so simple. All that had to be done was sit, listen, and let nature take its course."

Dick recalls Larry being angry about songwriters who wrote down to the public. He felt that people were capable of understanding better things than the juxtaposition of words like "slush" and "mush."

He also recalls that, at that meeting, "I heard for the first time about interior rhymes, feminine rhymes, triple rhymes and false rhymes. I listened with astonishment as Larry launched into a diatribe against song writers who had small intellectual equipment and less courage, the boys who failed to take advantage of every opportunity to inch a little further into the hitherto-unexplored in lyric writing."*

*In his introduction to *The Rodgers and Hart Song Book*.

That was Larry's permanent credo. "Don't have a formula—and don't repeat it."

Later, too, Dick would sum up that first meeting this way: "I was enchanted by this little man and his ideas. Neither of us mentioned it but we evidently knew we would work together and I left Hart's house having acquired in one afternoon a career, a partner, a best friend, and a source of permanent irritation."[*]

Their target was Broadway, but their immediate sights were on the Akron Club, which, at least, offered a platform from which the tunes could be heard. They were set to write the score for the club's 1920 production, *You'd Be Surprised*, with a book to be written by Dr. Milton G. Bender.

"Doc" Bender was a strange individual, a dentist who immersed himself in all the waters that cascaded through show business. Larry agreed to let him work with him on some of the lyrics for that next show. That, according to many, was Larry's first mistake.

Bender was an uninhibited swinger of his day, salacious and gross, leading a life that held, somehow, tremendous appeal for Larry. It certainly didn't appeal to many others, and not one of Larry's regiment of friends and admirers was ever known to share Larry's delight in associating with him.

Quite the opposite. . . .

Some of the kinder epithets leveled at him by people who loved Larry were "pimp," "leech," and "procurer." Doc Bender's name has become linked with Hart but hardly in a complimentary way. Some strove to explain it, charitably, as "a love-hate relationship." Almost all of Larry's friends

[*]Writing in *Theatre Arts Monthly*.

considered Bender a sinister fellow who wielded horrendous and ultimately tragic influences on him.*

While Bender labored over a libretto, Dick and Larry searched for a chance to place songs in a Broadway production. But they had no close connections with the big entrepreneurs, no publisher contacts. Larry's anonymous endeavors placed him among the unknowns, and both of them belonged to a group that was an anathema on the Great White Way—they were "college kids." They were unable to get themselves heard.

Again, the break came through the efforts of Phillip Leavitt. He possessed what he termed "an oblique sort of acquaintanceship" with Lew Fields, a famous comedian turned producer. Leavitt was "going with" his daughter Dorothy, whose popularity was enhanced by her beauty and brains. She was already lined up to be one of the dancers in the chorus of *You'd Be Surprised*.

Lew Fields had been a stand-up comic in a language-mangling act with Joe Weber. Their fractured English-German dialect rocked vaudeville and burlesque houses across the country with wall-to-wall laughs.

"I am delightfulness to meet you," said Weber.

"Der disgust is all mine," replied Fields.

They became a legendary Mike and Myer to the world, and while they changed their act at times, it always concluded with emotional good-byes, Fields telling Weber, "I hope you always look back on me as the habbiest moment uff your life," to which Weber replied, "I also vish to express to you—charges collect—my uppermost appreciation of der dishonor you haf informed upon me."

Finally, what they had said in fun turned sour. Dissent

*Wanting to know more about this man, I asked Howard Dietz, "Is Bender still alive?" "Bender was never alive," snapped Dietz. —CLAYTON

40

drove them apart; they worked their last year without speaking to each other except in the characters they portrayed onstage. It was then that Fields, a cultured man, turned to the production of Broadway musical comedies. The next one he planned, *A Lonely Romeo*, was in rehearsal when Leavitt asked him to meet Dick and Larry.

Besides producing and directing, Fields was playing the title role, and these multiple activities, Leavitt says jocularly, "exhausted him so much he was too tired to say 'No' when I suggested he listen to the hottest pair of songwriters since Gilbert and Sullivan."

Comparisons of that sort were very much the style in those days. Fields' son, Herbert, wanted to be a performer, but his father felt he was better suited to the writing profession. Unable to be taken seriously as an actor, but knowing his father's interest in new talent, Herbert lured him down to an obscure theater on the Lower East Side on the pretext of seeing "a second Edwin Booth." "Booth" turned out to be Herbert, and after the performance, Fields told his son, "Now I *know* you should be an author!"

The Fields family had a summer cottage on Franklin Avenue in Far Rockaway, Long Island. The producer agreed to meet Dick and Larry there on a Sunday. They walked with Phil from the railroad station toward the beach.

"It was a pretty long walk," says Leavitt, "but not too long for Larry. In his nervous, jerky way he drew up a line of strategy for the meeting. He was sure that 'Venus' would be immediately interpolated into *A Lonely Romeo*. He always loved best the last song he had written. He expected it to inspire Fields enough to ask Dick to play their entire repertoire. He would sing while Dick was at the piano and he would throw in a bit of acting for good measure.

"It didn't quite work out that way. Lew Fields didn't like 'Venus,' and though Larry was crushed, they did get to play

41

other songs, and one, 'Any Old Place with You,' registered big. Fields put it into the score of *A Lonely Romeo*, and it made pros of Dick and Larry. They had crossed into the magic realm of Broadway's professional theater.''

Otherwise, they were still amateurs.

Early in 1920, Doc Bender's Akron Club libretto was ready. *You'd Be Surprised* was billed as an "atrocious musical comedy.''

"By this time," Phil Leavitt relates, "the club shows were becoming more elaborate and expensive to produce while the talent retained its amateur standing. When the boys discovered that each girl in the chorus was a potential ticket seller, with relatives and friends willing to pay to see them, we encouraged large choruses. The club was more interested in selling tickets than in the charm, grace, and talent of the chorines. You can imagine the result. There were an awful lot of left feet in that chorus line. But the girls did sell our tickets and also worked themselves into a frenzy.

"Dick played the piano at all rehearsals and also with the five-piece combo during the performances. Even when the principals were rehearsing dialogue, Dick remained at the piano, improvising.

"Larry watched the leads go through their numbers, puffing on a big black stogie. I think he must have been born with a black cigar in his mouth and was never weaned from the habit. Every once in a while he scribbled something on a scrap of paper, either additional dialogue or new business for the actors. Often it was incorporated into the show.

"The play snowballed. Each scene started with just an idea; the shaping, lines, and denouement came later. If Dick happened to improvise a good melody, Larry would turn like a pointer and rush to the piano to hear it played again. If they both liked it, Dick would sketch out the notes on a staff sheet, and Larry would make his own lead sheet. Sometimes Dick would say, 'I think we need a waltz here,' then sit at the piano and play one.

"Instantly, Larry would start to build a lyric for it. They developed into a conglomerate—composer, lyricist, dialogue writer, situation developer, and play doctor, all in one.

"Character-wise and temperamentally, the boys were entirely different, but their thinking meshed. Their judgments of the theater and ambitions at that time were alike, and they spliced into one corporate individual. This was the hard-core experience that was so necessary in the development of their talents.

"Dick changed from a shy, diffident kid into a thoughtful and aware composer. That does not imply that he emerged from a chrysalis into a firebrand, but he developed sureness, confidence, and poise."

Although devoted to lyric writing, Larry was finding it difficult to concentrate and had to be trapped into meaningful labor, despite his early enthusiasms for a melody. "He took pride in a lyric when it was done; then he could be ecstatic," said Dick. "Once he got coerced into it, he worked rapidly—when I could find him. His lyrics were always intelligent; he reached for lines that went further than any that had been written up to then. He wanted to say, 'It's full of crap,' in one of our songs and I said, 'You can't say that.' He said, 'Why not? Everybody knows the word.' "

They discovered that they must be mutually dependent in achieving the proper balance of a song, so they agreed that neither one should ever insist his was the right way.

Although Dick didn't share Larry's sardonic views of their world in the lyrics he wrote, he gave in to his partner's rueful observations about romance, his professed indiffer-

43

ence to sex, his feelings about being unloved. These attitudes colored many of Larry's lyrics and figured prominently in his personal life-style. They contributed spicy dimensions and uniqueness to their songs, but it was also the beginning of differences between them and overtures of discords to come.

4

Where or, for That Matter, When?

MANY AKRON CLUB members at Columbia wanted to be involved with the Varsity Shows, a presentation of collegiate talent that enlivened the New York scene every spring.

Working speculatively against other teams, Dick and Larry concentrated hard, as if their lives depended on it.

Phil Leavitt collaborated on a book, Larry adapted it, and he and Dick wrote the words and music. Oscar Hammerstein II was chairman of Columbia's Play Committee, and he selected their submission for the 1920 production.

The April issue of the Columbia *Jester* heralded its coming with this poetic effusion:*

*Paul Gallico, who returned to Columbia after the war to get a degree as Bachelor of Science, handled the press relations for *Fly with Me*. He intended to become a doctor but preferred to be a writer. "I wasn't certain then that I would be good at writing or could earn a living at it," but of course, he was, and he did.

We have with us tonight, as Homer said,
A poor thing but our own, clept
Fly with Me. . . .

It went on to philosophize:
Sullivan's harp hangs mutely on Tara's wall,
The ink on Gilbert's pen has long since dried. . . .

It ended in practical fashion:
To prophesy is madness, but we'll say
There'll be four nights and cut-rate matinee.

An important feature was the Pony Ballet, danced by a troupe of enthusiastic males. Again, in the words of Phil Leavitt:

"You can imagine the setup, with the fellows dressed up as girls. They were all college students, they played it straight and serious, but the effect came through as a caricature—powdered and rouged faces with set smiles, awkward figures in blond wigs, distinctly masculine chins, points where there should have been rounded flesh, bones and muscles where there should have been gentle curves. It was indescribably funny. They were precision-trained in the dance steps, but when they kicked, their feet looked grotesquely large. Frequently, chest hair peeked through their costumes. Even if you were fooled by the padded-out shapes and makeup, it all fell apart when they joined in the chorus of a song. You expected a high treble chorus, and instead, booming bass voices came out. Well, a lot of people fell right out of their seats."

For their first Varsity Show, Larry wrote fourteen lyrics to Dick's melodies. "Peek in Pekin" was temporarily memorable, the audiences also enjoyed "Don't Love Me Like Othello, I'm Much Too Young to Die" in which Larry drew on his affection for Shakespeare, while "College on Broadway" had lasting qualities for the undergrads who still sing it at get-togethers on Morningside Heights.

The Varsity Shows were marvelous adventures. That particular period at Columbia, as Leavitt also noted, was a sort of golden era for all things theatrical, but in their hurry to make it on Broadway, few waited to graduate. Dick left Columbia's classrooms after two years, saying he had learned everything they had to offer. "Doesn't one always think that at the end of two years in school?" he asked.

Realizing that charm and bluff could no longer substitute for the real thing, he enrolled in the Institute of Musical Arts, which would become his true alma mater, the one he would always look back to with sentiment and appreciation. It is now the famous Juilliard School of Music. He studied harmony under Percy Goetschius, musical history from Henry Krehbiel, and ear training from George Wedge. He was a zealous student.

"I was as organized," he recalled, "as Larry was disorganized."

They continued to write the Varsity Shows and were inducted into Pi Lambda Phi, many of its pledges aspiring toward success on Broadway, among them Morrie Ryskind, Howard "Freckles" Dietz, and Herman "Mank" Mankiewicz. "It was," said Leavitt, "an inspiring climate for anyone who had a flair for the theater."*

Herb Fields had gone wholeheartedly into writing, and he teamed up with Dick and Larry. They planned a trinity of talent, each one contributing his ideas to the music, lyrics,

*In my research I believe I met 20,000 former Columbians who claimed they were at college with Dick and Larry. —CLAYTON. One of the 20,000, Morrie Ryskind, was expelled for making uncomplimentary remarks about Nicholas Murray Butler, who happened to be the dean. —MARX

and libretto as the creation of Herbert Richard Lorenz. Their first effort was taking shape, to be called *Winkle Town*, and their dream was to get Lew Fields to produce it.

Dick and Larry were happy to find themselves becoming more and more involved with Fields, who accepted some of their songs for his new production, *Poor Little Ritz Girl*.

He invited them to join the company attending the tryout in Boston, an overnight train ride from New York. Sleep came reluctantly in the midst of such excitement and anticipation. When Dick looked into Larry's berth next morning, all he saw was a jumble of blankets. It turned out that Larry was under them, slumbering so deeply that he didn't hear Dick call. When he woke up, the car was nestling in the railroad yards, and he barely made it to the theater in time.

That was all the comedy that enlivened the tryout of *Poor Little Ritz Girl*. Otherwise, there was no cause for laughter; it was clear that the show lacked the substance that made for success on Broadway. They had arranged to attend Camp Paradox that summer, so when producer Fields buckled down to doctoring the play, they went back to camp.

They were given special permission to return to New York for the premiere on July 27. There a heartbreaking disappointment awaited them. Between Boston and Broadway the producer had performed a monumental doctoring job. He had scrapped the book, rewritten it, and jettisoned seven of Dick and Larry's songs, replacing them with others by Alex Gerber and Sigmund Romberg. He was within his rights; there was no clause in composer contracts to prevent interpolations. As neophytes Dick and Larry were given no chance to voice any complaints.

The individual styles of Rodgers and Romberg made for a very uneven set of melodies. "Rommy," as he was called, was inclined to shmaltzy, melodic, old-worldish compositions. Complained one critic, "All his songs are variations of 'Liebestraum.'"

"He writes the kind of music you whistle going *into* the theater," cracked Howard Dietz.

Heywood Broun, a shaggy, unkempt bear of a man, critic of the New York *Tribune*, reported that "the more serious songs are from Romberg and they are pleasing but hardly as striking as the lighter numbers." Broun especially singled out "Mary, Queen of Scots" as a rollicking ballad, which had Dick's music but Herb Fields' words.

When camp tents were folded for the season, Dick, Larry, and Herb went back to work on *Winkle Town*.

Dorothy Fields remembers them "working like mad upstairs on the top floor of our house on Ninetieth Street. They had fresh, bright, wonderful ideas."

But *Winkle Town* failed to interest a producer, even though it had a lively, topical song called "Manhattan" in the score.

Dorothy thought the worst blow of all was that her father turned it down: "It was bad enough that the others wouldn't give them an ear, but there was the famous actor-producer sitting downstairs in his library on the second floor, ignoring them.

"They'd take their wares to diverse producers, who'd fix a baleful eye on my brother Herb and say, 'If you guys are as good as you think you are, how come your father isn't willing to produce your show?'

"Of course," she continued, "Pop came from an earlier era in which musical comedy meant just that—music and comedy. He didn't want a coherent libretto or a book show. He wanted music, yes, but the rest should just be gags, blackouts, and belly laughs, whereas Herb, Dick, and Larry were obsessed with the necessity of having a strong story."

49

Winkle Town was placed on a shelf; the manuscript would die there. The song "Manhattan," however, was destined for a considerable life of its own.

The Herbert Richard Lorenz trinity, disillusioned but undefeated, went to work on a new play, *The Jazz King*. Their spirits were low, and writing it came hard. It languished, for they worked on it only spasmodically.

Dick and Larry turned to amateur shows again and helped create *Say Mama!* for the Akron Club and *You'll Never Know* for the Columbia Varsity.

Recognition and acclaim were eluding all three, but Larry radiated hope and fun. Fraternity brother Robert M. W. Vogel saw him sashay onstage during a rehearsal of *You'll Never Know* in great good spirits. In it, he portrayed an outrageously campy Mimi in a burlesque of *La Bohème*. "I am La Bum!" he trilled to Vogel.

They went searching for other ideas, and early in 1921 inspiration struck. The movies had an enormous success in a rollicking production based on Mark Twain's *A Connecticut Yankee in King Arthur's Court*. The trio saw it on a cold winter day but emerged from the theater warmed by the notion they could turn it into a marvelous musical comedy. They were so excited that they went directly to the attorney representing the Twain estate.

There they met, as described by Dick, a "flinty-eyed" character named Charles Tressler Lark. In their naïveté, they allowed their excitement to be obvious, realizing belatedly that this was no way to acquire rights cheaply. To their astonishment, the attorney gave them an option on the book for free. However, although they discussed its treatment for music, they could not arouse producer interest. They were facing lean prospects but continued to write and stockpile songs. Larry and Herb put words to a melody by French composer Clapson. They called it "The Pelican,"

50

and when accepted for publication, it gained no prominence whatsoever among popular pieces of the day. It was intended to set the nation dancing, but hardly a toe responded. Its impact may be judged with these few lines:

> Shake it up better than jelly can,
> When you reel to this dance a la mode.
> Then you feel you're about to explode.
> He'll love you if you teach him
> To do the Pelican.

Deciding to concentrate on what might be a more salable subject, they elected to get *The Jazz King* into shape. Lew Fields showed interest but didn't press them to finish it. Discouraged by turndowns, they labored futilely for three long, painful years.

In the words of actress Helen Ford, 1922 to 1925 were "the bad years." Rodgers and Hart were meeting with so little success that Dick's father became concerned about his son's chances of earning his living as a composer. He urged him to find some other business that offered security and would set him up as a reliable young man able to support a wife and family. Dick embarked upon a lackadaisical search for new directions, finding it difficult to give up the dreams he had cherished since childhood.

Larry had no family pressures to make such a change. Although he, too, was standing lonely in the glare of producer indifference, he had no intention of turning away from the theater. Instead, he plunged into other aspects of it.

His friend Henry Myers literally incubated playscripts and remained unfazed by repeated failures to get them to Broadway. Such tenacity elicited Larry's admiration, and though suffering from some financial deficiencies, he informed Myers he would personally produce his newest, *The*

First Fifty Years. He elated the playwright even more with "great good news" that O.M. wanted to be the first investor and had given him a check for $1,500.

"But," added Larry, "right now, if we tried to cash it, he'd kill me!"

5

Where's What Rainbow?

IT WOULD BE Larry's fate to die early; his legions of friends would call it "untimely."

Few deaths are timely, all deaths are sudden, but his was called a "slow death." Some say he sought it, that he lost his urge to live, that his death was suicidal.

But even though these were the "bad years," Larry was full of life, and the end was two decades ahead. It was not only the tragedy of Larry's physical departure from this earth that still concerns his friends but the worry that the memory of his impish spirit, even the fascinating lyrics be devised, would also pass from sight as the years rolled on. Henry Myers was thinking all these things when he told us, "I firmly believe that Larry has got to be brought to life."*

*In addition to *Destry Rides Again* and other movies, Henry Myers was one of the writers of *Meet the People*, a successful revue in Hollywood in the late thirties and my first show. He lived a quiet, gentle life and died the same way in California in November, 1975. I remember him with gratitude and affection. —CLAYTON

In his apartment close by Greenwich Village, Henry was a willing interviewee among the many we talked to as we searched New York, Hollywood, London and other less obvious places for the men and women who knew Larry. It was fascinating to see them light up at the mention of his name.

Constant descriptions were; "Oh, what an adorable man!," "What a joy he was," "a delight," "a pixie," "always clowning," "laughing," "joking." "But underneath the clowning was great sadness," said Mabel Mercer, the first to describe him differently. "I loved him warmly, but he was Pagliacci," she said, then moved through the darkened room to her waiting accompanist in Fifth Avenue's plush St. Regis Hotel, to start her show with a thoughtful "Where or When."*

Others mused hesitantly that Larry was a tormented man, and we went looking for the reason.

Versatile author Jerome Lawrence invited an interruption in a crowded workday at his Malibu hilltop home that *Auntie Mame* built overlooking the *entire* Pacific Ocean.

"Unfortunately, I never knew Larry Hart—I never met him—but when I was growing up, I became aware of the tremendous impact of this man on lyric writing. A lot of people thought he overrhymed. I don't think he did. I think he *invented* some of the most fantastic new rhymes I have ever heard. The psychology of analyzing this man in his lyrics convinces me he was the minstrel of masochism.

"Part of it is that in the twenties and the thirties it was not what today is, which is the Age of the Uglies, when the Dustin Hoffmans or a Barbra Streisand can make it. Unless

---

*When I told Mabel Mercer I sang Jerome Kern's very last song in a revival of *Show Boat*, she chuckled, "I think I sang his first."—CLAYTON

you were an Arrow Collar ad guy or a Gibson Girl, unless you had that Princeton look. . . . Even with literary figures it was true, F. Scott Fitzgerald was handsome. And Larry wasn't. Larry was a little gnome and consequently he thought—and this is just a theory—but certainly in all his work was 'I hate me.' It was 'beat me.' It was 'I'm no good.' It was 'Nobody's heart belongs to me.' Always 'Spring is here, I hear.' These were the theme songs of this man's life. Anyone who would fall in love with a Larry Hart, he would think, there must be something wrong with him—he mustn't have any taste. *Every* lyric has some masochism, every single one.

"But there is *another* strain in this, which is a Jewish thing, and which is a Chinese thing, an Oriental thing which makes me always think the Chinese and the Japanese are the ten lost tribes of Israel. If anyone is complimented, you say, 'spit on it, it's ugly.' Don't tempt the fates. The I'm-no-good-kind-of-thing is the humility you are supposed to have so you don't tempt the gods—to get the hex off," concludes Lawrence.

It was difficult for many of Larry's friends to speak out affirmatively about these aspects, but clearly the mystery of the inner Larry Hart made him a very colorful human.

In his younger days Larry's war with himself was intense, and it forced him to seek forgetfulness in drinking. Liquor became an added compulsion, mixed with drunken companions. Larry was to be an object of both pity and scorn, he acquired habits that were unacceptable and unadmirable in his time, yet he emerges the more likable, and, in comparison to Dick, who comported himself with reliability, sobriety, and dignity, the more lovable of the two.

Dick was aware that he shaped up unfavorably by comparison. He often said, "The way you tell us apart, I'm the big son of a bitch!" (Years later, when he worked with tall Oscar Hammerstein II, he changed it to "I'm the *little* son of a bitch!")

Henry Myers had thought of writing *A Portrait of Larry Hart (As I Saw Him and I Think He Saw Me)*. He jotted down his recollection of characters, events, and conversations and then unselfishly asked us to take them "so people will know Larry better."

"Larry was my friend, for a long time my closest friend. We met at Columbia College, and I was in the group of his literary-inclined friends who met to discuss belles-lettres and read our works to one another. We met at his house on 119th Street, a place where people loved to gather—bright, articulate people, most of them with sights aimed at the theater. We were all part of the background of this still-formative period of his life. I'm one of them. We influenced him, and he, us.

"My mother (who was called Muzzy by everyone) and I lived at the Majestic Hotel on the tail end of a fortune she had spent, partly in an attempt to make a concert pianist of me. She had heard Paderewski play once and had no doubts that I could be greater.

"Muzzy liked the bohemian feeling of the literary gatherings at the Harts, as reported by me, and got me to invite the group to our hotel where she defended my music, not my writing. 'Why don't you like Henry's music?' she asked Larry accusingly. Larry, who had heard both, said, 'Henry's writing moves me. Henry's music does not.'

"Muzzy's concert dreams for me notwithstanding, my playwrighting went on and on and on. I wrote a play every day, or so it seemed. Ten years later that moved Larry to want to see something done with one of them. The traditional procedure of putting on a play was very important to

56

Larry, with all the time-honored moves and motions. If he had a religion, it was the theater. Mystical. . . .

"Somehow, somewhere, I had gotten up courage to submit my latest play, *The First Fifty Years*, to Margaret Wycherly, then starring in a Macdougal Street production. Her stage manager saw me hand my script to her. Driven by curiosity, he went into her dressing room when she was onstage, got it, read it, liked it, and took it to Larry. That was when he decided to produce it. It only required two actors, a man and his wife.

"Larry called on Miss Wycherly and told her he was going to produce our play and hoped she would play in it. She answered quite reasonably that she would like to read it carefully and be sure it was for her. She invited us to her Greenwich Village apartment for dinner Sunday, when she would give us her answer.

"When Sunday came, we learned that Miss Wycherly was a very good cook. During dinner Larry and I babbled compliments; then he steered the conversation to the theater, keeping it on a highly intellectual philosophical plane, a waste of time as far as I was concerned. At last, over the coffee, we got around to my play. Miss Wycherly brought out my script.

" 'I've made a few changes.'

"Like all playwrights who hear that for the first time, I felt chilled.

" 'Just in the dialogue,' she explained, and that was more chilling.

"She handed me the script. Every speech had been changed. *Every* speech! They waited for me to reply, but I didn't know what to say.

"Larry rescued me. 'I think Henry should take it home with him and study it. It's just wonderful for you to give him the benefit of your judgment and experience.'

"Outside, Larry pointed to the mangled script. 'We don't need her for that,' he said. Having lost the star we never had, he went to work in earnest and organized a producing company, composed of such of our literary group as could put up some of the $5,500 that he figured would be needed. Yes, $5,500! In those days you could produce a two-character one-set play for that. Particularly if you had snowed your O.M. into a $1,500 check that owing to an upturn in his fortunes, you were now permitted to cash. This, plus six other persuadable friends, constituted our entire group of backers, and they accompanied Larry everywhere and anywhere—seeing actors, interviewing directors and theater managers, renting scenery and costumes . . . everything. Bemused, pliable and amused, he named the organization Caravan, Inc.

"My chief difficulty was Muzzy, who was worried that Larry might not understand the mystical processes of play production as expertly as she did. So, over my loud objections, she phoned Larry, and his mother answered. No two mothers ever did a better job of attempting to upstage each other, but I think Frieda Hart got the better of it.

" 'I'm a little worried,' said Muzzy, 'that Larry doesn't know about scenery and programs and rehearsing and all that.'

"My Lori," replied Frieda coldly, 'knows everything about the theater.'

"Muzzy was reassured by a 'play doctor' whom Larry had hired. His addition to the staff didn't worry her, but it thoroughly upset me.

"Seeing that I meant to resist any kind of editing, Larry said to me, 'I see now, we'll have to *trick* you all the way through this production.'

" 'But isn't there some way,' I asked plaintively, 'that an

58

author can stop the production of his play if he doesn't like what's being done with it?' Then, for the only time that I can remember, he became furious, almost berserk. 'If you ever mention stopping this production!' he threatened. And I think he concluded with some especially dreadful way he would kill me.

"Still missing were a theater, a director, and a cast. The theater was especially elusive.

"After a string of turndowns Larry concentrated on getting the best director. And he got one of the tops, Livingston Platt. How? He just walked into his office in the Hudson Theater Building and let fly with a terrific sales pitch.

"Larry may have exaggerated, but my affection for him was certainly not dimmed by his calling me 'one of the great American dramatists.'

"Because of Platt, we got two excellent actors, Clare Eames and Tom Powers, and arranged for that charming little Princess Theater.

"We had a one-performance out-of-town showing in Allentown, Pennsylvania. Why, I don't know. One performance isn't enough if anything is the matter, and if you're in good shape, it dissipates the first-night excitement that should be saved for your official opening in New York.

"Our Allentown opening was enthusiastically received and everybody was optimistic, indeed.

"Larry liked it as much as anyone, but showed himself to be more of a realist than the others connected with it.

"'That,' he said, indicating Lent on the calendar, 'is what is going to lick us. We should close now and wait until next season to open, but I can't wait any longer; my nerves can't stand it.'

"We opened importantly before a swanky audience that could have graced the Metropolitan Opera House. All the first-string critics came, and most of the reviews were

59

raves. There were fifteen newspapers then in New York, and fifteen critics, who were in friendly competition with one another, and good writers themselves. Their names, for nostalgia's sake, and their publications:

Alexander Woollcott	*Times*
Henry Krehbiel	*Herald*
Gilbert Gabriel	*Sun*
Percy Hammond	*Tribune*
Heywood Broun	*World*
Charles Darnton	*Evening World*
Alan Dale	*American*
Kelcey Allen	*Women's Wear*
Arthur Pollock	*Brooklyn Eagle*
Robert Benchley	*Life*
Stark Young	*New Republic*
Jack Lait	*Variety*
S. Jay Kaufman	*Globe*
Leo Marsh	*Telegraph*
Burns Mantle	*News*

"Before the curtain went up, Larry said to me, 'I'd rather have a good review from Woollcott than from all the others.' During the intermission he said, 'Woollcott likes your play.' But we were a flop—not an out-and-out disaster, but not quite good enough.

"Business dwindled to such a point that I pestered Larry to do something dramatic, some romantic press-agent stunt I had heard would turn failure into success. I made such a nuisance of myself that one day he did come up with an idea: I should disappear and be reported among Missing Persons. That would get the police on the job. We'd be front-page news, and our press agent would plant stories about how creative artists like me are being driven to suicide. It seemed like a great idea, so off I went to a cousin of the Harts who lived in Paterson, New Jersey, to hide there until our aims were achieved. My signal to come back to life would be a telegram reading: 'It's a boy.'

"However, we had not counted on Muzzy's screaming hysterics after she consulted a lawyer and learned that our little stunt was illegal and I could be jailed for it. So the telegram was dispatched very soon after my 'suicide.' I thanked the cousin and went home. Larry later told some mutual friends, 'At least for twenty-four hours, I had some peace!'

"Inevitably, the show closed. But nothing good had happened in the meantime to the fortunes of Rodgers and Hart either; they were without a Broadway possibility of any kind, so Larry decided he wanted to direct one of my newest inspirations.

THE MACDOWELL CLUB
of New York City
108 West 55th St.

The Committee on Drama
announces
A MacDowell Club Repertory Presentation

"The Blond Beast"

a modern comedy

by

Henry Myers

Staged by Lorenz M. Hart

61

"Arthur Hohl and Effingham Pinto, two of the best of all American actors, did not disdain to take direction from Larry, who got 'Staged by' in the newspaper announcements. There was no mention of him as a lyricist.

"Larry was an excellent director; the actors felt and knew it, but he learned from them too. For example, Effingham Pinto crossed the stage during a scene, unobtrusively and without spoiling anyone's points—practically invisibly. Larry, the director, asked him admiringly, 'How did you get over there?'

"Milton Wynn, a lawyer, and Edwin Justus Mayer, a budding playwright who got to be pretty damn good, acquired the right to put *The Blond Beast* on Broadway. They were inexperienced and didn't know how to produce a play, but they were smart enough to know that. They were just fellows anxious to be part of the theater.

"To find a producer with more know-how (and money), they had a unique plan—they would give one performance in New York with the same cast, just as Larry directed it, and invite successful entrepreneurs to see this finished product, rather than have to guess at its virtues from a typewritten manuscript.

"It was a revolutionary type of audition. All the Broadway producers liked the idea and came to see what we had.

"Just as the curtain was about to rise, word went around that there might be an actors' strike, and every single one of those producers got up and left to attend an emergency meeting in David Belasco's office."*

The actors' strike did occur. The first stirrings had begun

* "David Belasco, dean of American drama, wrote or dramatized more than 100 plays, acted in nearly 200, and produced more than 300. His father figure on Broadway was enhanced by his clerical garb which prompted one pundit to describe him as "the only man in town who can go from his office to a costume ball without changing clothes."

back in 1896. Frustrations, hostilities, talked over, haggled over, agonized over, erupted in sound and fury. Bitterly fought on both sides, the strike tore the theater world apart. Business associations, love affairs, and friendships were strained, broken; many would never be the same again.

Alfred Harding, in his book *The Revolt of the Actors*, lists "What the Actors Had to Stand," and the most contentious was the absence of a standard contract. No actor could tell in advance what he would be required to do because each manager wrote his own contract, in which loopholes were many and, of course, in his favor.

There was no limit to free rehearsal period. Ten weeks for a straight play were not unknown, and musical productions might easily run into sixteen or eighteen weeks. Actors had to pay their transportation to jobs, and strandings out of town were frequent. No bonds were posted to guarantee salaries due in case of a sudden closing. Practically all players were required to furnish modern costumes, and sometimes period as well. This was a real hardship, particularly for women, who would invest a great deal in costumes adapted to a character, only to be dismissed summarily or not even allowed to open the play.

Backstage conditions were generally dreadful. Managers held the power of artistic life and death over their actor-employees. They invented a "satisfaction clause"; it was used to unfair advantage, and it struck a blow at the pride and ego of a performer. Dismissal was immediate, and there was no recourse if the manager decided that an actor was not "satisfactory."

The actors wanted a regulatory organization of their own; but the producers and managers fought hard, and they had strong weapons. Almost everyone concerned with one of the world's most glamorous occupations got into the battle. Broadway became an ugly field of theatrical civil war.

One army, the rebellious actors, became the Actors' Equity Association, officially organized in 1913. *The New York Review*, a voice for the Shuberts, attempted to dismiss it sarcastically: "An Actors' union is doomed to failure because the foundation upon which any sort of League must stand to be successful is absolute equality. It is quite absurd to suppose that any actor would admit that any other actor is his equal!"

The other army formed the Actors Fidelity League, and foremost among its members was actor-producer-playwright-composer, master of all these arts, George M. Cohan. He became fanatic against actors on strike. Typical of his anger was this advertisement he placed in the New York newspapers: "Before I ever do business with the Actors' Equity I will lose every dollar I have, even if I have to run an elevator to make a living."

The next day there was a sign hanging out of the office window of the Equity partisans: WANTED—ELEVATOR OPERATOR. GEORGE M. COHAN PREFERRED.

Cohan was very popular with the public, to whom he presented a benevolent look. But he was ill tempered in private, and success made him contemptuous.

However, the brouhaha subsided fairly amiably in September, 1919, the actors winning substantial gains and the producers pleased to clear the fire and smoke from Broadway in time to let the traditional fall season begin.

Leaders of Actors' Equity charitably forgave George M. Cohan and opened its doors to him. When he uncharitably rejected the offer, the victorious association honored him with a lifetime membership which enabled him to continue stage appearances. But he never forgave them, although he returned to acting and in the course of time would turn his arrogance on Dick and Larry.

The settlement of the strike came too late to help the

would-be producers of *The Blond Beast*. They never did get it off the ground.

"The strike seemed an extraordinary piece of bad luck for all of us," Myers added, "but heigh ho, supposing those fellows who ran out of the audition had sat through it and no one wanted it? What might *that* have done to our psyches?

"That setback caused Larry to discard his ideas about producing and directing and devote himself exclusively to writing lyrics. One never knows the ultimate consequences of bad luck of this sort, right?"

He joined Dick and Herb, and they finally persuaded Lew Fields to produce *The Jazz King* on Broadway. They had poured their hearts into it, feeling closely related to the plot, which dealt with a composer's struggle for recognition. It was actually a drama with music, needing only two songs supposed to ape cheap run-of-the-mill Tin Pan Alley effusions. Fields agreed to go ahead on finding that the title role was admirably suited to his acting talents. He was, however, a little short of cash, $1,000 to be exact. Larry's O.M. rode to the rescue, talking a friend into the investment. It came into New York as *The Melody Man*.

Its two songs, "Moonlight Mama" and "I'd Like to Poison Ivy," in accord with the plot, were not supposed to be hits. Both richly succeeded in fulfilling that intention; the show, too, was an unqualified disaster.

Many critics, in those days, tried hard to effect quotes in their reviews that would be bandied back and forth among sophisticates who loved derogatory epigrams. George Jean Nathan, mincing in appearance but never in his use of words, with definite ideas on all subjects, who once announced his candidacy for president of the United States, wrote: "The plot is not only enough to ruin the play, it is enough—and I feel I may say it without fear of contradiction—to ruin even *Hamlet*."

6

You Must Kick It Around

THERE HAVE always been instant Cinderellas reported in the theater, an electrifying performance by a player in a small part, an understudy who shines with greater brilliance than the star, an author who dazzles with a first play. It happens, of course. Success is everybody's ambition, but it can't be commanded: It has to be earned.

With each blow, Dick and Larry picked themselves off the dusty floors of the playhouses and set themselves for another try. They wrote a score for *Dear Enemy*, a play Herb had decided to write about the Revolutionary War. It was purely speculative. There was no certainty that any producer would want it. The story dealt with a legendary happening in that war when Mrs. Murray (of New York's Murray Hill) called on the young belles of the city to help her detain General Howe and the British troops so General Washington could make an escape. The leading role was Mrs. Murray's Irish niece, Betsy.

Actress Helen Ford had been out on the road in "a kind of

flop," she said. "I was living at the Algonquin Hotel, and one day, as I stepped out of the elevator, Herbert Fields was waiting to introduce himself and give me a script. He said if I liked it enough to hear the music, they would set it up for me. Well, I glanced at it, and before I read past my first entrance I liked it, because, for the first time in my life, I *had* a beautiful entrance. That's important to an actress!"

But the lack of a producer was a mighty void that had to be filled. She liked the play so much she volunteered to help find someone to put the show on. It wasn't going to be easy, especially after the crashing failure of *The Melody Man*. While Helen Ford took up her search, the desperately awaited spark that Dick and Larry needed to effect a change for the better finally ignited.

The circumstances were unusual and unexpected. Actress Edith Meiser tells what they were.*

"Early in 1925," she related, "all of us who played understudies and small parts for the Theater Guild got together and said, 'Why don't we get together and put on a small revue?' The guild, then in that darling small theater called the Garrick, was building this great big thing, which is now the Anta. It's a mausoleum of a theater. You can't play comedy in it at all. The guild was so busy with it that it didn't do what it usually did for subscribers. In the spring it always gave them a series of Sunday matinees and evening shows for free, but the executives didn't have the time to

---

*Fred Nolan is a delightful English leprechaun, author and historian of the modern musical scene for the British Broadcasting Corporation. He spent six years interviewing everyone he could find who knew Dick and Larry. He told us his passionate devotion stemmed from his own romantic successes whenever he murmured pure Hart into the soft pink ears of many lovely lasses. We are indebted to him for this 1974 interview and also to Miss Meiser for permission to use it.

get involved with them then. They were still raising money.

"Everybody gave balls in those days for fund raising, and everybody went, and they were full of fun, with everybody dressed to the teeth. All of us who were working for the guild—they had many plays, they sometimes had three plays going concurrently—we, the small fry, did takeoffs, not only of the Theater Guild plays but of other shows, and some of our material was written by the best comedy writers who were writing for the stage.

"We were kind of the pets, we young people, so we said, 'Why don't we put on a revue like *The Grand Street Follies*?' That was a topical revue that did takeoffs, a small, satirical revue. We said, 'We'll do one for the guild, all we need is to find someone to write the music and lyrics.'

"Romney Brent and I were appointed a committee. We were supposed to go around and talk to people who could write music.

"I was going to write the lyrics. But one doesn't know what one doesn't know when one is young.

"One of the great backers of the guild was an enchanting old gent named Ben Kaye; he was always very good to us youngsters. By that time we had talked to a lot of people, including Peter Arno, the cartoonist for the *New Yorker*, who thought of himself as a songwriter."

"Mr. Kaye suggested that Romney and I talk to a young composer he knew named Richard Rodgers. He told me that day, 'He's the son of this very well-known doctor, and his father has said that if he can't really get started, he's got to go off and into a serious business and stop this theater nonsense. See if he wouldn't like to write the music.'"

"This was February," she went on. "We were already in rehearsal with the sketches; we were working like mad. There were no rules or regulations with Actors' Equity about how long you rehearsed. None of this nonsense about unions and guilds. We all did everything. We did all kinds of strange things.

"Romney and I made an appointment with Rodgers to see if he would be suitable.

"I borrowed my mother's furs to make an impression," she remembered, "but Romney had a date with this beautiful, beautiful Oriental actress, Anna May Wong. Well, if you think I could get him to break that to go see Dick Rodgers, well, not at all. So off I went.

"I was living in a little walkup on the East Side. It was in February. I can remember it exactly. I can close my eyes, and I'm there. I went across town to West End Avenue, which was very elegant. Big apartment houses, a nice place to live. We were having a February thaw. Everything was dripping. The air was soft, but there was still snow on the ground, and I could see across the river, which was very hazy, kind of dreamlike.

"This elegant apartment had an enormous foyer and an enormous grand piano. Dick was waiting and said, 'I'll play you a few of the things I've done for the Varsity Shows up at Columbia.' So he did, and told me, 'I did these with Larry Hart, who is a friend of mine.'

"I said, 'Well, you know I have the ideas for all the songs, so I will naturally be doing some.'

"He played some songs from other shows he had done. I wasn't terribly impressed. Then he played 'Manhattan.'

"I flipped!

"I knew this was an enormous big hit number. You know, sometimes God sits on your shoulder, you know something that is way beyond anything you should know. And . . . so . . . I pulled myself together and said, 'I think you're going to be our boy. Can you do the whole show or do you just want to—?'

"No. He wanted to do the whole show!

70

"There were a couple of numbers that had to be interpolated, so I said, 'We'll get together, and I'll write the lyrics.' I had done a few in my college days.

"I went back to the Garrick Theater where the kids were
rehearsing and said, 'I have found the boy!' He came down
and played 'Manhattan,' and they all felt as I did about him.

"We began working together on several numbers to fit
into sketches until he said, slowly, tentatively, 'You know,
Edith, I generally work with a guy called Larry Hart. Would
you let him try a few of the ideas we've worked out?'

"I said, also slowly, tentatively, 'Well, all right,' you
know, thinking . . . hmmmmm. But then he brought in Larry's lyrics.

"Well, I did have the sense to know I was 'way outclassed
. . . but 'way out! Well, these lyrics began to float in, you
know, to all these ideas we had. They were so absolutely
sensational! I can remember Larry Hart coming into the
Garrick Theater on this whole backstage, this little bit of
an almost dwarf of a man. I've always said he was the
American Toulouse-Lautrec; really, he was that kind of
personality, but *enchanting!* He had such . . . what is now
called charisma. He had such appeal!

"It was funny. He was beginning to be bald even in those
days. He had this funny head, this enormous head, and very
heavy beard. He had to shave twice a day, and a big cigar
that always stuck out of his mouth, and he would always go
around as though washing his hands. This was his great gesture!

"Of course, we *adored* him. I mean Dick we were terribly
fond of, but Larry was adored. He was a pet; he was something very, very special. That is not to downgrade Dick at
all, because we were terribly fond of Dick, too. But Larry
was someone you wanted to protect, in a funny way. This
funny little ugly man who was so dear. . . .

"He lived always for today . . . yesterday didn't exist . . .

71

tomorrow, who knows? He was the real Laugh, Clown, Laugh. Always fun, always gay, light, a sparkling conversationalist. But you wondered. . . .

"I've written some lyrics in my time, I sit down with a rhyming dictionary. But Larry? Never!* It was purely out of his head. He had one of the most beautiful full vocabularies of anyone I've ever known. Triple rhymes were no problem to him. They just happened, they were nothing.

"The way Herb Fields got into the show. . . . That first time I saw Dick he said he wrote some songs with him also and showed me a picture of himself and Dorothy Fields being very cozy on a piano bench. I can remember seeing that picture to this very day, with her beautiful legs and all of that, y'know.

"Both boys desperately wanted Herb to have something to do with the *Garrick Gaities.* We suddenly discovered there was no one connected with the show who knew how to tell us how to do dance numbers. So Herb came in. He had never been a dancer, but having been with all of his father's shows and knowing what the one-two-three kick steps were, well, you didn't have to be an awfully good dancer. He taught us the dance routines for the songs, and then he did a couple of sketches.

"That," said Miss Meiser, "was how the *Garrick Gaieties* came about." Intended to be performed for just the week beginning Sunday, May 17, 1925, New Yorkers stormed the theater and even made standing room difficult to get. Everyone connected with it became the toast of New York.†

---

*Larry once told an admirer, "It's easier to think one up than look one up."

†Among those who went on to fame from *Garrick Gaieties* were, in addition to Rodgers, Hart, and Fields, Romney Brent and Miss Meiser, Sterling Holloway, Betty Starbuck, Philip Loeb, John McGovern, June Cochrane, Sanford Meisner, Libby Holman, Alvah Bessie, Lee Strasberg, Harold Clurman, Sam Jaffe, and Morrie Ryskind.

The Theater Guild quickly scheduled a regular Broadway showing. The following week it began a run that lasted more than 200 performances.

Most critics greeted the show enthusiastically, but there were the usual disagreements among them. Burns Mantle (*Daily News*) said, "The music and lyrics are well above the average Broadway output." Richard Watts, Jr. (*Herald Tribune*), qualified that with: "The music is pleasant and the lyrics are serviceable, if frequently obvious."

George Jean Nathan (*Judge*) trod lightly past the words and music, only acknowledging that one song, "Butcher, Baker, Candlestick Maker" was "fairly diverting."* He said, "The show's singing is bad, its comedy is poor, its dancing is commonplace, its pictorial quality is nil. . . ." He grudgingly admitted it contained one amusing sketch called "Mr. and Mrs."

Morrie Ryskind, who wrote that sketch, lives in Beverly Hills, and he told us, "I've never forgotten it. It got the biggest laughs you ever heard, and not because of any of the writing. Here's what happened:

"It opened—as almost all those sketches opened— y'know, a woman is asleep in bed in darkness. A clock strikes one o'clock, and some guy sneaks in with his shoes off. It's the husband.

"In this one, the woman puts the light on and says, 'Calvin Coolidge! Where have you been to this hour?' Well, the idea of a guy like Calvin Coolidge standing up there, Calvin Coolidge staying up to one o'clock. They laughed for fifteen minutes! I don't think they heard one word of the sketch; that's why I'm saying it didn't matter what they did. The writing didn't matter; the woman would start to say some-

*The song that diverted the erudite Nathan was not the work of Rodgers and Hart; it was an interpolation by Ben Kaye and his friend, Madame Mana-Zucca, opera singer and musician. Christened Agusta Zuccaman, she twisted the syllables of her last name to give it an exotic flavor.

thing, and a guy in the second row would start laughing again. When you had a guy like Robert Benchley in the audience, how he roared! I don't remember to this day if that sketch was funny."*

Larry had celebrated his thirtieth birthday while *Garrick Gaieties* was in rehearsal. His mother was the only woman who had figured importantly in his life.

His detachment from other women raised the eyebrows of many acquaintances. His friends had various—and often conflicting—opinions.

"Now and then you hear," said Henry Myers, "a baseless and offensive innuendo about Larry and homosexuality. No, Larry was not queer! He liked girls, the more beautiful, the better, and he was quite crazy about one when he was at Columbia. He never spoke to her about it. He never spoke to her at all, but he agonized over her to us.

"He was afraid she would laugh at him, for Larry was bothered that he was such a short man, bothered is not an adequate word—it was his lifelong tragedy. Another very attractive girl whom he admired was marrying a friend of his, and they asked him to be best man at their wedding. He accepted and was the life of the party at the wedding. While he was in that happy state, I said to him, 'Larry, why don't *you* get married?' With a sudden surge of unmistakable bitterness, he replied, 'Yes, I could get a stepladder and get married!'"

But Edith Meiser said, "Larry had a tragic life because he had to carry his ambivalence. He was terribly fond of tall girls . . . and of course he was fond of boys, too. That was his biggest unhappiness."

*Lyricist Ira Gershwin supplied us with the end of the sketch. Coolidge says he was at a party. Mrs. Coolidge asks, "What party?" and Coolidge replies, "The Republican Party!" BLACKOUT!

74

In 1925 Larry was too busy and too happy to be concerned with what people thought about his lifestyle. He and Dick were solidly back in show business. *Garrick Gaieties* wasn't all they had going for them. Helen Ford's effort to raise the curtain on *Dear Enemy* was paying off.

It was the apex of the thriving postwar period. The bad years for Dick and Larry were over.

At least, for the time being.

7

Cheer in My Arms

SHE WAS Helen of Troy, New York, and would become Dick and Larry's first leading lady, the very first actress to interpret a role that they, with Herb Fields, had shaped for Broadway.

Married to George Ford, a handy man at all phases of theatrical production, she was dainty, energetic, and appealing. In height, she was about the same as Larry.

She learned her craft in a variety of plays. She could sing and dance and act and didn't allow marriage to roadblock her career. In fact, two weeks after their wedding George Ford went on the road with a show of his own while she went to New York to look for one. They didn't see each other again for six months.

Helen replaced a flashy redhead, Francine Larrimore, in Rudolf Friml's operetta *Sometime*. "The general opinion of Miss Larrimore (not necessarily mine)," opines Helen, "was that she was so bad she couldn't even walk to music, much less dance. When she was fired, she took out her frustrations by ripping all her beautiful costumes to shreds!

"There were two Hammersteins connected with *Sometime.*; the producer, Arthur, who was a cad, and his nephew, the stage manager, Oscar II, who was a darling. He helped me get the part.

"Another one of my early shows was *For Goodness Sake*, and the rehearsal pianist was George Gershwin. I sang the first song he ever had interpolated into a show, called 'Tra-la-la.'

"Years later Ira Gershwin wrote a whole treatise on the fact that I was supposed to have sung the worst song George ever wrote!*

"When George Ford and I married, we agreed that we would write each other a letter every day that we were separated. He kept that promise. I wasn't that good, but I did write him a lot about *Dear Enemy* because I had fallen completely in love with Betsy, my part, and I was determined to get George involved in it, too. He says I kicked him into the show, and I did, too!"

George Ford was an imposing individual who grew up in show business and remained with it all his life. He had an important tie to American history: An uncle established a circuit of theaters in the Southeast, one being Ford's Theater in Washington.

He was an excellent biographer, and in his book *These Were Actors* he recounted the adventures of his ancestors, the Chapmans and the Drakes, who initiated showboat and minstrel acts and pioneered the theater in the Far West.

He was out West himself, but his indomitable wife was

*Ira Gershwin verified that Miss Ford sang the first song his brother George interpolated in a show, but he says it was "Waiting for the Sun to Come Out" in *The Sweetheart Shop*, and "I did not write any treatise that it was the worst song my brother ever wrote. How could I ever say a thing like that? George would have run me out of town."

determined to play *Dear Enemy*, even though help from him wasn't available.

"I really wanted to do that show," she said, "in spite of a lot of discouragement from the managers I knew around town. That was before *Garrick Gaieties*, and no one had heard of Rodgers and Hart and Fields but I believed in them. The problem we had, auditioning for money, was beyond belief.

"We auditioned all over town. . . uptown, downtown. . . on Seventh Avenue for the cloak and suiters, sometimes at Dick's place because I was at the Algonquin, and the Fields' place over on West End Avenue was so crowded with family—lots of fun, but lots of family, too. Tremendous!"

Miss Ford stopped for a thoughtful moment. "Something just occurs to me. . . . I suppose there are people who don't know about auditions for backers. In those days they were almost entirely unknown because many producers like David Belasco put up their own money.

"But producers who needed to raise capital had to inveigle actors and singers to give a sample of what the show would be about. It could be magic, and it could be hell—a real emotional experience.

"We had the most fun at Larry's place, although that had nothing to do with auditioning. We gathered around the big round table that always had a white cloth on it—they still had gaslights!

"Larry loved his family, even though he teased them a lot, especially his father, who was, I guess, at least Larry said he was, a petty crook! Well, I think he *must* have been kidding because he also used to say his father was in partnership with. . . who was that famous whore-mistress? Polly Adler!

"There was so much enthusiasm in our meetings, excite-

79

ment, we didn't discuss the play very much. That was already written; they had it. They also had twenty-five thousand dollars backing money, but needed another twenty-five. I blithely offered to get that for them, having not even the foggiest notion how one did it. In my naïveté I asked everyone I knew, or met, connected with our business and, not surprisingly, raised none.

"One day, coming out of the elevator at the hotel, a gentleman stopped me with a fairly proper salutation, 'Miss Ford, how lovely to see you again.' I knew we had met but couldn't for the life of me place him until he mentioned Toronto, and then I associated him with a closing-night party there. At this point he noticed I was carrying a script which was, of course, *Dear Enemy* (which went everywhere with me) and I told him it was the new musical I was going to do. Not pausing for breath, I said, 'Do you happen to know anyone who would like to invest twenty-five thousand dollars in it?' and he said yes, that he might know someone and could we have dinner to discuss it?

"Well, I refused, of course, almost rudely. But in a most gentlemanly way he persisted, suggesting lunch, and I guess in the back of my suddenly cunning little mind I realized I wasn't being very bright, so I suggested tea. Being about twelve years old in the sophistication of my thinking, I am sure I had no intention of making the Supreme Sacrifice for the Show, but if I had, I was doomed to embarrassing disappointment, because Mr. Robert Jackson, my host, was the brother of my husband's roommate at Dartmouth, a serious and successful businessman. He was completely captivated by the theater, and that very day he put up the twenty-five thousand we needed.

"However, while I was getting that half of what was needed, the *other* half disappeared. Some gangster said he would put it up, and I guess he changed his mind. Nobody argued with him, and maybe it was just as well for me because, in those days, when a gangster backed a show, he usually had some cutie he wanted to play the leading role.

"Undaunted, or maybe just a little daunted, we went auditioning again. We thought we had one backer in a rosy-cheeked happy little man, but he brought his rosy-cheeked fat little wife, and she was not so happy over 'the lady who does all the singing who is too pretty,' and that money flew away. Would you believe it, we did about fifty auditions?

"Ultimately, the happiest of situations developed. My husband came in off the road and liked the show and said he would put it on."

George Ford remembers the day. "Dick Rodgers said to me, 'I've been at work on this two years, and I haven't made hardly a cent. I put two songs into a show for Lew Fields, and I'm going to quit music. I've got a job, I can go on the road selling children's clothes. If something doesn't happen, I'm going to do it.' That's when I decided to put it on, right there."

Helen Ford adds, "Then everybody sat down and talked a lot, with the result that Mr. Jackson put up all the money and George produced the show.*

"He decided to try it out in Akron, Ohio, where he could have a theater for free. Free, that is, if I would play *The Gingham Girl* again, a show I'd had some success in and for which George volunteered me, saying I would do it without any salary. Really, my husband's generosity with my talents sometimes was quite overwhelming and a bit hard to take."

George Ford says, "We went through a hard time with the

*It turned out, according to Miss Ford, that Mr. Jackson was ready to put up all the money right from the start, but he so enjoyed the auditions that he didn't tell us that until he saw that we weren't going to get it from anybody else.

play at first; it never caught on on the road. Across the street in a vaudeville house, a lady was doing the shimmy, and they were standing in line! I was quite pessimistic about taking it to Broadway."

Dear Enemy, retitled *Dearest Enemy*, opened in New York on September 18, 1925, while *Garrick Gaieties* was still doing sellout business. It was an instant success. The critics said, because of these two new hits, "Move over, everybody!" The *Times* reported: "The full- toned quality of the music has more than a chance-flavor of Gilbert and Sullivan."

It was also a personal triumph for Helen Ford, but it was not achieved without differences between the star and the composer. She says, "Dick hates sopranos, you know."

The theater has known many wars between sopranos and tenors, but a battle between a soprano and a composer, especially when the lady is a coloratura, can be awesome.

Henry Myers said, "Helen Ford's voice had a phenomenally high range. Not just a high note now and then. It *stayed* up there—what musicians call high tessitura. This precipitated a running fight between her and Dick, who, whether he knew it or not, wrote for Larry's voice, which is to say, no voice at all."

Helen had a similar complaint.

"I had a terrible time with Dick, with my high voice. Our falling-outs were always over his keys because he wrote his songs for Larry to sing, and if it were in another key, it sounded wrong to him, I swear."

They sounded right to the reviewer of the New York *Telegram* who wrote: "We have a glimmering notion that someday [Fields, Rodgers, and Hart] will form the American counterpart of the once-great triumvirate of Bolton, Wodehouse and Kern."

To call Bolton, Wodehouse, and Kern "once-great" was

82

indicative of the changing times. Nineteen twenty-five was to become known as the year of the "debacle of idealism," so while *Dearest Enemy* was a hit, it was, nevertheless idealistic and overly sentimental. Dick and Larry weren't happy with that; they foresaw the coming of a more sophisticated era and the demise of the "Moonlight and Roses" type of song, which they despised. They were beginning to think ahead of their time.

The city of Boston was famed for its puritanical past and austere present. *Dearest Enemy* was booked there after Broadway, and Larry was told repeatedly to "tone down" some of the words of "A Little Birdie Told Me So," considered too risqué for Boston.

Part of the Larry Hart phenomenon was the gift of writing lyrics anywhere and about anything. Less phenomenal was his altogether-human hatred of change.

When he voiced his resistance to the Boston edict, he had the complete support of Helen Ford. She had been doing "A Little Birdie Told Me So" for a year, successfully, and her memory was automatic, matching her actions to the words of the song. Changing the lyric made for a difficult change in its delivery.

But puritanical censorship was stern and inflexible, so finally, on closing night in New York, as Helen was packing up, Larry burst into her dressing room, shouting, "Have I got a lyric for you!" and waved a roll of toilet paper, which bore the "toned-down" words. Helen said he did it on toilet paper to startle her and amuse himself.

"Imagine," she says now. "That's the basis of a whole TV commercial today. An entire family is on television writing notes to one another on that 'stationery.' " But in 1926, rhymes on toilet paper were pretty shocking.

Indications of great changes in art, customs, and mores could hardly be ignored, they were all around. New materials were available for architecture, and men like Frank Lloyd Wright were making full use of them; H. L. Mencken was rousing the intellectuals with his caustic pokes at romantic authors; playwright Eugene O'Neill was being hailed for his vital, if depressing, exposures of human failings; art collectors were turning from the bland output of British and American painters to embrace the outrageous nudes, in strange eye-compelling colors of the French moderns. Electrifying to Dick and Larry was bandleader Paul Whiteman's "Experiment in Modern Music" at Aeolian Hall in New York, at which George Gershwin, four years younger then Larry, just three years older than Dick, shook the world of modern music with his *Rhapsody in Blue*.

In those changing times, it was apparent to thinkers around the country that rebellious young people, the World War I generation, had become disillusioned with their own rebellion and were looking for new freedoms through the arts. It made Dick and Larry resolve to break with the sentimentality that had shackled musical comedy—the soft, even maudlin themes of Victor Herbert's operettas and, for that matter, the hitherto-hallowed effusions of Bolton, Wodehouse, and Kern. They began to seek free expressions in musical comedy. It wouldn't be easy. It would take time, but *Dearest Enemy* was a turning point on a road that would lead, ultimately, to *Pal Joey*.

8

Sell It Back to the Indians

BROADWAY HAD a new team. They weren't household words yet, but there was recognition in theatrical circles of songs by Rodgers and Hart. That was another step up the ladder.

Recognition brought them a publishing offer from prestigious T. B. Harms. Until *Dearest Enemy*, Max and Louis Dreyfus, owners of that firm and kingpins of Tin Pan Alley, showed magnificent indifference toward them. Dick played "Manhattan" for Max when it was included in the score of *Winkle Town*, only to receive a shrugging rejection. But now the Dreyfus brothers *wanted* to publish their music. Although he had previously harbored resentment at what he considered heartless treatment, Dick accepted for himself and Larry.

He knew that they were defenseless in a jungle dominated by the publishers. Many publishers copyrighted material in their own names, and youngsters like Dick and Larry could get nowhere with protests.

85

However, the Dreyfus brothers were different. They were true father figures who gathered musical protégés to their huge estate at Brewster, New York, and to which they invited them for weekends and encouraged and assisted them, in many ways as well as financially.

Even aside from that, it was the right decision to let Harms publish their music. It put Dick and Larry between the sheets with the best contemporary show composers; it gave them importance and was a further indication that Dick had a superior business sense. He was determined to protect all aspects of his music, the way it had to be played, and his right to own it through the years ahead, it is hoped, into infinity.

Larry left business matters to his strong, forward-thinking partner. He had no sense of the value of money and none of Dick's painstaking interest in safeguarding their material. He scribbled his rhymes on margins of magazines and newspapers, theater programs, backs of crumpled letters, and toilet rolls. He threw away anything he decided was unusable, but luckily for him, his finished lyrics went on to the copyright bureau with Dick's music.

Business-wise beyond his years, Dick took command of this partnership. In these early stages, Larry called him the General. Later he would refer to him as Teacher or the Professor. It was as if the seven-year difference in their ages had reversed; the younger partner was the decision maker.

The association with Harms paid off almost immediately. Jack Hulbert, a versatile British performer and producer, brought his revue *By the Way* to New York. He was doing well with it, costarring with his wife, Cicely Courtneidge.

The vigorous pace of Broadway's musical comedies excited Hulbert. He wanted the score of *Lido Lady* written by Americans and asked Louis Dreyfus to help him.

The Hulberts were a gregarious couple. They enjoyed giving parties, and Dreyfus, always among those invited, brought with him various teams whose work was published under the Harms banner, recommending that Hulbert choose one of them. Consequently, there was much playing and singing at these parties, with Jack Hulbert mixing his conviviality with careful observation. He later wrote, in his autobiography,* "A couple of these young chaps were outstanding and only too pleased to make the trip."

In London, according to Hulbert, "my two American college boys did some splendid work, especially with 'Atlantic Blues,' sung delightfully by Phyllis Dare, who was the leading lady I engaged to carry the love interest, and with 'Here in My Arms' which I sang with her."

Dick and Larry, of course, were "the two American college boys." They did not see eye to eye with Hulbert on some matters, including the choice of the leading lady. Her selection dampened much of their enthusiasm for the whole venture, although Hulbert wrote, "Miss Dare was a beautiful young woman and brought charm and elegance to the show in contrast to the comedy."

Dick and Larry didn't think very much of the libretto which marked Hulbert's first venture into a book show. They felt they were connected to an impending flop and, unhappy about that, left London for home just as soon as their work was done, even before opening night.

Jack Hulbert saw things differently, and described their departure in this way:

"When the time came for our two young American friends to return home, I thanked them heartily for their excellent contributions to *Lido Lady*, expressing the genuine pleasure I had had in working with two such amiable chaps

---

The Little Woman's Always Right (London: W. H. Allen Publications, 1975).

and wished them the best of luck when they got back to America. It was one of the maddest things I ever did. I'm certain they would have worked with me on future shows had I offered them a contract. I should have signed them up then and there and I'm sure they would have played ball. Within a few years they revolutionised the world of musical comedy. I was entirely unaware that I was working with one of America's greatest composers, Richard Rodgers, and that dynamic little enthusiast, Larry Hart, one of her best lyric writers."

They were assuredly a songwriting team by then; their method of operation became routine. Such combinations always develop their own ways of working, the manifold paths that lyricists and composers travel generally sort themselves out in time and that was how it was with them. Dick first mapped the direction the tune would go.

He said, "I didn't need a piano. I didn't wake up in the night screaming for a pencil. I could write songs sitting at a desk; melodies were always coming to my mind."*

In a *New Yorker* profile, Winthrop Sargeant wrote that the Rodgers quality of composition wasn't hurt by lack of toil and suffering, that even classical music was full of composers who tossed off melodies "as easily as they tied their shoelaces." Sargeant tells an anecdote of how Rossini, "too lazy to get out of bed to retrieve a manuscript that had fallen to the floor, composed an entirely new aria instead."

Dick played his new tunes, and Larry wrote the words almost as fast as he heard the notes. To outside observers, the speed with which they worked was fascinating. Larry's rhymes were tricky and ear-compelling; he was likened to those originals, as T. S. Eliot defined them, "who, in their own day, make language new."

*In a radio interview.

But in an interview, Dick said, "Larry wouldn't work unless I was in the room. I would try to have a tune ready to play him because this was one way to seduce him. If I played him a tune that he liked, it would force him to work. But he wouldn't work without the tune."

Larry's supreme carelessness extended to many aspects of daily life, and that included questionable sartorial elegance. Dick handled that for him, too, saying, "I take him by the hand, lead him into the children's department of any good store, and have him fitted out from head to toe—a very short distance!

"At that time he didn't care how he looked or how he lived or where he slept," reported the composer, "but he certainly cared tremendously about the turn of a phrase and the mathematical exactness of a rhyme."

"How he lived" was the big problem that Larry presented to Dick. Later it would grow worse. "He was not easily controllable," was the way Dick put it. "Much of the time he was not even findable."

This didn't improve. Director Josh Logan, many years later, said, "Dick was always shaking a finger at him and rightly so, because Larry was always playing hooky. He was like a small boy who was running away—always truant. You could walk down the street with Larry, and the conversation was going great; then you would look to the right instead of the left, and suddenly Larry wasn't there. He was like Houdini—he just wasn't anywhere."

Logan would soon learn, as Dick already had and almost anyone who walked down a street with Larry would, that he had probably spotted a tobacco ship and dived into it. He always needed cigars or a light for the one between his teeth because he never carried matches. The eternal fire available in a tobacco shop drew him like a moth to a flame.

Sometimes he disappeared into a barbershop. He never

89

learned to shave himself, and he always looked as if he needed a shave because his beard grew very fast. Edith Meiser said, "Even whe n he was very young, he had a barber shave him twice a day." Sometimes the people he left went back looking for him, but he was hiding under a wet towel in a barber chair and wouldn't reveal himself. "It always seemed like a great joke to Larry," said Logan.

This was an abomination to Dick, who felt the sting of losing time on a project in work. Dick didn't go for such jokes at all; he took work much more seriously. He also differed very much from Larry in after-dark pastimes. Dick loved the company of girls, but he enjoyed secret romantic places where the rest of the world didn't intrude.

Larry's preference was for speakeasies, crowded oases on Manhattan's side streets where entrance was gained by peering hopefully through a small grille in the door, giving the customary password, "Joe sent me," until constant attendance made the face familiar. He loved these places and mingled easily with wild and colorful characters, vigorous men with their ardent women, living hard and fast and drinking that way too, loudly and blatantly showing their resentment of the Prohibition law.

Going from one speakeasy to another, "making the rounds," became almost obligatory, a part of Larry's presence in the city's night life. Some nights he and a retinue of newfound friends headed for the larger clubs, where the doors were open but the liquor was just as strong, served in tea and coffee cups.

New York's bootleggers abounded, its racketeers less visible than their Chicago contemporaries. They didn't make as many headlines, but in private they could be just as lethal. A bullet from Jack "Legs" Diamond's snub-nosed revolver in Manhattan was as fatal as one fired by Al Capone's sawed-off shotgun on the Windy City's South Side.

90

Texas Guinan welcomed Larry almost nightly with her rowdy "Hello, sucker!" He was a regular follower of the one-time film, now nightclub queen as she moved from one address to another. She constantly fought the federal men who sought to restrict her liquor sales, a running battle that required the dexterity of a cowpoke on a bucking bronco. As fast as the law padlocked her club, Texas opened a new one, sometimes right next door, for such were the eccentricities of Prohibition enforcement.

Billy Rose put "Maybe It's Me" and "Where's My Little Girl?" into the show at his Fifth Avenue Club, and Larry dropped in constantly to hear them. Listening to one's own confections is a sweet pastime to most songwriters; Dick could enjoy it, too. Larry loved it.

On Washington's Birthday, 1926, Larry and Doc Bender were in the Fifth Avenue Club and Rose suggested they go with him to a party at the Earl Carroll Theater. The invitation read "From Midnight 'Till Unconscious!" It promised to be the kind of affair that Dick, even if asked, would not have attended, but the sort of revelry that no matter what complications might have arisen, Larry wouldn't have missed.

Samuel Marx was there through the entire affair. He describes himself ("not modestly but accurately") as being the traditional cub reporter, wide-eyed, idealistic, raw, and new to the business of writing." He had replaced Mark Hellinger as one of the two who constituted the entire editorial staff of *Zit's Theatrical Weekly*. The Carroll party was one of the first assignments given him by its editor, Paul Sweinhart, and even this was done somewhat dubiously.

Sweinhart regretted losing Hellinger and relentlessly dwelled on his defection to the important New York *Daily News*. He considered that the act of a traitor and an ingrate, even though Hellinger made an immediate success on the

News and gained a well-deserved reputation as a Broadway columnist, distilling sob stories from chorus girls' tears.

The office of *Zit's* was on the second floor of the Earl Carroll Theater Building, which was convenient for covering the story. Sweinhart, on assigning it to Marx, issued a last-minute command: "Get lots of names! Names, names, names! That's what sells papers!"

"Late that night," recalls Marx, "I walked self-consciously through the stage door that had a sign painted over it, 'Through this portal pass the most beautiful girls in the world!'"

It led onto the stage where scenery from Carroll's earlier evening's production was piled against a wall and now a huge bar with food and drink stretched clear across the width of the theater. Jovial bartenders, with painted red noses, were on duty throughout the night.

Three canvas portraits hung overhead. George Washington was labeled the customary "Father of Our Country." A ferocious likeness of a Texas banker, William R. Edrington, was captioned "Daddy of Our Theater." He was the backer that made Carroll's productions possible, "an angel," in show business parlance. A third canvas, depicting Carroll, simply said "The Great Man."

Earl Carroll was an extremely important Broadway character. He was tall and slim, with longish straw-colored hair, hanging back over his high dome. He always spoke in soft, velvety tones. His annual *Vanities* featured music he wrote himself, augmented by comedians and girls. Between editions of his revue he presented dramatic plays in the theater that carried his name.

He had lofty views of himself. "You can call me the man with three shining eyes," he said and identified them as Imagination, Illusions, and Ideals. All three were on display that night.

"I set up my observation post in an aisle seat," says Marx, "and followed instructions to get lots of names. My pencil and note pad attracted everyone."

Among those present, Harry K. Thaw was making a rare public appearance since being released from prison. He had shot and killed famed architect Stanford White over showgirl Evelyn Nesbit, but escaped the maximum penalty with a plea of temporary insanity.

Peggy Hopkins Joyce was another guest, celebrated for her swift succession of marriages, divorces, and incidental affairs. Her heavily bejewled arms were covered from wrist to elbow with diamond bracelets, popularly referred to as her service stripes. She was performing in *Vanities* under a serious handicap—no talent. She was not the leader, however, in the matrimonial sweepstakes of that day and those nights. Playboy-millionaire Tommy Manville, also at the party, had that honor; he aquired eleven mates, whereas Peggy Joyce stopped at four.

Another big name was Vera, Countess Cathcart, on "shore leave" from Ellis Island, where she was incarcerated on her arrival from England. She was charged with "moral turpitude" by the Immigration Department, sufficient cause to restrain her temporarily from entering the United States. "Moral turpitude" was a brand-new phrase for feature news writers who made Countess Cathcart an overnight celebrity. Although she would charge into obscurity with the same speed, she was the cynosure of all eyes that night, as she sat regally in a stage box, haughtily viewing the proceedings through a diamond-studded lorgnette.

Everyone could see that the party was going to be a success, right from the start, a night to throw away all inhibitions.

Carroll, clad in his ever-present artist's smock, announced that there would be a Charleston contest with a beautiful chemise the grand prize. The syncopated rivalry was lively and exciting and grew more so. At its conclusion a generous donor unexpectedly supplied chemises for winner and losers alike, if they would wear them. Some thirty girls disappeared into the dressing rooms and returned in pink underthings that were now overthings. It added considerable tang to proceedings already bubbling with a champagne atmosphere.

Larry was having a marvelous time, ignoring an early call for a rehearsal for *The Girl Friend*. Unexpectedly conscientious, Doc Bender insisted that Larry leave so he'd be able to function at that time. Larry was almost childlike in his plaintive desire to stay, but Bender dragged him out, saying, "This hurts me more than it does you!"*

A photographer's booth had been placed in the lobby, curtained off to give the subjects complete intimacy. Staid industrialists and prominent show business personalities were observed rushing for it, hell-bent on acquiring tangible souvenirs of themselves with a chemise-clad cutie. To get to the booth, they had to pass the spot Marx occupied with pen and paper. None was concerned with anonymity; it was an unending chorus: "Get my name in!" Their names in the paper at such a glamorous affair would provide a status symbol, something to show the boys. "Hey, kid. Get my name in! Be sure you spell it right." That was what the editor wanted, too. Names, names, names.

It was nearly 5 A.M. when a plugged-up bathtub was moved forward from where it had been half hidden in the wings. Waiting rather vaguely near it was a tall walleyed,

*Caricaturist Al Hirschfeld is one with guarded praise for Bender and understood this action. He told us, "He was a con man, but he could get things done, and he looked upon himself as Larry's agent."

pie-eyed girl wearing one of the gift chemises. Carroll invited everyone to toast the health of "the birthday boy," his backer, William Edrington, with champagne to be poured into slippers by a naked girl.

Meanwhile, the tub was set on wooden sawhorses and Earl's two brothers, Jim and Norman, who didn't look like him or each other, filled it from casks containing an amber liquid. A stack of satin slippers was placed beside the tub. About a dozen men, led by Carroll, lined up for drinks.

The girl was helped onto a chair, her torso hidden by a bath towel as completely as if it were behind a curtain. She dropped her chemise and, still protected by the towel, stepped into the tub. She passed out a few potions to the waiting men and then passed out herself. Instantly, Carroll summoned his helpers who carried tub, girl and all, offstage.

"As I watched this," says Marx, "I suddenly remembered I was a reporter and needed to know who she was. But the girl had been hustled into a locked dressing room. Carroll's stage manager, Herman Hover, identified her for me, and the name Joyce Hawley was the last in my notebook.

"As I was leaving, I saw that Bender managed to get back to the party—alone.

"I arrived in the office late the next day and wrote the story. There had been no mention of the party in the late editions of the dailies, and editor Sweinhart had no way of knowing there was anything but a routine yarn in the offing, and I must admit I didn't either.

"I wrote a conventional piece, mentioning that Earl Carroll always enjoyed showy spectacles and this one came up to his usual standards. Knowing its illegality, I carefully skirted the mention of alcohol and merely hinted at it for the sophisticated reader to sniff between the lines.

95

"Naturally, I got all the names into it, and with each one was a delicious side item telling what the person was doing when noticed among those present.

"I concluded with this simple paragraph: 'The final moments of the party featured the rather sordid spectacle of a Greenwich Village model, Joyce Hawley, naked in a bathtub, dispensing drinks to those guests willing to partake of them!'

"My chore being done, I dropped it into the editorial drawer on the boss' desk. 'Casting pearls before Sweinhart' was how my fellow reporter Gordon Kahn liked to describe that action. Later that day, as was his custom, the editor reached casually into the drawer. My back was to him. Suddenly, a terrific explosion almost knocked me off my chair. It was a roar that shook the building.

" 'MARX!'

"He was almost incoherent. My yarn was on top of his desk and he was hitting the last paragraph so violently with his finger that it must have hurt for hours.

" 'You mean this?' he sputtered. I nodded.

" 'You saw it? You saw this yourself?'

"I nodded again. 'I certainly didn't make it up,' I replied, aggrieved.

" 'And you call yourself a reporter,' he choked. 'Get back to your desk and rewrite! I want this bathtub stuff up front. New lead! Here! Take it down!' He thought a moment, then pointed dramatically out into space. ' "The Bacchanalian revels of ancient Rome were eclipsed on Broadway Monday night when Earl Carroll sat a Greenwich Village model, stark naked, in a bathtub filled with champagne. . . " and so on. You work through the rest of the party in the same way, see? I'll let you take it from here. Oh, my God, I hope you can!'

"I pleaded that it wasn't accurate, the bathtub bit was a

fleeting moment, possibly shocking to some, amusing and perhaps revolting others—only a few approached the girl in the tub, and no one saw more than her head and shoulders. I felt that, in print, the episode would appear rougher than it was and likely cause enormous trouble for Carroll. 'One shouldn't bite the heart that feeds you,' I said virtuously.

"Granite-faced, unmoved, he pointed to my desk.

" 'Write.'

"I wrote. It was a low moment. Columns by Hellinger and Walter Winchell were on the street; both had been at the party and said nothing about it. It would be my unwanted distinction to break the scandal. Still unmoved, Sweinhart suggested that we all get down on our knees and pray that we would be out first. 'It will be the scoop of the ages,' he said. 'What a triumph for a weekly paper!'

"His hopes and my worries were both shot down. Phil Payne, managing editor of the *Daily Mirror*, had cleverly waited for his rivals to be thoroughly circulated before he came out with his last morning edition. It had the largest headlines ever seen up to that time and a front-page picture, synthetically contrived, showing a nude girl in a bathtub and a number of lascivious gents drinking out of slippers. I was scooped, making me the happiest reporter in New York.

"Then, for Carroll, all hell broke loose. New York's other tabloids, the *News* and *Graphic*, charged into the melee. Obviously chagrined at being scooped, they called on the protectors of public morality to penalize the producer and padlock his theater the same as lawbreaking nightclubs.

"*Zit's* had not yet appeared, handcuffed to its later publication date. But I was busy. Oh, was I busy! Phone calls were stacked up with the same voices that had said, 'Get my name in!' now begging, 'Keep my name out!' Too late.

"Others must have been in agony over the pictures that

97

were taken in the booth. Their publication would have undoubtedly shocked the country. But apparently sensing problems ahead, Carroll made a dash for the photo lab, seized the negatives, and destroyed them.

"The clamor in the press was so great that District Attorney Emory R. Buckner reluctantly (by his own admission) brought charges against Carroll. I was among those called before the grand jury, a disappointing witness because I couldn't testify that alcoholic beverages had been served—I didn't drink any."

But many who were selected from the voluminous list of names supplied by Zit's could and did. Carroll swore that he served only ginger ale and later said bitterly he had "lied like a gentleman to protect his guests." That they did not do the same for him, he complained, was a disillusioning jolt in humankind.

True, he might have got off scot-free if his guests had also been willing to "lie like gentlemen," because when he was sentenced to a year in the Atlanta penitentiary, it was not for offending the national sense of propriety, scandalizing the bluenoses, or even violating the Prohibition law. He was found guilty of committing perjury.*

Bender needn't have worried that Larry couldn't function

*In keeping with the intent of this book to be an anecdotal account of the days of Rodgers and Hart, Marx recalls these late happenings in connection with the Earl Carroll bathtub party:

"On a June day, twenty years later, Carroll and I lunched together in his showy theater-restaurant on Sunset Boulevard in Hollywood. We were in a private section of the club, behind a glass partition. A rapturous female audience was there to watch a radio broadcast of Queen for a Day. Carroll spoke of the ornate birthday parties he gave himself each year at his hillside home. 'You must come to my next one,' he said, in his soft, cultured voice. 'It will be a masquerade—with lots of girls.' It was as if the sounds of 1926 were echoing through the canyons of time, but two weeks later he was gone, killed in an airplane crash in the Pennsylvania hills not far from where he was born. One of his loveliest showgirls, Beryl Wallace, died with him."

after a night on the town. He could and did. He was becoming a real night prowler. The Carroll party was the last time Bender would be able to restrain him.

As for rehearsals of *The Girl Friend*, Larry was in constant attendance, busy, busy, offering assistance everywhere. Typical of old-timers, Lew Fields tried to inject some favorite but ancient jokes into the show. Larry was vociferously opposed, battling the producer on this front when Herb Fields was finding it difficult to stand up to his insistent father. Dorothy Fields recalled seeing the battle rage. "They won out," she said, "and Dad's old chestnuts went back into his files to wait for the next show, when he'd pull them out again."

Larry's energies amazed Dick, who said, "I saw him write a sparkling stanza to 'The Girl Friend' in that hot, smelly rehearsal hall when the chorus girls were pounding out time steps and there was the usual noise and confusion. In half an hour he fashioned something with so many interior rhymes, so many tricky phrases, and so many healthy chuckles in it that I just couldn't believe he could have written it so fast."

But Larry wasn't standing around waiting for praise. When the chorus lined up to dance to the show's lively songs, he jumped alongside the girls and did the routines with them!

"It was reported that after the bathtub party, two well-known stage mothers gossiped that Carroll promised Joyce Hawley one thousand dollars and a job in *Vanities*. 'But all he gave her was twenty dollars!' 'Only twenty dollars for sitting naked in a bathtub!' exclaimed the other, aghast. 'Where was her mother?'

"To reinforce my memory of the party, I went to the New York Public Library to get a copy of my story in *Zit's*. The newspaper section dredged out a faded cardboard folder which contained that historic account. When opened, it was discovered that the paper on which *Zit's* was printed was of such poor quality that it had completely disintegrated. Only a quantity of brown dust remained."

9

Nobody's Heart Stood Still

RODGERS AND HART had developed a warm relationship with Lew Fields, affection for George Ford, and a continuing romance with the Theater Guild. (The second edition of *Garrick Gaieties* didn't match the success of their first but out of it came "Mountain Greenery," a song that would be long remembered.) Love affairs between producers and creators aren't vital to smooth the rough waves that batter a new production, but they help. In the autumn of 1926 Dick and Larry signed to write a score for Florenz Ziegfeld.

The glamorous image of Ziegfeld painted by his press agents bore little resemblance to reality. The self-proclaimed "glorifier of the American girl" was a ruthless, driving, demoniacal character. To know him was to dislike him.

He was a dapper man, a fastidious dresser, adorned in blue shirts and pleated brown shoes. He sprinkled himself generously with perfume and spoke with the twang of a rusty guitar. Socially, he was the soul of courtesy. In business he was utterly lacking in a sense of fairness.

Although Ziegfeld's reputation as a showman towered over that of Earl Carroll, they followed similar paths. Ziegfeld had his annual *Follies*; Carroll had his *Vanities*. Carroll had a theater bearing his name, and Ziegfield was about to follow suit. Both presented revues and other types of musical entertainment.

Ziegfeld's greatest success was the enchanting *Sally*, about an Irish lass. He decided to follow it with *Betsy*, in which a Jewish mama would be portrayed by a *zoftig* young singer and vaudeville headliner, Belle Baker.

Dick and Larry's alliance with Ziegfeld meant a temporary break from Herb Fields, who was busily writing the libretto of *Peggy-Ann*. As often the case, their music was ready before the book. They figured quite rightly they could write the words and music for *Betsy* before *Peggy-Ann* needed their concentrated attention.

Betsy was a disaster from the start, with Ziegfeld claiming "he was talked into it," an extraordinary statement since the showman was a firm believer in his own independent greatness. Its star, Belle Baker, was unhappy during rehearsals. Her son, Herbert, then only in his teens, remembers what she did about it.

"My mother was a great friend of Irving Berlin's," he told us. "Berlin wrote 'Always' and 'What'll I Do?' for her when she was in vaudeville. Dick and Larry had one called 'This Funny World' for her to sing in *Betsy*, but she didn't like it, and the night before it was to open at the New Amsterdam Theater she called Berlin and asked him to come over to our house. She was in despair, literally weeping on his shoulder. He said he had an idea for a song, but he couldn't get a bridge for it. He played the first part; it started with two notes, then four, then five and then three. Berlin only played with one finger and kept thumping those notes over and over while I was upstairs trying to sleep. They just kept trying to find a middle for it, and all of a sudden they got it.

102

Then he kept thumping through the whole song over and over while he put words to it. Of course, you know, he called it 'Blue Skies.' Early the next morning he and my mother played it for Ziegfeld, who turned it over to an arranger, and it was ready to go by the time the curtain went up.

"In the rush to get it ready, nobody told Dick and Larry. It was an oversight, but it wasn't very nice. The audience went wild about the song, and my mother had to sing it twenty-seven times! On the twenty-eighth she went absolutely blank and forgot the lyrics. Then Berlin stood up in his seat and fed her the words. It was a great moment in the theater, but Dick and Larry didn't talk to my mother for ten years."

Larry quipped, "This is Broadway's blue period," for they had a hit song, too—"Blue Room"—in *The Girl Friend*. That was having a year's run, while *Betsy* played only thirty-nine performances. Florenz Ziegfeld was quoted as saying he was glad to see it close. Dick and Larry were, too.

Even without it, they were well represented on Broadway, for *Peggy-Ann* also opened in New York the same time that *Betsy* did, Christmas week, 1926, and that show was set to run well into 1927.

Alexander Woollcott, the droll town crier, reported that the light and imaginative variation of Cinderella was "like a chapter out of *Alice in Wonderland*," and, because echoes of the bathtub party still sounded in the press, declared, "I would fain suggest that *Peggy-Ann* is something more of Lewis Carroll than Earl."

Within a month, Dick and Larry sailed for England with a number of matters in view. Their departure from New York was a triumphant one, with plenty of parties and press notices.

They had been wrong about *Lido Lady;* Jack Hulbert had

produced a definite hit at the Gaiety Theatre, London.

Although they failed to enjoy their first trip to England, their precipitous departure at that time would strongly affect Dick's romantic fortune. Dorothy Feiner was on the ship that took them to New York, having toured Europe with her parents. They discovered they had met years before, although "she was then two months old and I was a young man of seven," Dick loved to tell. "It wasn't a case of love at first sight."

On that voyage home, he found Dorothy tall and beautiful, possessing charm and sophistication and a stunning sense of humor. Their reunion on board ship was like the sounding of a note which became an harmonious chord.

Dick and Larry went back to London to see for themselves what made *Lido Lady* a success and why, even with a standout song, the show didn't contribute more to their growing reputations. That song, "Here in My Arms," was borrowed from *Dearest Enemy*, which, because of its American flag-waving plot, would never be seen in England. Borrowing a song from one show to put into another was a bonus that not all songwriting teams could enjoy, but with their enormous output, Dick and Larry could move songs around when they needed them, hopskipping and jumping from show to show. "It's like they dipped into a grab bag," observed an envious songwriter, "and always came up with a prize."

They had other objectives in England besides catching *Lido Lady*. They wre writing a score for a Charles Cochran Revue, *One Dam Thing After Another*, scheduled for late spring. Also, Lew Fields was to stage the London production of *Peggy-Ann* in the summer. For these events, Dick and Larry rented a service flat on St. James's Street, close to the theater district. This time they settled down to what would be a highly enjoyable visit to the British capital.

It was especially attractive to Dick, and he in turn was deemed very attractive by London. Although both were asked to the social affairs that went on constantly in Mayfair, only Dick was lionized. Handsome, with gracious manners, he drew people to him, mainly girls, girls, girls.

Larry was less favored. Songwriting teams are likely to say it was ever thus—the fellow who plays the piano at parties is king, while the one who writes the words stands aside, ignored, and hopes when the curtain goes up to wear his crown.

They were true New Yorkers, a special breed who believed Manhattan was their planet. There was nothing provincial about them; they were rooted in its excitement, stimulation, and electric atmosphere. They would have been content with fame in their own hometown, but they were becoming well-known citizens of the world, even if they had no desire to conquer it.

They had a song, "Paris Is Really Divine" in *One Dam Thing After Another*, and Dick and Larry crossed the Channel to see if it really was.

The genesis of a song that has become a famous legend started there and followed Dick and Larry through constant tellings and retellings, until Dick claimed that he flinched whenever he knew it was about to be repeated. But as often happens through repetitions, stories become distorted. For this account of it, we can claim absolute veracity. Thanks to musicologist Alfred Simon, director of light music for New York's station WQXR and coauthor of *The Gershwins* and *Songs of the American Theatre*, we have the words of Rita Heiden, to describe just what happened.

"The actual lowdown on it was," said Miss Heiden, "that a friend and I were traveling in Paris, and Larry was with Dick on a trip to Europe.

" 'You cannot leave without seeing Versailles,' said Larry. We drove there during the day in a taxi, and because we were going to the opera that night, Larry was thinking ahead. He told the driver to wait.

"We spent most of the day there, and on the return trip, Larry egged the driver on to greater speeds, something unnecessary if you know Paris taxi drivers. It was a much-used road, very rough. Traffic was heavy and I tried to tell the driver, over Larry's head, to slow down.

"The two boys were sitting on the jump seats riding backwards and they didn't see what was coming. Anyway, a truck came straight at us. My friend and I in the backseats of the cab saw it loom up at a terrific speed. It missed us by inches—there weren't more than *inches* between us. After it went by, I let out a deep breath and said, 'Oh! My heart stood still!' Larry gulped, 'That's a great title for a song!' and Dick chuckled nervously, 'You son of a bitch.'*

"And that is the gospel truth. I promise you it is absolutely true, and if you knew anything about Larry, you'd know this was typical of him.

"So, sometime later, I don't know, my friend and I were in North Africa and we got a telegram saying, 'Come join us in London. We've got a show running and we're writing another one.' So we decided to go.

"They met us at the boat; we didn't fly so much then. They engaged rooms for us at a hotel. We went to the theater that night and Oscar Hammerstein was there and gave a party afterward. At something like two thirty in the morn-

*Later, in the flat on St. James's Street they shared, Dick found the note in his little black book—"my heart stood still"—so he wrote a tune for it. He called Larry in and said, "I have a tune for your title," and Larry said, "What title?" When Dick told him, Larry said, "I love it, but I never heard of it," and sat down and wrote the rest of the lyric. It took him only an hour at the most, but Dick stood over him, to make sure he wouldn't disappear.

ing, we were walking up St. James's Street, where they had their flat, and as we walked by it on the way to our hotel, Dick said, 'You've got to come upstairs.' I said, 'No, at this hour that's ridiculous,' and he said, 'There's a special reason.' We argued awhile, but then we went up. Dick took me by the hand and led me to the piano and said, 'There's the special reason.'

" 'Oh, come on, Dick, you just wrote another song,' I said. 'Is that all?'

" 'Look at the music,' he said.

"I did, and the title was 'My Heart Stood Still.' "

When they went into the theater for rehearsal of *One Dam Thing After Another*, Dick sat down to the piano in the orchestra pit and played "My Heart Stood Still" for producer Cochran and the cast, including its sparkling star, Jessie Matthews.

Jessie recalled for us: "C.B. said, 'I like it, but we've got to have a verse. Where's the verse?' "

Larry Hart, who was sitting in the stalls, his hat tipped back and with his inevitable cigar, ran down the aisle. "You want a verse! You want a verse, right?"

He pulled an envelope out of his pocket and, leaning against the proscenium, started to scribble.

"How do you like this, babe?" and he handed me the envelope. I held the envelope in my hand and read out loud an amusing little verse about hating boys in my Heathfield schooldays.

"Jolly good," said Cochran. "The song's going to suit Jessie." To my immense joy I was chosen to sing "My Heart Stood Still."*

The appealing Miss Matthews inspired Larry to dream up

*In a letter to Clayton.

an idea for another show in which she could sing their songs. The theme of eternal youth was a popular one. *Black Oxen*, by Gertrude Atherton, was an international best-seller, and *The Makropoulis Secret*, by Karel Capek, was onstage in many parts of the world.

Larry's notion was to do a play about a young girl who pretended to be many years older than she was and the romantic problems such a masquerade made for her.

Cochran wanted to do it, but Dick and Larry were too busy to write the libretto, so Benn W. Levy was engaged.

It was to be called *Ever Green*. Dick and Larry agreed to do the score, but it would take three years to reach production. They had a much more pressing matter at hand while they remained in England. It was to find an English girl to play *Peggy-Ann*.

Summer nights of 1927 were forerunners of what would later earn the British capital the designation of "Swinging London." Cafe Society, as a term, had just been invented; parties followed parties in a nightly parade. American correspondents bombarded their newspapers with accounts of these star-studded doings, putting special emphasis on their leader, the dashing Edward, Prince of Wales, who would later renounce the throne for the woman he loved. When Dick taught the prince "My Heart Stood Still," David Ewen wrote that Edward helped make the song better known and more popular than ever. It was an accidental publicity coup. One evening at the Royal Western Yacht Club in Plymouth, Edward requested bandleader Teddy Brown to play it, but Brown didn't know it, so the prince sang the entire number, verse and chorus. The band picked up the melody; the incident was widely reported in the newspapers and proved the making of the song.

Americans were playing a big part in London's social life, and many strove hard to show their importance. Britons howled with delight at an innocent remark by silent movie star Corinne Griffith when it was suggested that a group of partygoers finish off the night at the *Kit Kat,* the most popular club in London. It was sure to be packed with humanity from front door to kitchen, and the Prince of Wales, who was in the party, warned that they might not be able to get a table.

Miss Griffith indicated her husband, film producer Walter Morosco. "Of course we can," she said. "Walter knows the headwaiter!"

Blond, svelte Dorothy Dickson was a spectacular success in the role of *Sally.* "Every time I walked into a place," she told us, "the orchestra struck up my song, 'Look for the Silver Lining.'"

She was told that Dick and Larry wanted her to play *Peggy-Ann,* but she was not impressed. She said, "In fact, I was quite condescending about it."

She had a particular liking for music of Ivor Novello. They shared warm personal feelings, too. However, as one of England's brilliant homosexuals, Novello told her wryly and sweetly, "But for a kink at birth, we might have married."

Miss Dickson was introduced to two Americans at a party but didn't catch their names. "It was at the Guinnesses," she told us. "It was a brunch or lunch for about twenty, in honor of a Japanese prince visiting London. One of these charming young men sat down at the piano to play some of his own songs." She realized it was Dick Rodgers and thought to herself, "Why, he's actually quite good."

That led to her accepting the role of Peggy-Ann, which helped make her internationally known. She married Carl Hyson, who was her dancing partner, and while they were on a trip to New York, a story about them attracted the attention of corpulent Alec Woollcott, critic and columnist of the New York *World,* a celebrity of importance in his own right. Broadcasting on the radio as *The Town Crier,* he told the story twice, over the airwaves in his beguilingly gentle voice and writing under the title of "Shouts and Murmurs." He called this "A Christmas Story."

"I refer to Dorothy Dixon and Carl Hyson, a gracile couple," and went on to relate that "in a now-forgotten December" they lodged in New York's Algonquin Hotel. But they had no job in sight, and their credit was suspended. Unwilling to accept defeat, they elected to stay for the prestige of the hotel's address, where they could see and be seen. The day before Christmas they could afford only a loaf of bread and a hunk of sausage, which they smuggled into their room. However, they lacked ordinary utensils, "not a napkin, a fork, no butter, no salt, no pepper, not a dish," detailed Woollcott. But Miss Dixon had a bright idea: They would order a dish of soup and count on the hotel's custom of bringing up a full paraphernalia. It meant an outlay of fifty cents, plus tip, but they decided it was allowable for Christmas, although it strained their meager budget. Finally, the feast devoured, they haughtily phoned for the waiter to clear away the debris, and as he was doing so, Hyson, in an elaborately casual manner, asked for the check.

"No check," said the waiter.

"No check?"

"There are no checks tonight," was the reply. "This is Christmas. Guests can order anything they like, and it's on the management. You are the only couple who didn't order the whole darn menu. We decided you were on a diet. Well, good night and Merry Christmas, Mr. Hyson. Merry Christmas, Miss Dixon."

"Well, it's a good story," says Clayton, "But I became curious about it. I wrote Miss Dickson (grossly compounding

110

Woollcott's error by spelling it Dixon—as he did), and I received an answer that O. Henry might have enjoyed. Here it is.

ERIC BRAUN ENTERPRISES
Press Representatives
36, Michelham Gardens
Strawberry Hill
Twickenham, TW1, 4SB.

Miss Jan Clayton
Los Angeles,
CALIFORNIA, U.S.A.

Dear Miss Clayton,

Dorothy Dickson has asked me to reply to your letter of April 1st. and to apologize for the delay in replying; she was out of town when it arrived.

Mr. Woolcott produced a very inaccurate version of the "Algonquin" story, besides spelling D.D.'s name wrong!* What happened was: Carl Hyson had just lost 15,000 pounds in a poker game, and Dorothy, shocked, and feeling let down, accused him of having ruined her Christmas by such improvidence and said that not a penny was to be spent on seasonal fare. As a punishment she sent him out to the nearest delicatessen to buy a couple of sandwiches, which would have to serve as their Christmas dinner, pointing out that they would have to practice strict economy for a long time to come, as he had lost all their savings at one hand of poker. It wasn't until the next time they ordered a modest meal from the hotel kitchens that the chef sent up his regrets

*Note Mr. Braun's spelling Woollcott. Was that on purpose?

111

that they had not availed themselves of the traditional Christmas dinner on the house! In point of fact the lesson had its effect, and Carl never gambled seriously again. Actually, throughout their dancing career they were highly popular and well paid, so Mr. Woolcott's picture of them as "struggling," while it may have tugged at the heart strings, was another inaccuracy. Nice story though it was, I think Dorothy's is better, besides being authentic.

Best of luck with your book; D.D. sends all best wishes.

Yours sincerely,
Eric Braun,
P. R. O. for Miss Dickson

Dick and Larry returned to New York soon after Dorothy Dickson agreed to play *Peggy-Ann*, and meanwhile, Lew Fields had arranged with a British producer to restage the show in London.

Six years had passed since Fields rejected *Connecticut Yankee* when Herb, Dick and Larry proposed it. The idea was set aside, and their option, given them for free, had lapsed.

Now they needed a new project, its being agreed that it had to have the approval of all three to go forward. They met constantly but Larry was always late, if he appeared at all. "It was becoming impossible to start him working," Dick mourned.

He bounced in so late one day that Dick and Herb came down really hard on him. Petulant, he rejected all their ideas.

They wondered icily if he had some idea that they would like. Cornered, he came out with "*Connecticut Yankee!* That's what I really want to do!"

112

Hesitantly at first, then gaining momentum, he danced around, rubbing his hands together. He pointed out that it could be a breakthrough in musical comedy construction, it was the opportunity he and Dick had hoped for at their very first meeting, it offered them a chance to use their intellectual equipment, it gave Dick opportunity to write music of ye olden and modern times, Herb to have fun mingling up-to-date slang with ancient Englishe, while he could let go with unusual rhymes that would also mix the languages. The others caught his excitement and, by unanimous consent, agreed that *Connecticut Yankee* would be their next project. But the option had lapsed.

Lew Fields had never read the Twain book, but he was embarking on a weeklong ocean journey to England, so they delivered a copy to him aboard ship. Then they went back to attorney Lark to arrange a renewal of their option. Their fortunes had changed, and "flinty-eyed" Lark knew they could afford to pay. He granted the option again, but it was no longer for free—it required considerable cash.

That deal was just concluded when a cable was received from Lew Fields in London.

He still didn't like it.

Larry was thirty-three years old when he, Dick, and Herb were forming *Connecticut Yankee* into a musical comedy. Thirty-three was getting up there, but still there were no women in Larry's life, even though Frieda continually hinted her hopes that he would find a bride. Naïve as ever, she had no knowledge of his inner torment, and Larry was determined she would never know.

Unlike some of his contemporaries—Noel Coward and Ivor Novello, to name only two—who breezed through life flaunting their gay spirits, Larry agonized over his and, at soul-searing cost, hid his feelings from all but the few who

113

had to know. It was as if he lived "We have met the enemy, and it is us."

In the spring of 1927 the Harts made a typical Manhattan safari. They moved a few blocks away to a large terrace-duplex apartment at 320 Central Park West.

Parties went on there with as much zest as when they lived "uptown."

Larry was throwing these soirées. His father no longer intruded on them. There was a scandalous rumor that the O.M. was finding pleasure in quarters other than his own; the popular way of whispering it was to say, "He's wearing a path in the rug to the maid's room." That was widely said but never in the open, so there were never any denials.

The household was large, the staff continued in greater numbers than needed, and Frieda was satisfied to occupy her own quiet niche in the background. Actual running of the household was taken over by Mary Campbell or Big Mary, as she was called. A black from the Caribbean, "she cooked Jewish food better than anyone," declared Irving Eisman.

Few of those invited to the Harts were likely to forget Big Mary. She had a vinegar flavor to her opinions and never hesitated to express them. One of the much-circulated stories about her was when Josephine Baker, the St. Louis-born black who made good as a chanteuse in France, asked for "café au lait, s'il vous plaît." Big Mary looked her up and down and said, "Why don't you speak with the mouth you was born with!"

That celebrated guest could afford to overlook the remark. Miss Baker had just rejected a maharaja who offered her her wieght in diamonds if she would marry him.

The parade of dinner guests marched through the household at a quickening pace. Many of the repasts were scheduled on a spur of the moment, and some were planned, most casually. George Ross described one of these in an interview in the New York *Times:*

"If Mary is a dogmatic and dictatorial servant, people familiar with the Hart eccentricities don't blame her. For example, the question of how many she is to expect for dinner is forever a mystery to Mary up to the very last minute. A favorite tale goes that Larry telephoned Lawrence Riley, the playwright, and invited him to a meal. 'About seven?' asked Riley, who keeps a daily calendar. 'Doesn't matter,' Hart replied, 'bring as many as you like.' To Mary's disgust, Riley never showed up, nor did Larry."

Dinner was merely the takeoff point for his night's revels. Dick now began to show real impatience with his partner's ways. If they were to work at eleven in the morning, he started putting in calls for Larry at ten.

Big Mary would answer the phone and dutifully rouse him, but he would go back to sleep like a child. After a third repetition of this, Mary was inclined to turn picturesque. On the fourth call she was heard to yell heartily into the bedroom, "Mr. Larry, it's Mr. Dick again, and it's goddamn time to get the hell *up."* If Teddy had a job in a show, she allowed him to sleep one more hour. *"Workingmen* can sleep longer," she said with a glower at Larry.

Frieda put up with a lot, too, no question. The parties— oh, the parties! Larry was happiest surrounded by multitudes, or perhaps it is more to the point to say he was *not* happy when alone. To isolate his rooms from those of Max and Frieda, he installed a massive door that stifled sound. Leonard Spigelgass said it was made of steel. His parties started "from scratch" at midnight. Larry wandered among his guests, of which there were dozens, past four in the morning. Mostly, they were temporary friends who enjoyed his unlimited alcoholic largess.

Margaret Case Harriman wrote: "Whatever revelry enlivens his evening, Larry Hart generally begins work next morning while he is dressing, sorting out crumpled fragments of paper which his mother periodically removes from his coat pockets and places on his bureau. These contain lyrics written the day before or perhaps a week earlier and the probability is that Larry composed them in a traffic jam or in a Turkish bath or while waiting for an elevator somewhere."

Doc Bender had tied himself to Larry so closely that it was difficult to see one of them without the other. Debauchery was a way of life with Bender. He kept a coterie of homosexuals around. Also, his business association with Larry gave him access to many he would not have had otherwise. He had no scruples against shooting at "sitting ducks," kids who were available because they hoped for chorus jobs.

He augmented his allure by continuing to act as a theatrical agent while he pursued his calling as a dentist. He conducted auditions of new talent while patients were in his chair.* He played the piano reasonably well and on occasions left his patients to provide accompaniment to some singer in search of an agent. Larry often contended, laughingly, that piteous cries coming from the deserted person in the dentist chair were caused as much by suffering eardrums as Bender's orthodontia.

Larry was always amused by Bender's antics. He had an open invitation to Doc's nighttime parties at which orgiastic sex and perversions were chic. These festivities amused Larry, too; he gave every indication of hugely enjoying

---

*Years later Betty Comden and Adolph Green drew on their knowledge of Bender to write a similar character in their brilliant musical comedy *Bells Are Ringing*.

them, although not participating. Larry's sexual interests were very private to him.

Socially, the Rodgers and Hart families rarely mixed. The contrast between their ways of life was apparent to all, especially to themselves. Dr. Rodgers and his wife were too restrained and well bred ever to speak out their opinion of the goings-on on Central Park West. Max Hart had no such inhibitions; he described the Rodgers ménage on West End Avenue as "like Frank Campbell's Funeral Parlor, beautiful but dead!"

Dick at this time was cutting down dates with all but Dorothy Feiner, and that romance was progressing as smoothly as his music for *Connecticut Yankee*. The words and the melodies for the Twain classic were completed by the time Lew Fields returned from England. His direction of *Peggy-Ann* had been well received, he was complimented by the customarily reserved British press, and so he felt in a mellow mood toward its three creators. He consented to a reading of their libretto of *Connecticut Yankee* and hearing of the score.

This time he became excited by it, and his objections melted away.

He shelved other plans in order to concentrate on its production, scheduled for out-of-town tryouts in October, and the New York opening early in November, 1927. A partner, Lyle D. Andrews, owned the Vanderbilt Theater; this eased the problem of finding somewhere to raise the curtain.

Even before rehearsal started, Dick and Larry agreed to write a score for a play that Charles Dillingham intended to do on Broadway with the delightful madcap British comedienne, Beatrice Lillie. Miss Lillie had heard Jessie Matthews sing "My Heart Stood Still" and insisted that she introduce it in America. Dick and Larry were horrified. Jessie

117

Matthews was a romantic ingenue type, Miss Lillie was a zany clown, whom they admired enormously, but this song was certainly not right for her. They had to be devious and diplomatic, so they told her it was woven into the story of *Connecticut Yankee.* However, she was determined, and this put them in a bad spot. They weren't sure it would be in *Connecticut Yankee,* after all, because they had agreed not to unveil "My Heart Stood Still" in America until *One Dam Thing After Another* had closed, and it showed no signs of ending its run in London. They were caught between an insistent star and a persistent hit on the other side of the Atlantic. To extricate themselves, they ended up having to buy back, at considerable cost, the right to have it sung in *Connecticut Yankee.* In effect, they bought something they already owned, but it wiped out the problem encountered with Miss Lillie.

Still another song in *Connecticut Yankee* was giving them trouble, or rather, the producer was giving them trouble about another song. Lew Fields wanted to eliminate "Thou Swell," which, in the opinion of Larry and Dick, was a sure hit. For the first time they challenged the right of a producer to drop their song. Dick took the lead in the fight.

He persuaded the producer to give the song one chance—just try it on opening night. It was Dick's custom to conduct the orchestra at premieres and on that evening, November 3, 1927, he lifted the baton in the pit of the Vanderbilt Theater, and the show began. Although his back was to the audience, he later said that during the singing of the song he knew it was the hit he had been sure it would be.

And so was *Connecticut Yankee.*

The glow that suffuses artistic vindication, the exhilaration that comes with a great theatrical success and the dazzling lights of public acclaim brightened the world of Rodgers and Hart.

Dick, with his feverish desire to release the melodies still within him, felt this was the time it could all happen. Now he could realize their earliest hopes, now the way was clearing, the dreams that were born the day he met Larry could be fulfilled. There was no limit to where they could go.

The words Larry spoke that first day still had a burning effect on Dick, who was always conscious of his partner's battles against the conventional; his music and his own views reflected this. They were completely in tune as artists, and the time had come. Whatever they wanted they could achieve.

IF. . . .

If Larry would change, if he would conform, if he would be *findable*, if he would only make some effort to adjust his disorganized life to harmonize with the dependable one that Dick lived.

It was a very big IF.

10

Somebody's Heart

THE EXUBERANCE that characterized Larry's Old Man began to dwindle in the late 1920s. Recurring illnesses took a slow toll on Max Hart; then cancer struck and melted away his chubby frame.

He lingered, usually gentle, in spite of the pain. But then, suddenly, he would rant at his misfortune and shout, "Why me? Why me?" as if to make his voice reach the ears of God.

He rallied just before the end, contemplated all that he had seen and known, and was apparently satisfied. He bade the world farewell as if tossing life over his shoulder. "I haven't missed a thing," were his last words.

O.M.'s death, in contrast with his life, was quiet. Few of the notables and not-so-notables who attended his late-night parties knew that he was gone. Larry hated obituaries to the point of obsession, and even his close friends didn't know his father was dead until they heard it mentioned obliquely weeks later.

He and Frieda, affectionately entwined all their lives,

drew closer than ever after O.M.'s death. He lived at home with her; she was his date at the theater and he proudly escorted her to the proper parties to which he was invited. But after he took her home, he headed out to the profligate nights on the town that he now preferred.

It was an expression of his affection, too, for O.M. and awareness of Max's roving eye that inspired the words Larry wrote for a song he called "Life With Father." A duet for a mother and son, it was enchantingly introduced by Ray Bolger and Benay Venuta:

VERSE

HE

Won't you step into my parlor, said the spider to the
 fly.
Like him, I'm meek; that's my technique.
I learned everything from Father, who apparently
 was shy.
They thought he was a sheep, and then the wolf
 would leap. . . .

Chorus

I used to love my life with Father.
He was pure in his mind, but his actions were very
 free.
When I walked down the street with Father
He was only a mouse, but a louse in the house was
 he.
Not a stingy man, but rather he was lib'ral as could
 be.
When girls got sick of life with Father
He was generous enough, so he handed 'em down to
 me.

122

SHE
I used to love my life with Father.
He was terribly sweet, though he wasn't exactly
  bright.
A tired man all day was Father,
But he'd walk in my room like a flower in bloom at
  night.
When romance began to bother, in his eye a gleam
  I'd see.

HE
I'm glad you loved your life with Father
'Cause the gleam in his eye
Was the reason for little Me!

Harry Ruby was tall, dark, and straight-backed, with a nose that suddenly turned straight down. A songwriter-playwright with a droll sense of humor, Ruby was fanatical about baseball. He loved to don a uniform and work out with a professional team. His partner was short blond Bert Kalmar, a magic buff. Kalmar was always performing sleight-of-hand tricks; he was very good at them, but he couldn't make the bad libretto of *She's My Baby* disappear. "Pitching a show at the public is like pitching at Yankee Stadium," Ruby told Dick and Larry, who were writing the score. "You've got to have the stuff to make it to the World Series."

Dick and Larry had nothing to do with the "stuff" in the book. Kalmar, Ruby, and Guy Bolton had written *Lido Lady*, which turned out so well; Bolton's abilities were impeccable, and being the Englishman in the trio, he came in to supply flavor to the deadpan delivery of Beatrice Lillie.

But nothing worked for *She's My Baby*. Ironically for Dick and Larry, their best song in it was called "You're

123

What I Need." An unsuccessful show was precisely what they didn't need.

She's My Baby ran so briefly that Ruby explained, "We needed God in the bullpen, but He was on a road trip with another team."

Charles Dillingham, although an important producer, preferred the social background of Fifth Avenue to the showy climate of Broadway. He rarely strayed far from the conventional. *She's My Baby* fitted perfectly into that genre, and its lack of novelty accounted for its early demise. It reinforced Dick and Larry's belief that it was risky to play it safe.

But they had no choice because Lew Fields was another with little taste for experimentation. His *Present Arms* was still another exercise in the usual, about a United States marine in love with a titled English girl. Herb Fields was the author.

Busby Berkeley, who had staged the dances in *Connecticut Yankee,* was called on for a repeat in *Present Arms.* He shaped squads of boys and girls into machinelike formations, innovative and exciting. Hollywood was beckoning him, but he stayed on to play an important role onstage and sing a duet, "You Took Advantage of Me," with Joyce Barbour. Her career took off from there; she became a star in New York and London, while Berkeley's unique style of platoon dance direction carried him to the top of his profession in Hollywood.

In March, 1975, nearly a half century after *Present Arms,* Marx and Clayton called on Joyce Barbour at Denville Hall, a home for retired actors, a two-hour train ride from London. The mission: an interview with a former Rodgers and Hart star.

It is a spacious, lovely old building of gray stone with typ-

124

ical English lawns and high hedges. Several ladies, chatting near the front door, were willing to act as our reception committee. Clayton remembers that this is how the interview with Joyce Barbour went:

"We were escorted to the drawing room (it just had to be) to await her entrance. Her husband, Richard Bird, was also at the home. Dickie Bird, as he was and still is generally known, was a star of the British theater, too.

"As we waited for them to appear in the drawing room, one of the first persons we saw was an immaculately outfitted gentleman in a well-pressed but shiny tuxedo, shoes glistening, a bright-red rosebud in his lapel, and white silk muffler around his neck. Sam said he was perfect casting to grace one of those fine parlors in Mayfair, the kind that Somerset Maugham, Frederick Lonsdale, or Noel Coward wrote about when they fashioned their popular society dramas. Perhaps so, but I kept peeking around for the rabbits.

"He wore heavy makeup and sat absolutely motionless beside a telephone, as if waiting a call he was sure would come from some producing manager or casting agent, one that would beckon him back to the footlights. He was surely ready. After granting us a gracious nod, allowing us to wait with him, he remained motionless and also emotionless. I kept wishing with all my heart that the phone would ring for him, but it didn't. Well, of course, there was still time; it was only eleven in the morning!

"Joyce Barbour was pleased and bewildered; she was vague and noncommittal about Dick and Larry but remembered well and was *very* positive about the charms of Howard Dietz and George S. Kaufman. She was happy and content to be living out the last act of her life at Denville Hall. . . . with no particular memoirs of Broadway and *Present Arms.* But Dickie Bird had an entertaining story to tell: 'I was in New York when Joyce was doing that play, and during her matinee I went to a vaudeville show at the Place Theater. . . . ' "

He returned, he recalled, to pick up Joyce backstage after her show and found her in conversation with Dick and Larry and another young man. They wanted to know how he liked all the acts he had seen at the Palace.

Mr. Bird was *not* enchanted with the American variety show. He particularly disliked the headline act, "a couple of blokes," Weber and Fields, who had come out of retirement for this final stage appearance and, in Mr. Bird's opinion, would have been better advised to stay where they were. "Dreadful, really dreadful!"

Larry and Dick egged him on to a harsher and more devastating critique, and when he finally ran down, they grandly introduced him to the "other young man." He was Herb Fields, son of Lew Fields!

"And what a gentleman Herbert was," concluded Mr. Bird. "He said he never really cared for them either!"

Like *She's My Baby, Present Arms* was distinguished by its lack of originality, "a cross between *Hit the Deck* and *Good News*," summed up Brooks Atkinson of the *Times*. George Jean Nathan declared he had stopped hoping to find anything that excited him in any musical show on Broadway. Extending his bitter reflections to women and endearing him to none, he said the sex should pattern itself after these same musical comedies: "Easy to look at and if you don't hear the words it won't make any difference!"

Dick and Larry determined to make another effort to escape the humdrum. They found a novel that had "something different" to say—a theme that permitted them to have fun with sex. It was *The Son of the Grand Eunuch*, by Charles Pettit.

Larry was especially taken with it, and when they procured the stage rights, he exclaimed, "It's got balls!"

He paused, reflected, then fell apart, laughing uproariously. "My mistake! That's just what it hasn't got!"

Helen Ford was becoming known as "The Star of the Rodgers and Hart Stock Company," following *Dearest Enemy* and *Peggy-Ann*. She had been placed under contract by Lew Fields and was in Europe on her first vacation in four years when she received a cable from Herb, asking her to read the book. Although she missed the world of the theater and yearned to get to work, she cabled YOU ARE CRAZY TO DO THIS FORGET IT.

Soon after, another cable reached her, to come back at once because they had a new play ready for rehearsal. "Herb didn't say what play," she recalled. "Of course, I hurried home and then found out it was that book. They were all keen for it, including Dick. It was a long time afterward that he claimed he didn't like it. But I didn't like it from the beginning, and I told my husband I didn't want to do it.

"George said, 'Don't even *start* rehearsal. Be fair but firm. Tell them the minute you walk in that you are not going to do it.' That's what I did, but the boys were ready to go into rehearsal and sweet-talked me into going along with them, at least to open in Philadelphia while they looked for a replacement. Of course, they never found anyone. I know damned well they didn't even look for anyone. But while I didn't mind so much that Dick and Larry deceived me, what hurt me was that Herbie got me into it, because Herbie loved me."

The story was set in the time of the Tartars in Peking. The grand eunuch was raised to his enviable position in the emperor's court after an unenviable conversion—i.e., castration. Before the operation he was permitted to conceive a family, so that the honor could be passed on to his son.

127

That son was the hero of the play, who, in this case, revealed a revolutionary distaste for the advantages he was about to inherit. Married to the lovely Chee-Chee, he preferred to continue his marital course without the mutilation his eminence required.*

In spite of her constant appearances in their plays, Miss Ford's skirmishes with Dick didn't slow down one bit. As far as she was concerned, it was a battle to the cadenza, to get her keys raised so that her lower voice could still project.

The pitch of one skirmish was raised even if the keys hadn't been, to the point that Dick came to the theater before a matinee and said, "Helen, I stayed up most of the night changing your keys and reorchestrating. . . . Now will you be happy?"

"Of course I was happy to hear that," related Helen, "but I have perfect pitch, so when we got to that number I knew not one damn note had been changed—I was still growling in my lower voice. After the performance Dick came to my dressing room and actually asked me how I liked it. I was so mad I sputtered. . . . I couldn't get any words out so I just threw my hairbrush at him. Hard! And hit him! I wasn't a bit sorry.

"Then Dick wrote a coloratura song for me in *Chee-Chee* because he thought I adored high notes. It had lots of those, but it didn't fit into the show at all. No, Dick and I didn't get along too well."

The reviewers were generally unkind to *Chee-Chee*.

Charles Brackett set the key for their remarks in his *New*

---

*Some of the fun in the show was supposed to come from hearing a baritone turn into a falsetto tenor. A wit suggested the score be drawn from Tchaikovsky's *Nutcracker Suite*.

Yorker magazine notice: "The joke of the theme has become pretty tedious before the curtain is up ten minutes, and is practically intolerable before the evening is over."

A visiting English critic, St. John Ervine, wrote in the New York *World*, "Nasty! Nasty! I did not believe that any act could possibly be duller than the first—until I saw the second!"

The opinions of the people who were involved with *Chee-Chee* were also at variance.

Phil Leavitt said that his father invested in it. "I read the book, Dorothy Fields read it and loved it, and I loved it. It was a beautiful show; it would be beautiful today; it was very much ahead of its time." But Helen Ford still asserts, "It was a mistake right from the beginning."

Unusual invention had gone into it; the score was fitted into the background more than ordinary musical comedy music. Only one song survived, "Moon of My Delight," for which countless auditioning singers are grateful. Although Dick and Larry still wished mightily to push into a daring world, *Chee-Chee* was not the vehicle for it.

While it seemed that musical comedy audiences of 1928 weren't ready to accept the unconventional, possibly there was another reason. The theme and details of *Chee-Chee's* plot weren't easily understood by theatergoers of that day. Many reacted like one of the Leavitt family's friends, a polite lady who laughed appreciatively and applauded enthusiastically but, when the curtain came down, asked "What *is* a eunuch?"

It ran less than a month, the shortest life of any of Dick and Larry's professional shows.

11

Ten Cents—or Less—a Dance

HISTORICALLY, 1929 was the beginning of the end of the long era of peace, prohibition, and prosperity. In March of that year Dick and Larry were represented on Broadway by *Spring Is Here*. The libretto was by Owen Davis, whose prolific works dotted the theatrical scene with comedies, dramas, and musicals. It was not one of his auspicious items.*

It had little impact on the critics. The *Herald Tribune*'s Arthur Ruhl branded Larry's lyrics "Of the usual Broadway pattern, 'You need romance, someone in pants' being characteristic." George Jean Nathan, never a Rodgers fan, took a subtle swipe with "his score is the poorest he has turned out in a long time."

Nathan was wrong.

Dick created beautiful, romantic songs for the play,

---

*Dick and Larry wrote two songs titled "Spring Is Here." The popular one is from *I Married an Angel*.

among them "Yours Sincerely," "Why Can't I?" and "With a Song in My Heart." Such tenderness wasn't surprising, for he and Dorothy Feiner were deeply in love.

Larry's contributions bared some of his inner yearnings, especially his preoccupation with unrequited love. His long-suppressed conflicts were mounting within him. What Edith Meiser called "his ambivalence" was starting to torture him horribly. He could hide it under his façade of gaiety, but Dick knew it, could see it, and was worried by it.

Dick had concerns of his own, but of a different nature. And, of course, relating to music. He knew he couldn't equal George Gershwin's dexterity at the piano or Oscar Levant's technique.

His competency at the keyboard was certainly good enough to please listeners. He played well enough for them, but the wish for perfection and failure to attain it irked him. He would have loved Gershwin's virtuoso ability.

George's brother, Ira, remembers Dick standing beside a piano, looking directly at George's hands, and saying, "I'd give my right arm to play like that!"

"It was an expression he used frequently to indicate he wanted something, and I heard him say it about George's playing many times. I've never really been sure if he meant it humorously or not."

Listeners might not be transported to heights by Dick's playing, but they were certainly impressed, knowing he had created the melodies. His playing was on a par with Kern and Romberg. He was better than Irving Berlin, although it was not true, as widely believed, that Berlin played with only one finger. "He used them all," reported Sidney Skolsky, "badly!"

Actually, Berlin played only in the key of F sharp and wisely made life simpler for himself by having a keyboard made which mechanically transposed every key to F sharp.

Dick had many rivals, in addition to Kern, Romberg, and Berlin. Cole Porter was back from Europe and rising rapidly on Broadway. Brilliant, neurotic Vincent Youmans was being hailed as "the composer's composer," drawing forth dynamic sounds from melodies derived from single notes. All were on their way to earning fortunes with their melodic inventions.

Dick was intrigued with Arnold Schoenberg's cautiously propounded theory of a twelve-note serial system of composing, instead of the standard eight, known to musicians as the "tone row." Dick told friends that it could open up new channels for songs he hoped to write, and he would love to try it. But he never did. Schoenberg, often called "the archmodernist," went only a short distance forward, and it never gained popularity. Phil Leavitt admired Dick's vision of his own limitations.

A devotee of ballet and classical music, Leavitt is also an observer of the contemporary field of musical advancement. He believed Gershwin to be the best of the Broadway composers, and in fact, many learned students of that scene consider Gershwin superior to Schoenberg. In 1929 it was known that he was working on an American opera, based on the novel *Porgy* by Dorothy and DuBose Heyward.

"In spite of the fact that Gershwin's music may well live for a longer period, and it probably will, Dick was right," says Leavitt. "He did what he wanted to do, and that, after all, is the essence of life."

The perfectionist in Dick was a tangible thing. It was and always would be important to him that his music be played correctly. He was inflexible about that.

His music was arranged by Robert Russell Bennett, a master at his calling. Bennett's services were in demand from the entire elite corps of Broadway musical comedy composers, especially when the autumn months ap-

133

proached, for their shows all aimed for September and October, the traditional start of the theatrical season. Bennett didn't exactly share the sense of excitement that punctuated Dick and Larry's view of those nights when a solid phalanx of new offerings lit up the sky over Broadway.

"Orchestrating is the loneliest and most miserable thing in the world," he commented. "There's never enough time to finish the orchestrations of a musical comedy. Dick, at least, makes it easier for me. First, he improvises. He sits down and writes a piano sketch, a complete piece of music, harmonies and all. He'll say 'I hear a little strings here. . . .' That's the extent of it. Kern could do this but didn't. Berlin didn't even write the notes."

The Rodgers and Hart offering in the fall of 1929 was *Heads Up!* Originally called *Me for You*, it was a disappointment in its tryout; it closed for repairs. Dick and Larry were not involved in the rescue effort—no new lyrics needed to be rewritten; no additional melodies composed. Two of their songs were thrown out immediately.

They still had to endure producers who cut their songs, sometimes rightly but more through personal dislike or for petty reasons, faulty intuition, or ignorance. Dick and Larry had to accept these rejections, but it was a kick in their creative pride. And it hurt.

Knowing their protests would be overruled, these amputations instilled strong feelings in Dick that someday they should produce their own shows and maintain control over songs that were eliminated. Although only twenty-seven, he could see himself correctly: He had attained stature as a composer; he had power in his grasp. It was a heady feeling, one that served to excuse the strong and often ruthless attitude he would assume—when he was ready to seize the chance.

That ambition to produce his own shows was born out of

frustrating experiences with Lew Fields and the worst of all, Florenz Ziegfeld.

The stock market began to sag and finally sank with a rush just before the November premiere of *Heads Up!* The world was plunged into the Great Depression. Money for risk ventures, personified by show business, dried up. Dick's producing ambitions had to be indefinitely postponed.

Heads Up! achieved a fair run on Broadway after undergoing a vigorous doctoring job. The London production fared less well; it closed in two weeks, as could have been predictable since its plot dealt with bootleggers and Prohibition. They were subjects of little interest among people who couldn't understand any law that was a denial of the right to quaff a pint or, if one chose, a barrel.

Reluctantly, Dick and Larry agreed to write for Ziegfeld again. Their experience with *Betsy* had been soul-searing, but they were optimistic enough to hope the second time would be better.

Simple Simon was made to order for zany Ed Wynn, who coauthored the book with Guy Bolton. But Ziegfeld didn't like anything Dick and Larry wrote—from the opening note. He said their songs were "too highbrow," and threw out six of them.

"Why can't you fellows write an ordinary song?" he complained. "Why are you always so fancy-shmanzy?" They went away furious and came back the same day with "Ten Cents a Dance," the hit of the show.

Simple Simon ran four times longer than *Betsy*, but that brought little joy to Ziegfeld. He was not one to display gratitude to others. When a play was successful, it was all his doing; when it failed, it was entirely the fault of others associated with it.

Later, with wry comments spiked with a dash of bitters,

Dick and Larry could take their own chops at Ziegfeld. "His talent for self-congratulation was a marvel," reported Dick, "and the envy of his fellow egomaniacs." Larry said, "Flo's definition of a non-sequitur is *anything* that doesn't relate to him."

Bouncy Bernard Sobel masterminded the producer's public relations for some years, an unrewarding job. A typical example of Sobel's problems was the time he worked valiantly to secure newspaper headlines revealing that Ziegfeld was sailing for Europe. Although it was unlikely to quicken the pulse of readers, Sobel managed it and then received a cablegram from shipboard THANKS FOR SNEAKING ME OUT OF THE COUNTRY!

Ziegfeld seemed to have a natural antipathy toward respecting obligations. (After his death it was discovered he owed hundreds of dollars to a newsboy who peddled papers outside the New Amsterdam Theater.) He withheld royalties that were due Dick and Larry. Long before he paid up, the collaborators agreed they would never write for him again.

Dick and Dorothy were married on March 5, 1930, in her parents' Park Avenue apartment. The ceremony was performed by New York's chief rabbi, Stephen S. Wise, who held an exalted position in American Jewry. He was seated once in the middle of a family group at a dinner party.

"You should be at the head of the table," said a guest.

"Wherever I sit is the head of the table," said the rabbi.

The end of bachelorhood and his entrance into matrimony fitted Dick's image and the ordained pattern of his life. It was right for him, it was part of the American dream, and he was cast in a starring role: He had youth, success, fame and a beautiful girl who truly loved him and gave him encouragement and inspiration.

Larry Hart was down at the other end, the American

nightmare. There was no woman in his life, none on the horizon. He was unable to shake the portrait he had of himself as dwarfish and misshapen. His personal disorganization leaned heavily toward the erratic. He spent money recklessly and without regard to how, where, and on whom. He gave lavish gifts, purchased from Tiffany or Cartier, to new acquaintances, many of whom disappeared out of his life with the same suddenness that they appeared. He was "taken" by Doc Bender mercilessly, according to almost everyone who knew them. It wasn't unusual for Larry to hand "Doc" a $100 bill and send him out for sandwiches for an impromptu party. Bender would return with $20 or $30 worth of food, but give no accounting. "Look," Larry would say, with a grin, "no change!" Bender joined in the mirth but never gave him back any money.

Belatedly, Larry became aware of fashions and style. But it didn't matter that he now had his linens, handkerchiefs, even his underwear made to order and by hand. "Dressed from head to toe in faultless bad taste" was how the suave Armenian novelist Michael Arlen described Larry when they met at Louie Bergin's Tavern on Forty-fifth Street. Bergin's, Sardi's, and Tony's speakeasy constituted the midtown circuit that Larry frequented almost daily, moving from one to the other, taking on a subtle alcoholic load as he went. He could hold his liquor well at this time; gregarious friends encouraged him to drink up, up, and up.

Charley MacArthur, the stunningly attractive newspaperman turned playwright, also an habitué of Manhattan's speakeasies, observed Larry in a new, dazzling outfit and quipped, "Sartorially, you leave practically everything to be desired." But MacArthur loved Larry.

Although Larry was deeply attached to his family, he was never able to assume his father's place. The widowed Frieda mothered him and Teddy.

Teddy was struggling with his acting career, the recipient

of more promises than jobs, usually from producers seeking favors from Larry. When the promises were kept, Teddy was given small parts and isolated lines of dialogue. Sandy Sturges, widow of movie director Preston Sturges, said, "Teddy could never remember what a director told him to do but he could recall the script perfectly. Most scripts said, 'Front and center,' so when Teddy had to say a line he would move up front and center, say the words, and go back to his former position, but because of his round clownlike face, appealing smile, big eyes, and little-boy size, audiences loved him!"

Larry promised Teddy he would create an outstanding role for him in one of their future shows. But it had to wait, for Dick and Dorothy were in Italy on their honeymoon and Larry was to rendezvous with them in London where *Ever Green* was reported ready at last.

The three of them shared a flat at York Terrace, a tranquil neighborhood near Regent's Park and not far from Madame Tussaud's Wax Museum and the Royal Academy of Music.

Knowing Larry's forgetful ways, Dick reminded him that certain aspects of London life differed greatly from those of New York. Among them was the tendency of the English to use water sparingly. Larry found that inconsistent, for it was falling from the heavens continuously, but he promised to conform to local custom, no matter how quaint.

Not long after that, however, he turned on the taps in the bathtub and then forgot and left his section of the apartment unattended. The running water damaged the apartments below and almost flooded York Terrace. The episode did little to improve British-American relations.

Larry and Dick were impatient with the slow pace of London production, especially reflected in producer Cochran's attitude, when he decided to put back the presentation of *Ever Green* until later in the year. The postponement was not unhappily received, for Dorothy was pregnant and she and Dick wanted their child born in America.

That trip to England proved pleasant but unprofitable. Profligate as ever, Larry needed money, while Dick felt that fatherhood demanded a higher income. In depression-ridden 1930, with the full impact of the Wall Street crash revealed, only one place on the map of the United States appeared to be feeling no pain: Hollywood.

Out-of-work men and problem-laden women were finding escape in the movie theaters, where rays of light from projection machines dazzled the populace, offering forgetfulness from reality.

"The Jazz Age" had ended. The new climate of depression was, of course, very different, but financial travail, engulfing the world, seemed more bearable with music in the background. Screen entertainment provided it. Leaving Dorothy in New York, Rodgers and Hart headed for the movie capital with a contract and high hopes.

In a requiem to "The Jazz Age" critic-columnist Heywood Broun wrote a remembered and repeatable quote: "It was wicked and monstrous and silly. Unfortunately, I had a good time."

12

Dancing off the Ceiling

THEY HAD CONTRACTED to do three films for First National, a studio operated by Sam, Jack, and Harry Warner. The brothers had introduced Vitaphone, ending the long era of silent movies. They prospered mightily by their jump into the new medium.

Hollywood was jumping, too—making movies in daylight and "making whoopee," as a popular expression went, after dark. Parties were big, swank, opulent, and pretentious. Dour Oscar Levant warned Larry that "under the tinsel of Hollywood lies the real tinsel." Levant, too, had transferred his musical talents to Hollywood but didn't share anyone's optimism about filmland. When a young actress told Levant she had just been given a long-term studio contract, he asked, "What did you do, break a mirror?"

Dick and Larry would have reason to remember Levant's bleak utterance. Although they were teamed with Herb Fields, their first movie, *The Hot Heiress*, was a slight, banal concoction. Most of the people involved in the making

141

of it came from nonmusical backgrounds, violating the first law of entertainment that musicals should be made by people who *know* music!

But they had no say in production dictates, and while others did the preparatory work, they joined in the gaiety that whirled dizzily around them.

They wrote four songs for *The Hot Heiress*, a meager output for them, but with their usual rapidity, which disconcerted the Warner brothers, who suggested they take more time. Moreover, their songs were judged too sophisticated, which was similar to Ziegfeld's complaint, and this irked them. Sophistication in both words and music was indeed their aim.

The director assigned to *Hot Heiress*, Clarence Badger, was more adept at guiding melodrama than a musical film. The title role went to Ona Munson, a pretty girl with limited experience. Ben Lyon, a personable young New York actor, drew the lead opposite her.

In those new times when the movies were first capturing sound, cameramen filmed from inside a huge windowed box. Such encasement was to prevent the noise of camera mechanism intruding on the spoken dialogue and the songs sung on the set. These primitive methods and their own inexperience in the medium made Dick and Larry understandably edgy.

Ben Lyon told us, "Ona Munson and I were sitting near a live microphone that fed into the booth when we saw Dick and Larry climb inside to explore. The mike was there so the director could talk to the cameraman. Seeing an opportunity to play a joke, Ona and I started a dialogue that went like this: 'How do you like those two guys, Rodgers and Hart, coming out here and thinking they can write music for our movies?' Ona caught on, and the two of us leveled several jibes at them. Of course, they were hearing every word we said.

"Out of the corner of my eye I could see Dick and Larry, inside that box, reacting to this.

"We piled it on until suddenly, Dick bounced out absolutely livid, with Larry right behind him. Nothing we could say would convince them that it was all meant in fun. Dick was mad as hell, and Larry, who was a much sweeter guy, wasn't exactly sure we were telling the truth either. Larry didn't talk to me for weeks, and Dick has hardly spoken to me since."

The Hot Heiress hardly made a ripple in the flowing stream of movie musicals, at a time when such films had enormous novelty and the public had an insatiable appetite for them.*

It was an unpleasant experience, and while Dick and Larry found the medium intriguing, they had no chance to show what they could really do with it. But the zaniness of Hollywood opened up to them the delicious possibility of a stage musical. Herb Fields was at work on one when word came from London that *Ever Green* was ready at last.

Dorothy Rodgers finally braved the four-day train trip to California despite her imminent motherhood. But on her arrival she was told to turn right around and go back to New York, for Dick and Larry were sailing for England.

Ever Green was to be tried out in Glasgow. C. B. Cochran was excited by Larry's marvelous idea that the play's many changes of scenery would be enhanced by use of a revolving stage. He ordered a giant carousellike mechanism from Germany, stipulating it had to be in Glasgow *two weeks* before opening night.

It wasn't. No one knew where it was. Frenzied cables passed back and forth. Suspense mounted because the scenery, especially designed for the device, had to be installed

*The two remaining films they were to write for First National were canceled by mutual consent.

on it. Finally, it arrived at the theater *three days* before the curtain was to go up.

A new Cochran show was an event, important enough for the London *Daily Mail* to assign its critic, Harold Conway, to cover it. He met Dick and Larry for the first time and told us what happened then:

"When that huge mechanism from Germany was installed in the King's Theatre in Glasgow, it didn't work right, and panic descended on the entire company. It looked like it couldn't be used at all, which meant interminable stage waits would disrupt the flow of the plot. To cover these, Larry had to add new lines; everybody had to spend hours learning them; the cast slept in the seats of the theater and on the floor. It was October and freezing. Cochran caught cold, and so did I. Mine was worse. I came down with bronchitis and was put in hospital.

"To be hospitalized when you're on an assignment is a rough go, but what happened, well, I'm still emotional when I talk about how Larry Hart devoted himself to me, a stranger. He came to the hospital and took a room near me; then he sent off my dispatches to London for me. Somehow, he managed to do some of his own work while looking after me. A marvelous man, I never knew anyone like him."

Jessie Matthews, the captivating nymph who was the inspiration for Larry's idea, scored sensationally with "Dancing on the Ceiling," the song that Ziegfeld had jettisoned from *Simple Simon*.

The downs and ups of Rodgers and Hart's professional experiences were never better illustrated than by their success with *Ever Green*, so close after the uninspiring *Hot Heiress*.

C. B. Cochran had the ability to stage musical shows with all the know-how that early moviemakers lacked. Despite an old show business adage, "Never tamper with success," British film producers tampered hard and often when they translated *Ever Green* to their medium. Dick and Larry were not involved with the movie; they had returned to New York because Dick was anxious to rejoin his pregnant wife.

Even the spaced-out title was contracted to one word, *Evergreen*, and only three songs from the play remained in it. A saccharine ditty, "When You've Got a Little Springtime in Your Heart," was interpolated and plugged *ad nauseam* throughout. The plot of the movie was radically changed from that of the play. Miss Matthews reenacted the leading role of Harriet Green, the girl who in the film pretended to be her own mother (in the stage version, she pretended to be her own grandmother), with the play's locale, Paris, switched to London.

Jessie Matthews had things to say about both productions, as well as some frank observations about Dick Rodgers. Miss Clayton, observing that the star had written a book of her own, wrote her about it.

"Thank you for your letter," replied Miss Matthews. "The name of my book is called *Over My Shoulder*, taken from the song in the film *Evergreen*. It was written by darling Harry Woods, who had only one hand, the other one was a stump, but boy! could he write and play songs. I think he also wrote the classic song from the *Evergreen* film, 'When You've Got a Little Springtime in Your Heart.' Perhaps you can check.*

"I can tell you one nice story of the film, which was directed by Victor Saville, who was very brilliant but very temperamental

"I was standing in front of the camera, wrapped very closely from the neck downwards to my ankles in gold

---

* She's right; he did.

lame to show off the figure of Harriet Green, when on the set came the dress designer and an argument started between him and Victor.

"The next thing I saw and heard, the designer was screaming at Victor and tearing up all his sketches and yelling, 'If your film is as good as these are, you'll have a bloody good film!' Victor was yelling back, 'They are not the designs I passed, and I'm going to the head office to get you the sack!' Meanwhile, I am still standing under the hot lights, unable to even hobble one foot.

"About fifteen minutes went by, and Victor came back, picked up the pieces, and put them onto a table. Then he said, 'You were present when we looked and decided on the designs. Look at them!' and he brought the table across to me to look at and said, 'Well?' I said, 'What do you want me to say?' and he said, 'The truth, of course,' to which I replied, 'You did pass them; the only difference is that he's colored them!'

"Victor then started *yelling* and went behind the camera, saying, 'Even my leading lady is against me now!' I yelled back, 'If you've anything to say to me, say it to my face, and I'd walk off your set, too, but I can't bloody well move!'

"Victor picked me up in his arms and laid me on a couch and said, 'Get her some tea, quickly!' He looked at me whilst I was drinking my tea, and I said, 'You realize you've got to go say you're sorry and get that boy his job back.'

" 'Okay,' said Victor. 'You win.'

"The boys on the gantry applauded after Victor left the set, and one guy yelled down, 'The taming of the shrew in reverse, eh, Jessie? Good girl, keep up the good work.' Victor had an unfortunate manner when talking to anybody who was not an artiste, but the very good sense to understand that to get what he wanted was the gentle approach,

146

and it worked every time, especially with me. Bullying tactics or rudeness in any form just makes me *freeze*, and a curtain comes down, and they *get just nothing from me!* *It's not being obstinate,* it was my early training from great impresarios like C. B.* and André Charlot that had laid down for me gentle handling, and giving me always a free hand to create before he put his word in.

"I'm sorry to say that the first toughness that crept in was when Richard Rodgers was helping in producing the stage show of *Ever Green* when I was bullied to distraction by Rodgers, Benn Levy, and my darling C. B. Cochran.

"Ada May was doing her damnedest to get the part of Harriet Green away from me, and I was going through the unpleasant publicity of my forthcoming marriage to Sonnie Hale. He had just been divorced and Evelyn Laye, his wife, cited me.†

"C.B. had become enamored of Ada May, so he sided with her and tried to make the divorce problems an excuse to take me out of the show. He said he wanted *either* Sonnie or me, but I stuck to my contract and said we rise or fall together. It was Ada May at the back of it, because C.B. may have been many things to many people but loyalty was one of his best traits. He was besotted by her, and she sat in at every rehearsal. Of course, she didn't get the part, and Sonnie and I did the show together."

"It's strange that Dick Rodgers didn't understand artistes.

*Although most of the girls called Cochran "C. B." or "Charley," others referred to him with a more affectionate nickname. Of them, the producer's wife told a friend, "Whenever I hear a girl call my husband Cocky, I know she has been to bed with him."

†I am happy to report that Miss Matthews, in her letters, has never called him anything but C. B.—CLAYTON

"Anyway, a nice story is that he sent Victor Saville a wire about the film. It read: "I wish we had thought of the story.'"*

Mary, daughter of Richard and Dorothy Rodgers, arrived in the world on January 11, 1931. One week later a very young and pretty little girl from Valley City, North Dakota, "arrived" on Broadway. Harriet Lake† made her stage debut in *America's Sweetheart*, the comedy they conceived in Hollywood. "All I remember of Larry Hart is a little short man who used to be there," Miss Lake said. "I remember Richard Rodgers, who scared me to death. He was a very stern man, very, very stern.

"I auditioned for *America's Sweetheart*, but it seems that Richard Rodgers didn't want me. It was Larry Schwab who absolutely insisted that I be in the play. Laurence Schwab and Frank Mandel were the producers.

"Actually, I can't speak with any authority about Rodgers and Hart because I was so young and under my mother's thumb. Everything was her decision, and all I did at the au-

*In 1962 Jessie Matthews was in New York. She wrote us, "I told my American brother-in-law that I'd love to see Dick Rodgers, and he said, 'Over here, kid, we just pick up the phone and ring there.' This I did, and I arranged to see Dick in his office. He greeted me very warmly outside his office, and then he invited me in. I said, 'Do you mind if my brother-in-law comes in, too?' and, to my horror, he said, 'Well, it's all according to what you *want*.' I replied, 'I don't want anything, I've just called to see you and to talk of old times, if you've the time to spare.' Then he was very effusive and charming, and things were going along fine until I mentioned the name of Larry Hart. Then Dick leaped from his chair and started banging on everything that was in his way and said, 'Oh, God!' 'What have I said that's wrong?' and he said, 'Nothing, nothing. I'm so goddamned furious that even after all these years he has the power to still irritate me to death!' Strange, Jan, isn't it?"

†Miss Lake went to Hollywood after *America's Sweetheart*, and movie tycoon Harry Cohn changed her name to Ann Sothern.

dition was sing a song, and Larry Schwab thought I'd be divine in the part, and I got it.

"I played a country bumpkin kid, which I looked exactly like, who comes to Hollywood and becomes a big star. The only thing I can remember about the whole play is that in the first act they pushed me into a fountain, and I always had a wet fanny every night. How funny that's all I can remember about my first show!"

Time magazine called Miss Lake "a lovely synthesis, one part Ginger Rogers, one part Ethel Merman." George Jean Nathan, whose choice of Rodgers and Hart hits continued to give him a batting average of zero, favored "Sweet Geraldine" and "Innocent Chorus Girls of Yesterday." Both passed swiftly into oblivion. He took no notice of the song that registered the biggest hit, "I've Got Five Dollars."

America's Sweetheart was the last collaboration of Rodgers, Hart, and Herb Fields. Although the playwright would continue his career in Hollywood and New York, with many superb hit shows to his credit, the mythical character Herbert Richard Lorenz passed into history, when, in 1932, Dick and Larry gave Hollywood a second chance.

And vice versa.

13

Love Me Tonight and Thereafter

THE SECOND Hollywood experience began auspiciously. Although they had a contract for one picture only, it would star Maurice Chevalier and comely, red-haired prima donna Jeanette MacDonald. She had switched to a movie career after some incredibly inept Shubert musical comedies. One of her featured roles on Broadway was in a show called *Boom Boom*.

Making *Love Me Tonight* at Paramount was exciting and innovative. Dick worked closely with director Rouben Mamoulian, a knowledgeable music lover who, unlike more egotistical members of the movie-director breed, welcomed the composer's notions. Until then, the camera and microphone worked simultaneously, in a method known as direct recording. Its disadvantages were that it anchored singers close to the mike, and they were unable to make natural moves.

In *Love Me Tonight*, Mamoulian, in combination with Dick, perfected a system of prerecording songs which allowed singers to mouth the words and pretend they were singing as they were being photographed. This has since become standard. With the sound track off their minds, singers happily concentrated on the camera and how they looked, especially in a love duet nose to nose, unafraid of facial distortion, open mouth, or broken eardrums.

Dick was always sensitive to singers and singing, musicians and his music. He felt his tunes were lost when they were jazzed up. He was unhappy with variations by soloists or bands. Mamoulian was another who adhered strictly to the called-for tempo.*

Jan Clayton was directed by Mamoulian when she created the leading role of Julie in the original Broadway production of *Carousel*, and this is her description of what it was like to work with him:

"He was called Mamoo irreverently only by those who revered him. His direction is a very personal thing because to him each member of the cast is an individual performer. He handles large groups magnificently because he acknowledges no 'chorus' per se. Each performer, whose name he knows early on, is directed specifically to have a personality and purpose all his own. It's beautiful to watch the growth.

"Mamoo directs by suggestive monologue, too. That is to say, in the middle of rehearsal he may choose to stop, call a halt to everything while he tells a seemingly rambling story, but which will illustrate an important point. He is a consummate teller of tales, with that beautiful articulateness nicely garnished with a Continental accent. His illustrator of points, more often than not, is Michelangelo, whom he admires enormously.

"He has with him at all times a tiny gold whistle, used

---

*One of Dick's most delicate melodies is "Lover," from the score of *Love Me Tonight*. Peggy Lee, whose frenetic recording of that song landed on the hit parade, foolishly asked Dick how he liked it. Icily, he replied, "It's a waltz, you know."

discriminately, given him by Greta Garbo (that romance only mysteriously and gentlemanly hinted at), and a long, slender cigar. The cigar is with him so much that he eschews the conventional ashtray in favor of a water bucket. (I had the bucket painted gold. Two carats.)

"Ferenc Molnar was in New York during the rehearsal of *Carousel*, and it was with great excitement, not to say trepidation, we learned the author of *Liliom* (on which *Carousel* was based) was coming to our first run-through.* Actually, as a cast, I must admit we were completely insensitive to any importance and significance of Mr. Molnar's seeing his play adapted to music or how it could affect the Theater Guild, Rodgers and Hammerstein, Agnes DeMille, and Mamoo. No, we just wanted to make our entrances, try to remember a third of what they had all taught us, and bump into each other as little as possible.

"Mamoo interrupted us as infrequently as possible, but he was, of necessity, in evidence, a whistle here and there. I believe it was a three-cigar rehearsal, and the bucket was tripped over only once.

"At the end of a most successful run-through, Mr. Molnar courteously and enthusiastically complimented the guild, Miss DeMille's dances, Mr. Rodgers' beautiful music, Mr. Hammerstein's book and lyrics, then turned to our director and said, '*But*, Mr. Mamoulian'—a visible sagging from him—'*but*, Mr. Mamoulian, you smoke too much!'"

Love Me Tonight made Hollywood much more livable to Dick and Larry. They settled down to more movie work, taking another assignment from Paramount, to write songs for George M. Cohan's first talkie, *The Phantom President*.

The Rodgers family of husband, wife, and infant daughter

*It was a coup that Molnar chose Rodgers when he had turned down Puccini.

153

rented a Beverly Hills house, and Larry moved in with them. Dorothy, chic and intelligent, had a sharp wit and superb poise; she fitted perfectly into her role as wife to one of America's newly successful composers.

Dick's bachelor life had been romantic and varied, but his nature was such that he welcomed the pleasurable discipline that marriage brought to him. It made for a mighty contrast and underlined the dissimilarity of his life-style with that of his writing partner. Dorothy became Larry's friend; he adored her and she tried to protect him from himself and others, but she, too, was limited by his odd hours and even odder acquaintances.

The motion picture colony still included unusual characters who had flocked there in the gold rush that followed the invasion of sound. Hollywood was a happy hunting ground then, making use of all sorts of ill-fitted people as it sought to conquer the technique of talk. In the early thirties, when Dick and Larry returned, that lunatic fringe had been replaced by legitimate experts on voice, articulation, noise, and decibels. However, some kooks and weirdos, out of work and with time on their hands, remained, and Larry had an uncanny knack of meeting up with them.

"Larry was a fey creature," observed Rouben Mamoulian. "He was out of this world. I have never seen such a combination of innocence, true innocence, that could produce such sophistication of lyric."

Frieda came west to keep house for him, and rented a mansion on North Bedford Drive in Beverly Hills, not far from where the Rodgerses lived.

It was a large and stately house, typical of the opulence of the neighborhood. The street was quiet and serene until Larry moved in. His companions arrived noisily and at outlandish hours.

"Don't you *ever* mind these hordes descending on you?" Dorothy asked Frieda.

The gentle little lady, whose hair was now snow-white, thought about it for a moment, then said, "Well, maybe once, when Larry brought home Paul Whiteman's band."

Not even the most intimate of Larry's friends knew if a wife could have brought a peaceful, organized home life to him—or him to it. But he certainly admired and envied the world that Dick and Dorothy brought to each other. Dorothy's cool elegance epitomized the desirable lady to him. Added to that, Frieda always let him know that she considered marriage the ideal state.

According to Teddy Hart's wife, Larry longed for a family of his own. "He would have been completely happy at the head of a big table," said Dorothy Hart, "with his wife at the other end and a lot of children on both sides.

"In his own immediate family, when there were aunts and uncles and cousins visiting, he made a point of staying home, playing cards with them. If he was going to be late for dinner, he always called his mother to tell her. It was true that he might, just as dinner was about to be served, decide to take a shower and keep everybody waiting. But when they did finally sit down together at the table, he charmed them so that they would forgive him anything."*

He was finding himself lonely in the crowds that he sought, collected, and demanded around him. "He was," says chanteuse Mabel Mercer, "the saddest man I ever knew."

To acquaintances less sensitive than Miss Mercer, he showed a cherubic, pixielike face and indulged in little private jokes that amused him.

In one of these, played on brother Teddy, it reversed itself, and he became its victim.

Teddy was playing in a Broadway show, and Larry sent him a telegram CAUGHT YOUR SHOW LAST NIGHT YOUSE WAS

*In a BBC interview.

TERRIFIC. He signed it GEORGE BERNARD SHAW. Teddy didn't catch on, agreed with Shaw's presumed opinion, and showed it to everyone. Larry, amused and chagrined, didn't have the heart to tell him the truth.

Arthur Marx, son of the great Groucho, recalls that, as a little boy, he woke up one morning to find he and his sister, Miriam, had been moved by their parents to a back bedroom while they were asleep.

They also lived on Bedford Drive, and Groucho discovered that a dilapidated Ford with no license plates had been parked all night in front of his house. Arthur remembers that the whole of Beverly Hills was living in a climate of fear of kidnappers. Movie stars believed their children would be prime targets; a near neighbor, Marlene Dietrich, employed round-the-clock guards. Groucho was also alarmed because a dilapidated Ford with no license plates was as out-of-place on that exclusive street as if a diplodocus strayed in from the Mesozoic era and settled there. The Beverly Hills police also viewed it with suspicion and decided to leave it where it was, under discreet surveillance.

However, no kidnappers appeared, and the police finally towed it away. *Two years later,* according to Groucho, he was at a Mayfair Club party, dancing with Ginger Rogers, when Larry danced by and asked him, "What did you ever do about that old Ford that was in front of your house?" And danced on.

Groucho puzzled over this around the dance floor until they passed again. "How in the hell did you know about that old car?" They lost each other on the floor for a while before Groucho was startled to hear Larry whisper at the back of his neck, "I put it there."*

---

*"I consider myself something of an authority on comedy," Groucho told us, "but if that's funny, the joke escapes me."

Ever since the actors' strike George M. Cohan had kept a chip on his shoulder as a mark of antagonism against almost everyone connected with the entertainment world. He never warmed up to Dick and Larry or, for that matter, to any of the movie people connected with *The Phantom President*.

It might be attributed to the same syndrome that affects a pilot who rides as a passenger in a plane; he believes his is a much surer hand at the controls. Cohan was, of course, a skilled producer, director, author, and songwriter. His melodies were sweet; his lyrics reeked of sentimentality and patriotism. He had no rapport with the sophistication of Rodgers and Hart. He hated doing *The Phantom President* and later told an interviewer, "If given a choice, I'd rather go to jail than Hollywood." Five years later Dick and Larry would go to war again with Cohan; the battlefield would be Broadway.

Their next movie was *Hallelujah, I'm a Bum*, a story with elements considered relevant to the Depression. Its authors were Ben Hecht and S. N. Behrman, two polished gentlemen of letters whose salaries came close to $10,000 a week. This could be 10,000 reasons why it was difficult to empathize with the hardships of those days.*

However, both were articulate and inventive and pounced on several other sources of material, putting together a presentable combination of research and plagiarism. Some of the critics found hints of *The Beggar's Opera*, others claimed a resemblance to a film classic *À Nous la Liberté*, but the most notable resemblance was to Charles Chaplin's various tramp characters. In *Hallelujah, I'm a Bum*, one of Broadway's best-known personalities, Al Jol-

*Hecht's unceasing mockery of movies and complaints about life in Hollywood finally elicited a scorching answer from Behrman, who said, "Yes, and all we get out of it is a lousy fortune!"

son, played Bumper, a hobo with a heart of pure gold, who returned the girl he loved to a friend who loved her, too. Dick and Larry's score was undistinguished except for one beautiful ballad, with sentimental melody and lyric combined, "You Are Too Beautiful." Larry was fascinated by Jolson, a super song stylist who could hold the stage of a theater as long as he pleased without tiring his audience or himself.

Director Lewis Milestone recruited Dick and Larry to portray infinitesimal roles in the film, Dick as a photographer and Larry as a banker. The director's expertise was insufficient to the task of getting outstanding performances from them. Any director's would have been. Larry's entire dialogue consisted of the word "No" which he spoke with dubious authority. Ben Hecht suggested that having created the role of a banker in a Depression-ridden bank, he should never play anything else.

That was not their film debut. Hard on the birth of sound films, they had made a musical short, *And Then We Wrote*, at the Paramount Long Island studio.

Early in the research of this book, Marx and Clayton decided to view that film. Forty-five years having passed since it was made, it would be an understatement to report that executive changes had occurred in the producing company during that time. However, a single member of the top echelon actually remained, Adolph Zukor, more than one hundred years old (he is credited with the line, "If I had known I was going to live this long, I'd have taken better care of myself"), was available but had no recollection of the Rodgers and Hart film.

Paramount could come up with no record of any existing print. We redoubled our efforts. Then Samson de Brier, aficionado of the cinema scene, collector of infinite memorabilia of movieland, alerted us that a print was indeed in existence and might, perhaps and just possibly, be seen.

However, in true cloak-and-dagger fashion, we were not to breathe this to a soul, simply wait for word that would be forthcoming, if we were patient, from an operator whom we began calling 007½.

The reason for secrecy appeared obvious. Ever since World War II, when film companies made their product available to the armed forces, pirated versions, some stolen outright, some converted to easily transported and easily projected sixteen-millimeter prints, appeared throughout the world. The loss of revenue to the producing companies, as a result of such skulduggery mounted into millions of dollars. Finally, various government bloodhounds took up the search, prepared to hand out stiff sentences to anyone caught with such movies in their possession. Obviously, we were about to be contacted by someone who had access to *And Then We Wrote*, most likely illegally.

It certainly seemed that way, when operator 007½ telephoned. Yes, he had the film, and yes, it could be seen. But not in the immediate future. The print, he whispered, was on the East Coast, and time and expense would be required. He thought he could get it back in California in a week. We agreed to wait, a very nominal willingness on our part, considering there was little else we could do.

The word came. We had passed a security check, and 007½ was revealed to be a well-spoken young man we now called Dapper Dan. He told us his expenses had proved heavy, and he would require $50. Expectation that we were being permitted forbidden fruit was too appetizing for us to quibble over exorbitant demands. Our rendezvous point would be in a certain booth in Musso-Frank's Hollywood Boulevard restaurant.

Dapper Dan was an enormously self-contained young man with an equally enormous appetite. We paid the check, our lunch amounting to about one-tenth of the total, while his, selected with fastidious attention to his gourmet

159

tastes, constituted the balance. Musso-Frank is one of Hollywood's most historic gustatory landmarks, but we doubt if its chef has ever been challenged as carefully to deliver such meticulously cooked manna. When luncheon was finally consumed by our guest, we followed his expensive sports car into the hills. Had it not been necessary to see where we were driving, it was obvious that we would have been blindfolded. A circuitous route was taken to a narrow little house perched behind a locked gate.

He warned us to sit quietly in the car until he signaled that the way was clear. We took advantage of his absence to check the tape recorder that Clayton had secreted in the trunklike portmanteau slung over her left shoulder, hidden there because D.D. refused our request to use it. It should be noted that, being absolutely upright in our dealing with those who could disclose secrets about Rodgers and Hart, we never made use of the recorder without asking and being granted permission. However, as Dapper Dan was the first to demand pay for his information, we felt righteously that we were entitled—*especially* after he had absolutely forbidden it.

We followed him down a rocky hillside, into a room crowded with old movie fan magazines, photographs of stars, and still pictures of ancient cinema classics. We squatted on fantastically uncomfortable chairs, while D. D. busied himself in the rear with a projector, his mastery of the machine not quite up to getting seeable focus or hearable sound. The machine was stopped, and after a ten-minute intermission, he announced that it was fixed. It was exactly as before.

Apparently warmed by his expensive meal and possession of our $50, D.D. unexpectedly gave permission for Clayton to record the movie's sound track. It was done, the tape picking it up with complete fidelity to its indistinctness.

160

The program cover of Columbia's 1920 Varsity
Show, *Fly with Me*. Eighteen-year-old Richard
Rodgers, Class of '23, composed the music.

1920—Donald Kerr and Elise Bonwit
dance in *Poor Little Ritz Girl,* first
Broadway show with Rodgers and Hart
songs. *Photo/Lynn Farnol Group, Inc.*

"The Three Musketeers," one of Rodgers
and Hart's earliest satirical songs, sung by
Philip Loeb, Sterling Holloway, and Romney Brent in *Garrick Gaieties,* 1925. *Photo/
Lynn Farnol Group, Inc.*

CANDIES
· CAKES ·
RESTAURANT

Mary Elizabeth

Music
Afternoon Tea and Dinner

Fifth Avenue at Thirty-sixth St.

LENA G. TOWSLEY
Photographer of Children
in their homes
regardless of location

Workshop: 10 East 30th St.
Phone, Ashland 0192
if no answer
Ashland 0354
New York

The
THEATRE GUILD
presents

The Theatre Guild Jr. Players

in the

Garrick Gaieties

Music by Richard Rodgers   Lyrics by Lorenz Hart

Production directed by Philip Loeb.

Settings and costumes designed by Carolyn Hancock.

Orchestra directed by Richard Rodgers.

ACT ONE.

"Soliciting Subscriptions"

In which we let you into one of the business secrets of an Art theatre.

Sterling Holloway, James Norris, Romney Brent, June Cochrane

"Gilding the Guild"

*In which we introduce you to Betty Starbuck and the Guild Gaieties Chorus;
(the girls are all college graduates and have undergone a course in the
higher mathematics, which accounts for their keeping time so well.)*

Betty Starbuck and Chorus

"The Guardsman"

by B. M. Kaye

(*With apologies to Franz Molnar, Alfred Lunt, Lynn Fontanne and
Dudley Digges.*)

Alfred Lunt, The Actor...Romney Brent
Lynn Fontanne, The Actress..Edith Meiser
Dudley Digges, The Critic...Philip Loeb

"Romantic You and Sentimental Me"

June Cochrane, James Norris, Edith Meiser, and Sterling Holloway

"Working With a Scarf"

Eleanor Shaler

continued on page x

*Two hours away
in Connecticut
on the Sound*
an old New England homestead
with the charm of 1840
and the comfort of 1925
welcomes a few guests (not
more than four) for quiet
restful week-ends
No alarums nor excursions
A pantry full of preserves
wide verandas and open fireplaces
Reservations may be made by personal
interview in New York City

For further information address
Hostess-resident
in care of
Offices of The Guild Program
65 West 35th Street, New York City

The program of the first *Garrick Gaieties* (June 8, 1925). *Courtesy of Hil-
degarde Halliday.*

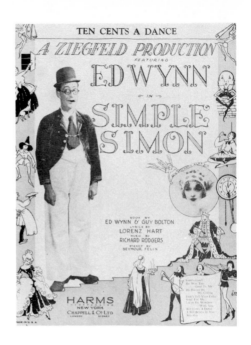

Peggy-Ann (1926); *Simple Simon* (1930); *Jumbo* (1935); *Babes in Arms* (1937). *Photo/Theatre and Music Collection, Museum of the City of New York.*

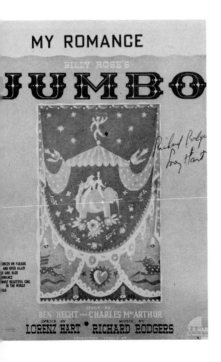

Their first big song hit was "Manhattan," and here are its writers—in Manhattan. *Mark Morris Photo.*

Helen Ford loved a "good entrance," and this is how she made hers in *Dearest Enemy* in 1925. *Photo/Photo-Times — Wide World Studio.*

Eva Puck helps milkman Sammy White train to ride in the six-day bike race in *The Girl Friend,* 1926. *Photo/Lynn Farnol Group, Inc.*

Dick lectures Larry for being late to a swank party.

"I forgot my pants," reveals Larry.

These are blowups from a 16mm movie. *Courtesy of Milt Larsen, Hollywood.*

Helen Ford points an accusing finger at Edith Meiser and other members of the cast of *Peggy-Anne.*

Helen Ford (left) in a dream sequence in *Peggy-Ann,* with Patrick Rafferty and Lulu McConnell.

The team of Fields, Rodgers, and Hart in real life.

The team in reel life—Marshall Thompson (Fields), Mickey Rooney (Hart), and Tom Drake (Rodgers) in MGM movie *Words and Music.*

Scenes from The 1927 Cochran Revue.
Top: Sonnie Hale, Jessie Matthews,
Morris Harvey, and Mimi Crawford.
Lower left: Greta Payne. Lower right:
Jessie Matthews.

The composer and the lyricist,
posing like businessmen, in 1927.
Photo/Lynn Farnol Group, Inc.

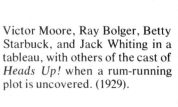

It's 1928, and Busby Berkeley,
Doremus Dore, and Charles King
cavort in *Present Arms.*

Victor Moore, Ray Bolger, Betty
Starbuck, and Jack Whiting in a
tableau, with others of the cast of
Heads Up! when a rum-running
plot is uncovered. (1929).

Ed Wynn, hailed as "the Perfect Fool," in the Ziegfeld production of *Simple Simon*, in 1930.

The imported German turntable permitted four simultaneous sets in *Evergreen*, 1930, all rooms in a seaside boardinghouse. Star Jessie Matthews shares the top bedroom, left, with Sonnie Hale. In the right top bedroom are Joyce Barbour and Eric Merivale.

The inverted chandelier is the setting as Jessie Matthews and Sonnie Hale are "Dancing on the Ceiling," from *Evergreen*, 1930.

California in the thirties—Larry Hart in Beverly Hills. *Courtesy of Richard Rodgers.*

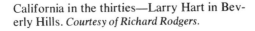

Paris in Hollywood for the 1932 movie *Love Me Tonight,* and Maurice Chevalier captivates Jeanette MacDonald with "That's the Song of Paree."

Myrna Loy also appeared in *Love Me Tonight* with Charles Ruggles and C. Aubrey Smith.

George M. Cohan was elected President twice by Rodgers and Hart—once as President Varney in the 1932 movie *The Phantom President* and again in 1937 as President Roosevelt in *I'd Rather be Right.*

Edgar Connor, Harry Langdon, Al Jolson, and Madge Evans in Rodgers and Hart's 1933 movie *Hallelujah, I'm a Bum.*

Jimmy Durante and Larry Hart at MGM studio for *Hollywood Party*. Howard Dietz —also a good man with a lyric —holds the other cigar.

Durante, pictured here with Lupe Velez, sang "Reincarnation" in *Hollywood Party*.

Durante, on the stairs, and Jack Pearl, as Baron Munchausen, confront a gorilla in *Hollywood Party*, 1934.

Paul Whiteman on his precarious perch for "The Circus Is on Parade" in *Jumbo*.

Back in New York, 1935, Jimmy Durante and Larry Hart enjoying the twists and turns of a new lyric for *Jumbo*.

Tamara Geva and Ray Bolger dancing to "Slaughter on Tenth Avenue," in *On Your Toes*, 1936. *Courtesy of Mr. and Mrs. Ray Bolger.*

The Brewster, New York, farm of Max Dreyfus, where the publisher helped Rodgers and Hart charge into the forefront of musical comedy songwriters. *New York Daily News Photo.*

Rodgers plays a song from *I'd Rather Be Right* (1937). Around him, left to right: Sam H. Harris, Larry Hart, Moss Hart, George S. Kaufman, and George M. Cohan.

Rodgers demonstrates the way he wants a tune played to a group involved with *I Married an Angel* (1937).

Vivienne Segal reminds Zorina in song always to "Have a Twinkle in Your Eye" in *I Married an Angel*.

Young Desi Arnaz bangs the bongo on his way to fame in *Too Many Girls* (1939). Diosa Costello is the dancer.

Dick Rodgers' important ballet, *Ghost Town,* was performed for the first time by the Ballet Russe de Monte Carlo in November, 1939, at the Metropolitan Opera House, New York.

Jack Haley shows a group of servants how to play golf in *Higher and Higher* (1940).

"I don't need a piano—I can write music seated at a desk."—Richard Rodgers.

Hart could write a lyric anytime, anywhere. All he needed was paper and a pen—and a cigar. *Photo/Mary Morris.*

Hart dashes off a lyric while producer Dwight Deere Wyman looks on.

Gene Kelly, as Pal Joey, spins a tall yarn to the skeptical Vera Simpson, played by Vivienne Segal. (Photographed during an actual performance, 1940.)

In the successful 1952 revival of *Pal Joey*, blackmailers Lionel Stander and Helen Gallagher confront Harold Lang as Joey.

Harold Lang, Patricia Northrop, Gordon Peters, and Vivienne Segal in the revival of *Pal Joey*.

Robert Chisholm, as King Arthur, and Vivienne Segal, as Queen Morgan Le Fay, in the 1943 revival of *A Connecticut Yankee*.

Vera Ellen and Jere McMahon dance in the 1943 revival of *Connecticut Yankee*, the last play that Larry Hart saw. *Photo/Lynn Farnol Group.*

Ronald Graham, as The-
seus, and Constance
Moore, as Antiope, in *By
Jupiter*, 1942–43. *Courtesy
of Mr. and Mrs. Ray Bolger.*

Right to left: Ray Bolger as
Sapiens, Benay Venuta as
Queen Hippolyta, and
Constance Moore as Anti-
ope in *By Jupiter*. *Courtesy
of Mr. and Mrs. Ray Bolger.*

This piquant note of recommendation is one of Larry Hart's rare letters.
Courtesy of Irving Eisman.

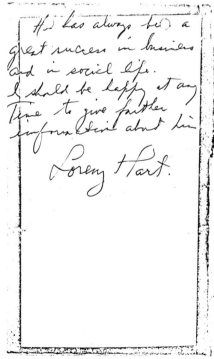

"It Happened in the Dark," probably Larry Hart's last lyric. *Courtesy of Irving Eisman.*

The movie is a monument to bad acting and inferior singing. Visually and orally, the acting talents of Rodgers and Hart merit the use of the word "embarrassing." "I can't truly remember that Dick was ever critical of my acting," notes Clayton, "but had he been, revenge would have been sweet. Here was an extraordinarily creative person in his own field setting mine back, well, only a century or two. Maker of melodies he is; thespian he ain't."

The day after we saw *And Then We Wrote*, a mutual friend phoned and said he knew where there was a print of it and the man who owned it was prepared to let us have it, on loan.

"He would have offered it ten days ago," said our friend, "'but some guy named Dan borrowed it and didn't return it until last night."

"What does your friend charge?" we asked.

"Oh," was the reply, "he doesn't charge anybody anything. He could get arrested!"

Writing songs for individual Hollywood producers made for a transient existence. After *Hot Heiress, Phantom President,* and *Hallelujah, I'm a Bum*, Dick and Larry took refuge under the glamorous parasol that Metro-Goldwyn-Mayer held over its employees. They signed a contract to work in the studio that proudly proclaimed "More Stars Than There Are in Heaven."

MGM was top of the heap, a glittering ivory tower, a walled-in Olympus, a mythical kingdom where the unbelievable was routine. Its people were untouched by the money troubles that wracked the outside world. Their parties were continuous.

Edgar Allan Woolf was a gourmet cook who spent more time over a hot stove than his typewriter. A scenarist with a huge shock of red hair, he was never happier than when his home was filled with guests. Dick and Larry went to

161

many Hollywood parties but rarely together. Since Woolf loved to have both of them, he always asked Frieda, and she asked Larry to take her, so usually both Dick and Larry came to his home.

He lived in a Beverly Hills mansion with a small brown and white dog picked up when he found him wandering dangerously on busy Pico Boulevard. Their attachment was mutual and beautiful. All the guests had to be introduced to the four-footed co-host, naturally named Pico.

Woolf was one of the studio's top gagmen, a creator of funny situations and one-line jokes. It was good casting, for he wrote blackouts and vaudeville sketches before coming to Hollywood. He authored the midnight revue being performed for the first time in the cabaret on Madison Square Garden Roof the night Harry K. Thaw shot Stanford White. That wasn't all that was tragic that night. Woolf's show was so bad one critic reported that "to call it downright awful would be a complimentary notice."

It was, in fact, so bad that, when the shots rang out, Woolf's mother screamed, "They've shot my Edgar!"

Woolf's Saturday night guests were a hodgepodge of stars, producers, writers, directors, and new settlers to Hollywood, like Dick and Dorothy Rodgers.

The living room of Woolf's home was a few steps below the foyer, and Dorothy, looking at the earlier arrivers, gazed quizzically at a woman clothed in terribly out-of-date raiment, a large tiara shooting skyward out of her henna-colored hair. It must be admitted that the woman appeared somewhat mummified.

"My God, who's that?"

Dick recognized her as a former Broadway star. "That's Mrs. Leslie Carter," he said.

"Isn't she *dead*?" asked Dorothy.

Edgar Allan Woolf's parties provided several memorable

moments like that. Among his guests, one night, were Hollywood's gossip columnist Louella Parsons and her husband, Dr. Harry Martin. "Docky," as his wife called him, drank too much and could barely stand when the party was over around 3 A.M. She belatedly discovered his condition and was horror-struck. He was a heavyset man, inclined to hostility when drunk.

"Please! Please help me sober him up," she begged. Wringing her hands, she urged that someone ("Won't anyone?") walk him around the block. She explained: "He has to operate early in the morning!"

Their first MGM assignment was a play from the Hungarian, *I Married an Angel*. Soon after they started on it, they had a visitor, their friend Larry Adler, a wizard with the mouth organ, a competent composer, and a knowledgeable stage performer. He had auditioned for *Garrick Gaieties*.

"I didn't make it," he said, "and I was terribly disappointed. This young fellow Larry Hart came over and said, 'Don't take it to heart, kid, it happens to everybody.' But I did take it hard. I couldn't stand not being appreciated at once. So later on, when I began to get jobs, I used to go around to see him, and he was always very kind. He was very nice.

"In 1933," Adler told us, "I was appearing at Grauman's Chinese Theater, and Dick and Larry invited me to see them at the studio. By then, as far as I was concerned, they were tops at writing show tunes. I had a chance to ask Larry, 'What lyric that you've written are you most proud of?' and this has got to be authentic because I could never remember the words if it wasn't. 'I'll tell you right away, and I don't even have to think about it. Listen to this. It's called 'A Cat Can Look at a Queen':

163

Though it may be dark at night
A cat can see
More than you,
More than me!

He almost fell off his chair laughing. He said he felt that was the best line and the funniest, not only that he wrote but that *anybody* ever wrote!"

But as he did to all who asked him, Larry was responding with the title and a sample of the last thing he had written. He may well have believed "A Cat Can Look at a Queen" was his best, or it could have been a private joke, made to order to laugh at alone.

Adler also felt that the studio was not giving Rodgers and Hart the respect that he felt they deserved. He said, "It was one of the saddest things I ever saw, the way MGM was treating them. They had them stuck in a little room. You felt they were the hired help, and they were being treated as the hired help."

On March 11, 1933, they completed writing the title song of *I Married an Angel*. It was late in the afternoon, but they were elated with the sound of it and wanted to try it on someone. They called Marx, who was the studio's story editor.

In his autobiography, *Musical Stages*, Dick relates his memory of that day:

"We were given a large studio [by MGM], in which to work and one afternoon, while playing piano for some friends, I suddenly heard a roaring sound and deafening crash, followed by the incredible sight of the piano moving away from me. We were in the middle of an earthquake! Luckily the studio was on the first floor of the building and we simply dashed for the nearest window and jumped out. The next day I discovered that the deafening crash I'd heard

164

was caused by a brick wall falling on an empty rehearsal hall adjacent to my studio. If the wall had fallen just a foot closer, we would have been killed."

Marx also remembers that incident but differently, and although there is nothing funny about an earthquake ("after all, this solid earth on which we depend to stay put is suddenly going somewhere"), what happened to him seems as farcical as it was dangerous. "I'm sorry to differ with Dick," says Marx, "because I dine out quite often on my version."

"Late that afternoon Dick called me and said he and Larry had just finished writing the song 'I Married an Angel' and asked if I would like to hear it. Would I? Well, naturally. I went down to the tiny space they had been given at the end of a long corridor in the ramshackle wooden building that housed the music department. Boxlike, the room was barely large enough to accommodate Dick, Larry, and a scratched-up baby grand piano.

"They had just begun the song when we heard a low rumble, seeming to come from the ground beneath us. It grew louder, and Dick stopped playing. 'What's that?' he asked. He didn't get an answer, we didn't have one, but then he didn't need one; the room started shaking wildly and, as he too remembers, the piano moved away from him and then came back, stopping beneath a very tiny window that was set about six feet above the floor. Outside was a narrow automobile road, so the window was locked and barred to prevent breaking in.

"This earthquake was a beaut; it continued to shake and roll for what was probably a very short time but seemed an eternity. All the lights went out in the building. I don't know if it was raining before, but now it was coming down in torrents. This combination of angry elements was scary enough, but we were far down the corridor and could barely see in the dark; I doubt if we considered running through it.

165

"Larry moved first. He scrambled onto the piano and struggled to open the window. It wouldn't budge, so he jumped down, picked up the piano stool and hurled it through the glass. Then he climbed back onto the piano and leaped out.

"Dick and I stood there laughing. One minute Larry was singing, and the next he had jumped out the window. But with that, a terrific crash shook the building, and I thought (as Dick did) that the whole place was coming down on top of us. He scrambled onto the piano and leaped out the window, and I followed him.

"We landed on wet roadway that had a layer of broken glass, and as we picked ourselves up, a car came along. The driver leaned out and asked with a kind of polite curiosity, 'What the hell is going on?' He had seen a piano stool fly through a window, immediately followed by one small, one medium, and one large man. He was justifiably mystified; it seems that one doesn't feel an earthquake while riding in a moving automobile."

A few weeks later Dick sat at the piano at Edgar Allan Woolf's home and played "I Married an Angel," while Larry sang it for the party guests. The plot of I Married an Angel was slight, a whimsical bit of froth about a heaven-sent angel falling in love and marrying an earth man. Two feathery wings sprouted between her shoulders, only to disappear after her first night in the nuptial bed.

Marx remembers that evening, too. He and his wife were sitting beside Frieda Hart and as Larry began to sing "Have you heard, I married an angel . . .?" Frieda whispered to them, with touching sincerity, "How I wish my Larry would marry an angel!"

Larry didn't, of course—no angel, not even an ordinary

166

mortal. He continued, at times, to escort his mother to Woolf's parties, sometimes leaving her there while he prowled the late spots. Woolf's parties came to a sad end. On his return home from the studio, Pico playfully jumped at him to greet him at the top of the stairs, causing his master to lose his balance and fall to his death.

Two incredibly handsome identical twins joined the entourage that accompanied Larry around the town, to the private parties and the late-night clubs. Like ever-present Doc Bender, the Rocky Twins became closely involved with Larry. Norwegian-born, and rumored to have been protégés of Adolf Hitler, they were pursued by international swingers of that day, admired as "male courtesans."

They were professional dancers, usually performing in drag. "They were beautiful boys but absolute madmen," said actor-dancer Bennett Green. "They loved to play unfunny jokes, phoning people all hours of the night just to annoy them. They were wild!"

Lee Gershwin, attractive and observant wife of lyricist Ira Gershwin, recalls seeing Larry give them expensive gold cigarette cases as gifts. "How they danced around the room!" and she too describes them with the same word: "Wild!"

That madness helped make them the toast of a bizarre group who loved the Rocky Twins so much that when they performed, they literally flung diamonds at their feet in the form of rings and bracelets.

Playwright-scenarist Leonard Spigelgass recalls that the Rocky Twins did a burlesque of the Dolly Sisters, two stately Hungarian beauties who performed an intricate dance with a a pair of Russian wolfhounds. The dogs pranced between the sisters as they turned and pirouetted about the

167

stage. The Rocky Twins imitated them with the same movements, the same elaborate costumes, wide-feathered hats, and tall, thin walking sticks. . . using a pair of mutts!

Spigelgass came to know Larry very well in later years. He holds vivid opinions of the people surrounding Larry.

"Wherever Larry went, he brought Bender along. He was a kind of comic, also a procurer, pimp, arranger. I never knew whether he liked me or not. I simply ignored him. To me he was something slimy, a worm."

Edith Meiser felt that Larry's downfall began at this time in Hollywood. She blamed the movie town for it. "Hollywood is a tough thing for anyone to take," she said. "It was too easy to be led up the woods. Everything was coming easy for him, but it was mostly his own emotional problems, plus alcohol. Dick couldn't ride herd on him; he had a family to raise; he had responsibilities."

One night Henry Myers dropped in on Larry, who was alone in a big house. "After a session of amateur philosophizing, it got too late and dark for me to want to drive out to where I lived on Palos Verdes, so he put me up for the night," said Myers.

"In the middle of the night he woke me up to say, 'I'm going to get a horse and carriage and go for a drive around the park.' All I said was 'Go ahead, I'll see you in the morning,'" and went back to sleep.

"I did see him in the morning. He was filled with excitement and plans for us to take a house or an apartment together in Hollywood. It seems I wasn't the only one he awakened in the middle of the night, but when he told others that he was going to get a horse and carriage and drive around the park, there was always a horrified attempt to dissuade him. Even though I was very sleepy when he said it, it seemed an eminently sensible and delightful idea and I

168

would never have thought of discouraging him. I believe that as much as he demanded constant companionship, the artist in him needed time for refueling, for contemplation or whatever purpose solitude is suddenly necessary to everyone and certainly to a creative person like Larry. The fact that I didn't try to talk him out of an impossible idea pleased him; he thought we could get along well living together. But he was not going to stay forever in Hollywood, and so nothing came of it."

And nothing came of Dick and Larry's work on *I Married an Angel* either. At least in Hollywood.

Through a series of events over which they had no control, the film was abandoned by MGM. Destiny played a large part in these happenings.

The aesthetic and often-ailing head of production, Irving Thalberg, suffered a heart attack. Those production reins were temporarily passed to Louis B. Mayer, who was strong-minded but sometimes needlessly panicked by outside suggestions. The Catholic Church was the most powerful, because of its strict views about the contents of movies, and it frowned on any that collided with its beliefs. It looked askance on stories dealing with angels and devils and particularly disliked those that brought them to earth instead of leaving them where they belonged. Mayer listened to a complaint from their emissary and jettisoned *I Married an Angel*, to the bewildered outrage of Dick and Larry.

Much of the score was done, which accounted for some of their resentment. But Mayer never read story material and didn't know the nature of their assignment until the church indicated its opposition. Ironically, the film's abandonment would eventually pay off for them because the work they had poured into it kept it fresh in their minds.

Stopping the film brought their labors at the studio to a temporary halt while another assignment was sought for them. That gave Larry more time than ever to pursue the bizarre. A favorite starting point was the Club New Yorker in the Christie Hotel on Hollywood Boulevard.

The star attraction was twenty-four-year-old Jean Malin. A tall, handsome brute, he was a superb female impersonator, but at the New Yorker he appeared in top hat and tails, red rose in his buttonhole. He called it his "class act" as he sang, danced, and thrust sharp cutting witticisms into the guts of Hollywood and its people. Malin's inclinations toward homosexuality weren't hidden, even in male attire. He was a favorite of the movie colony. The New Yorker was the "in" place.

Charles Chaplin, rarely seen in nightclubs, admired Malin's talent enormously and was frequently at ringside. Larry, too, made it a habit and joined the circle of Malin intimates who often accompanied him to his home after the show, where the parties continued. At one of these, Larry disappeared, and it was believed he had chosen to leave quietly, but in the morning Malin found him curled up asleep on the floor of the linen closet.

That spring, 1933, Prohibition was repealed. It had never been hard for Larry and his friends to procure liquor, but when the ingredients were legal, they were considerably safer to the digestive tract. That made for wilder parties than ever before.

The advent of warm weather moved the action out of the city area, and the nights came to life at the home of film star Lew Cody at Malibu. He had an impressive beach house with a lighthouse tower that served as a beacon to attract transvestites, homosexuals in drag, and lesbians in mannish outfits. Many were world-famous.

"Those parties did nobody any harm," contended a for-

170

mer chorus boy who went often with Larry but asked not to be identified. "If someone showed up and was shocked by what was going on, he left. You slept only with the person you wanted. Nobody was raped, for God's sake! It was understood that what went on was confidential, and you never saw a hint of anything in Louella Parsons or any other gossip column. That was an unwritten law. Everyone obeyed it! My God, if they didn't, there would have been scandals that Hollywood would still be buzzing over."

Malin moved from the New Yorker to the Ship Café for this summer. The new hot spot was on the Venice Pier, a few miles south of Malibu. His devoted clan of gays and heterosexuals followed him. There he did female impersonations, powdered and rouged, in stunning wigs and glittering sequined dresses. He mimicked prominent movie actresses so adroitly that he enraptured those who gathered ringside.

Larry was there regularly with his usual corps of hangers-on, as well as Broadway's throaty-voiced Tallulah Bankhead. Forceful and ever the trouper, she manifested little concern that her effort to be a star in talking pictures was meeting heavy going. Another of Larry's companions was William Haines, a stellar movie attraction about whom hints of homosexuality were spreading and would subsequently shoot down his screen career.

The Venice Pier jutted out from an amusement zone. Built to withstand heavy tides with the café and parking space at the far end, it was like a sturdy finger pointing across the Pacific, stretching beyond the breakers and over deep water.

On his closing night that summer, the place was jammed with Malin's admirers. He gave a sensational performance, a triumph all would have reason to remember. Then the star, with comedienne Patsy Kelly, climbed into his car. He

171

had to back it away from the pier edge but accidentally shifted the gear into forward position. The machine smashed through a low barricade and plunged into the ocean.

Patsy Kelly was rescued. She recovered after being in a coma two days. But the announcement on the club's electric sign, still lit, was eerily prophetic: JEAN MALIN'S LAST NIGHT!

There is no doubt that Larry succumbed to the erotic temptations of Hollywood, but Dick went there with him, worked with him, spent the same amount of time there, and it didn't affect him. He busied himself with music and let Larry dance to it.

Their assignment to a revue type of film, *Hollywood Party*, was as disastrous as *I Married an Angel*. It was an ill-conceived pot of celluloidic goulash. Producer Harry Rapf hoped to include all the famous stars of MGM in the cast. Dick and Larry wrote a special song, a seductive melody called "The Prayer," for platinum blond Jean Harlow.

> O, Lord, I know you're busy up there,
> I ask your help with a prayer
> So please don't give me the air . . .
> O, hear me, Lord, I must see Garbo in person
> With Gable when they're rehearsin'
> And some director is cursin'!
> So let me open up my eyes at seven
> And find I'm looking through that stewd-yo gate.
> I'll go walking in my movie heaven
> Where some exekative will say I'm great!
> O Lord, I know how busy you are,
> If I'm not going too far
> Be nice and make me a star!

172

But Jean Harlow never sang it. Again, the ubiquitous Mayer stepped in, previewed some of the incomplete film, and decided not to include any stars in *Hollywood Party* at all. With Harlow out of it, the song was dropped.

In the year 1933 it was believed that every movie had to have a theme song. The melody of "The Prayer" appealed to producer David Selznick, and he asked Dick and Larry to refashion the words to fit his picture *Manhattan Melodrama*. Larry wrote a lyric to match that title, and Dick performed some melodic changes. For a time it was actually called "Manhattan Melodrama" but then changed to "The Bad in Every Man."

The movie was an exciting one. In its climax Clark Gable, a murderer, nobly spurned an offer of life imprisonment and went to the electric chair. It might not be very true to life, but certainly had a gripping appeal. On a sweltering hot Sunday, late in July, it drew Public Enemy Number One, John Dillinger, out of hiding to see it at Chicago's Biograph Theater. "The Bad in Every Man" was the last song he heard; he was wiped out by G-man guns as he left the theater.

The film was a hit, but the song still failed to achieve popularity. Then music publisher Jack Robbins suggested they try another lyric, "something us common people will understand, y'know, a love song with June and moon and spoon!"

"How about 'Blue Moon'?" asked Larry as a gag, then nearly gagged when Robbins said, "Terrific!"

Cornered, Larry pointed out that the standard description of that celestial goal of lovers was silver, but that failed to move Robbins. Suddenly, Larry said, "Goddammit, I'll do it!" and he did, and "Blue Moon" became their most commercial song, and Larry always hated it.

When Thalberg returned to the studio he took on a new

173

film production of Franz Lehar's *The Merry Widow*, to star Jeanette MacDonald and Maurice Chevalier. Its director was the celebrated Ernst Lubitsch, creator of the droll studies in film technique known as the Lubitsch Touch. He was hardly two inches taller than Larry, smiled perpetually as if enjoying a private joke, and, like Larry, chewed incessantly on a cigar. They hit it off well, and he borrowed Larry from Dick to rewrite the original lyrics of Victor Leon and Leon Stein, already translated by Adrian Ross. However, *The Merry Widow* songs were so famous that Larry had to retain the titles and simply put new words to them. It was an easy task, taking him back to the schmaltzy material he concocted for the Irving Place Theater fifteen years earlier.

Their MGM contract expired, and in 1934, Dick and Larry happily returned to New York. The abandoning of *I Married an Angel* still angered them, and they hoped to acquire it for the stage. Larry's work on *The Merry Widow* received appropriate but inaccurate screen credit—Lyrics by Rodgers and Hart. That was because their contract tied them together, even when only one of them performed. "Blue Moon," although never part of a musical comedy score, was their outstanding achievement of the year 1933.

When they had left Broadway in 1930, they were fair-haired boys, White Way whizkids. They were shocked to find on their return that they were virtually forgotten. Many changes had occurred in their absence; producers they had worked with, including Lew Fields, had retired. They were up against an enforced creative drought.

Suddenly, to the delight of so many friends, Larry became intensely fond of a woman for the first time in his life. Nanette Guilford was singing at the Metropolitan Opera House when Herb Fields introduced him to her.

This is what she told us about how that relationship got started:

174

"Dick's father brought me into the world, and Joe Weber was my great-uncle. I knew Herbert very well, he was the one Fields that I knew, and I knew Dorothy, naturally. But I knew Herbert best of all, and we were awfully close friends. He brought Larry backstage.

"I was called the baby star of the Met. It was ridiculous, but I was fifteen when I went in, straight from finishing school. I was singing the smallest parts in the world. By the time I met Larry I was getting leads."

Larry's romantic feelings were sidetracked when she left the Metropolitan for a European vacation. Meanwhile, he was called back to Hollywood. The movies wanted more from Rodgers and Hart.

This time it was the Paramount Studio and a production called *Mississippi*. They wrote seven songs, smooth and easy-sounding, redolent of the Deep South.

Replacing the originally cast Lanny Ross was a rising young crooner, Bing Crosby, who sang their songs sleepily and successfully. He also sang Stephen Foster's "Old Folks at Home" which the caustic *New Yorker* called the brightest song in the score.

Mississippi was their last Hollywood effort. Larry, with his open heart and open pocketbook, took a few companions back to Manhattan to continue their revels there. On the whole, Larry had enjoyed Hollywood life and even believed movies would, in their use of music and dance, come to supplant similar stage confections.

Dick didn't share any of his partner's reactions. He cared little for its celebrated climate, its outdoorsy atmosphere, its sunshine, and, most certainly, its moonshine. Speaking of their years there, Dick would later say, "I hated them and will never know why we did them."

14

This Can't Be Love, or Can It?

IT WAS impossible for Dick and Larry to live in New York and be unaware of the existence of Billy Rose. He had cast a shadow over their lives ever since he materialized at summer camp to buy lyrics from Larry. Even when they didn't see him, they read endless stories about him in the press.

Ben Hecht, from whom words flowed like quicksilver, saluted Rose as "a song writer, cafe keeper and fame hunter who found invisibility painful. A celebrity, Rose was haunted by the fear of waking in the morning and, like an inverse Byron, finding himself unknown."

In 1935 the saga of *Jumbo* began. It began with a telephone call to Hecht and his writing partner, Charles MacArthur. The "Bantam Barnum," as Billy Rose enjoyed being called, wanted the playwrights to concoct "the biggest musical extravaganza in the history of the world." That call was a pleasurable surprise, made more so because Hecht and MacArthur described everything they wrote as "something like *Romeo and Juliet*," and Rose, in his phone call, said he wanted "something like *Romeo and Juliet*." "A likely story," rejoined MacArthur, or so he claimed.

But Rose meant it. That classic tragedy (with a happy ending) was exactly what he had in mind. He had a specific background for it, too.

Ever since he had utilized Larry's lyrical qualities and claimed them for his own, Rose had traveled high and low roads in quest of fortune and, of course, fame. He achieved a measure of both.

He strayed for a time along a byway from show business, detouring into a job as secretary to Bernard Baruch, then chairman of the War Industries Board. Rose could take shorthand and type with championship speed, accomplishments that endeared him to Baruch. The old man left something to be desired as a statesman (although reputed to be expert), but he was a financial prophet, an ability that appealed to the nation's political leaders and very much to Billy Rose.

By listening carefully to the pearls of monetary wisdom that issued from the lips of his boss, Rose left that job with a fantastic portfolio of stocks and bonds that spewed out dividends like oil gushers. He returned to show business with one of the largest egos ever seen on Broadway. Walter Winchell, whose ability to recognize massive egos could be considered expert in view of his own, announced that Rose had returned to the Broadway scene "now that he has won the war!"

However, in spite of his grand delusions and proved skill at thinking big, the diminutive showman's efforts to put on a Broadway hit never approached his Wall Street success. Neither did his determination to become king of the nightclubs. After nursing wounds suffered when the Fifth Avenue Club folded, he made another run for the throne, this time with a theater-restaurant called Billy Rose's Music Hall. Observing a law he claimed to have originated, "Never use your own money," he sought the backing of bootleggers for this venture. They seemed charming associates, putting their booze on the tables and their girls in the chorus. They became utterly uncharming, however, when Rose's Music Hall was unsuccessful. They lost all their easy-earned money, and Rose fled to Europe to escape their uncouth methods of showing displeasure.

Pushing deep into Mittel-europa, Rose came to rest at a hunting lodge owned by Baruch. He had no taste for the sport, so called, of shooting animals but spent his days and nights wandering the quaint mountain villages of inner Bohemia.

To the best of Rose's somewhat faulty recollection, he dropped into what he thought was a Hungarian zoo but found a play in progress that utilized wild animals. It was a boy-girl romance told against a background of feuding circus families. Recognizing its Shakespearean antecedents, Rose decided it must surely be considered in the public domain and therefore was part his, too. He hustled back to New York, inspired by the possibilities, to invoke the *Romeo and Juliet* line to Hecht and MacArthur. He also hired their press agent crony, Dick Maney, to publicize the project, now called *Jumbo*.

Maney went about his duties with considerable zeal. He announced that *Jumbo* required a theater big enough to accommodate a climax never before conceived, the shooting of an elephant named Jumbo out of a cannon. In an effort to make that fantasy come true, Rose rented the New York Hippodrome, then the largest playhouse on earth. "We are scouring Africa for animals bigger than elephants," said Rose complacently (according to Maney), "because the

179

Hippodrome stage is so huge I'll have to use elephants to simulate dog acts."

The Bantam Barnum or "Mad Mahout," as Maney preferred to call his employer, found enormous satisfaction in such a mammoth undertaking. *Time* magazine, in a cover story, reported that Rose was indeed raiding the circuses of the world for talent, signing up aerialists, bareback riders, clowns, and on through the alphabet to zookeepers. Maney kept the Rose name foremost in every item about the upcoming show, a service that his boss sometimes appreciated and always demanded.

Rose could read his name in the papers much more than the title *Jumbo*. He reveled in the activity of assembling all its sawdust components. He was so busy that it was only in an offhand way that press agent Maney learned of an important addition to the cast of characters involved. Dick Rodgers was an infrequent visitor to 21 West Fifty-second Street, once a speakeasy but now a popular and expensive saloon. Coming glass to glass there with Maney, who frequented it frequently, the composer asked, "Has anyone told you Larry and I are doing the music and lyrics for the show?" No one had. Billy Rose, entranced with the world of circus performers, had forgotten that detail.

Hecht and MacArthur also took matters lightly. They might become known later as "Yesterday's Playboys," but in 1935 they were at the height of success as authors, scenarists, and playwrights.

They were indeed a joyous pair, addicted to practical jokes and with imagination enough to convince people they had perpetrated outrageous pranks, even when they hadn't. Among the legends of their antics:

Once, calling on financier Otto H. Kahn, they were ushered into the library of that celebrated patron of the arts. While waiting, they autographed innumerable volumes, inscribing passionate outpourings "To dear Otto, without whose help this could never have been written, Plato" or "To Otto, in memory of our wild and wonderful weekend at Cape Cod, Shelley." Similar remembrances, if true, would indicate they profaned thousands of dollars' worth of classics.

They also claimed to have made their way into the apartment of much-married and much-divorced Peggy Hopkins Joyce. Finding the lady out, they filled her bathtub with Jello, then turned on the hot water and watched that basin become a huge portion of the aspiclike dessert. It made for a merry story, but *chefs-de-cuisine*, who should know, say you can't make Jello that way.

Ribaldry was also part of their activities, and their friend Charley Lederer, no mean jokester in his own right, recalled a visit to the theater with MacArthur when the playwright was loudly affected by the quantity of liquor he had consumed. He made obscene references to a prim lady seated next to Lederer until she rose in her seat and called for help. Seeing the theater manager and a formidable corps of ushers advancing on them, MacArthur, in a voice that carried through the auditorium, advised Lederer, "Quick! Put your hand up her skirt; we're going to be thrown out anyway!"

There were lunatic antics in and out of the Hippodrome throughout the making of *Jumbo*, and it would seem that Dick and Larry alone provided a semblance of sanity. The show was too big to indulge in any out-of-town tryout. Instead, a sign on the Hippodrome warned noisy Sixth Avenue, "Sh-h-h-h! *Jumbo* is in rehearsal!"

It continued rehearsals all summer of 1935. Billy Rose planned an August opening, then postponed it to Labor Day and was still in rehearsal eleven weeks and seven postponements later. Everybody who was anybody in New York saw the show during that period; it was the thing to do. Joan

Crawford and Franchot Tone, arriving from Hollywood, spent most of their honeymoon there, along with many other nonpaying celebrities. It was great fun to see efforts (not always successful) to keep tubby Paul Whiteman on the back of a horse while leading his orchestra through the melodic "The Circus Is on Parade." Or to watch the birdlike clown A. Robins trill his way through the Rodgers music. The theater was so huge (and electronic amplification unknown) that few heard his whistling, and not many in the audience heard dialogue clearly either.

Blue-ribbon society folk, out-of-work actors, Greenwich Village artists, and ordinary passersby freeloaded in such numbers that MacArthur observed darkly, "Billy isn't going to open the show until everybody in town has seen it." But Rose had more important matters to worry about: He was running out of his investors' money and still needed a quarter of a million dollars.

It was his open-door policy, however, that saved the situation. *Jumbo* might never have opened at all if Bernard Baruch, Herbert Bayard Swope, and Jock Whitney hadn't become excited by the spectacle they saw in rehearsal and bailed him out.

Charley Lederer was there, and he, too, made a contribution toward the betterment of a scene in the show. Watching comic Jimmy "Schnozzola" Durante try furtively to sneak Jumbo, the elephant, past a sheriff who was there to serve a writ of attachment, Lederer made this suggestion: "You could have the sheriff ask, 'Where are you going with that elephant?' and have Jimmy say, 'What elephant?'"

It provided the biggest laugh in *Jumbo* and still remains one of the classic dialogues when great laughs in Broadway shows are recalled. Hecht and MacArthur rewarded their friend with a line in the program: "Joke by Charles Lederer."

The elephant joke, as it came to be known, outlived the

182

show, and so did three memorable songs, "My Romance," "Little Girl Blue," and "The Most Beautiful Girl in the World." Larry wrote a knowledgeable lyric when the curtain rose on the play, depicting the vicissitudes of circus performers, set to one of Dick's matchless waltzes, "Over and Over Again." There could have been still another hit song in *Jumbo,* but although "Small Hotel" survived some rehearsals and won many aficionados, it had to be cut when the play ran too long.

Jumbo was unveiled before a paying audience just before Thanksgiving Day, 1935. Most of those at the premiere had seen the show. The critics liked it; garlands tossed in its direction included such bouquets as brassy, breathtaking, thrilling, bespangled, glamorous, happy (if haphazard), different, exciting, outstanding, gargantuan, bizarre, gigantic, lively, huge, great, and megalomaniac, which sounded like celestial psalms in the ears of Billy Rose! The discords were in the ears of the backers: *Jumbo* was too costly to show a profit. But it ran well into the spring of 1936, and by that time Dick and Larry had a new play, *On Your Toes,* which opened in New York the week before *Jumbo* closed.

Now Hollywood was a thing of the past. Even Larry would write "hate California, it's cold and it's damp." On Broadway a curtain would rise on a Rodgers and Hart show every evening for two straight years ahead. They had earned the right to believe Manhattan had been reconquered. They were headed again for the greatness Dick was so eager to reach.

Music ranks high among the most beautiful sounds in the world and may well be the most beautiful of all. Sweet, beguiling melodies were in Dick's head and spilling out of his heart. For sixteen years the words to go with his tunes had been dreamed up and magnificently supplied by one man.

But while Larry still had his gift for turning them out, it

183

was becoming more and more difficult to make him settle down. In the beginning he had been hard to find. Now it was getting impossible.

It was of secondary importance to Dick whether Larry's absences were due to inner torment or drink. What mattered was that he, Richard Rodgers, had limitless melodies clamoring to be born, that required completion with words. Larry's disregard of this need in his partner, however, gave birth to anger in Dick. Sparks were igniting that lit whispers along Broadway. Rumors of discord between them reached the New York *Times*, which printed it. That necessitated a denial, and The *Times* printed that, too.

Larry's friends staunchly defended him. "You may not know where to find him," said Henry Myers, "but you were always sure how to stood with him."

There were many songs ahead for the collaborators, but Dick couldn't foresee that; instead, he could see with great clarity that storm signals were flying.

There was justification for his angers, but he would be patient. However, even when set to music, a man's anger wants to be heard and can grow to peaks of rage and fury. It was only a matter of time.

15

Without a Song in My Heart

"IT WASN'T important for me to produce our own shows,"
reflected Dick, "but it was convenient."

Although they sought help from seasoned play doctor
George Abbott, Dick also said, "Our best books were the
ones we wrote ourselves."

"They had a lot of fun working together," Dorothy Hart
said in a radio broadcast, but then she thought about it and
added, "Most of the time."

Collaborations, like marriages, are not always what they
seem. Dick tried to make the fabric look beautiful, but the
fraying edges of their relationship couldn't be hidden.

"If you made an appointment with Dick for a Thursday
morning at ten," said producer Gene Rodman, "Dick would
be there five minutes early. If you made the same appointment with Larry, he might not show up until three Thurs-
days later."

"Larry was probably what we now call kinetic," said Bennett Green. "He was in perpetual motion; he never sat down. He liked small movie theaters, and often, when he disappeared, we would search them. In his Hollywood days he was fond of a sleazy one downtown on Main Street, and I remember finding him in the balcony, asleep."

George Abbott, working with them on the libretto of *On Your Toes*, was quick to praise Dick's methodical ways: "He worked without fuss and feathers. If he had a song to write, he went and wrote a song. No talk about the greater things in life."

But Dick said, "People don't seem to realize how much thought, preparation, and composing went on before I sat down at a desk or piano and seemingly became the 'instant composer.'"

Dorothy Hart bears this out: "People talked about how fast Larry worked. I could almost see the wheels turning, but before he wrote, he would be playing cards, or just sitting . . . and then the words would explode."

To avoid the diversions that New York City offered Larry, Dick took him to Atlantic City for a weekend, so they could concentrate on a new song for the upcoming show. Adolph Green remembers that and says, enviously, "Instead of writing only one song, they wrote three. When they got back to town, dear Lord, they said they felt rested."

One of the hits of the score was "Small Hotel," originally written for *Jumbo*. Larry's dummy lyric, written before the concept of a small hotel was considered, received wide circulation among their friends. It didn't need to make sense but it was a source of amusement. All dummy lyrics are simply words strung together to show how the rhymes should go.

186

There's a girl next door,
She's an awful bore,
It really makes you sick to see her.
She's got a forty waist,
But she's got no taste,
I know I sure would hate to be her.
By and by, perhaps she'll die—
Perhaps she'll croak next summer;
Her old man's a plumber,
She's much dumber.

Doc Bender was very much in evidence around the theater during rehearsals of *On Your Toes*. He claimed the art of the dance as one of his superior attributes and, bulky as he was, could twirl about in spectacular leaps and movements. He was clowning backstage with the dancers waiting to make their entrances in a ballet of Nubian slaves until choreographer George Balanchine called, "What's holding them up?" When they danced onstage, Bender was on the end of the line, kicking in unison with the ensemble.

Larry, of course, was the most amused of the spectators and was moved to parody. . . .

Looking through the window you
Can see six slaves and Bender.
Bender's on the end-a—
Lucky Bend-a.

"Doc Bender was weird," said Larry Adler. "The reason that dummy lyric was good is that it was subtle. Bender loved orgies, and you had to understand what Larry meant by 'Bender on the end-a.' Bender on the end-a was what Bender damn well wanted.

187

"He was a lousy dentist. Larry is supposed to have said to him, 'Look, you're such a lousy dentist that I think you would make a very good agent.' Well, he was a lousy agent too, but not for Larry. The reason I say that is that he was the only one who could make Larry sit down and work. You see, Larry felt that lyric writing was hard work and resented it very much if anyone said it was easy. He was known to snap in irritation, 'The words don't just jump onto the page, you know.'"

It was Larry who persuaded George Balanchine to enter the musical comedy world.

Balanchine banded a group of Russian dancers together in Petrograd in 1923. One year later they excited enormous attention in Paris and worked there with the famous Sergei Diaghilev for four years. Then, after a season with the Ballet Russe de Monte Carlo, Balanchine organized the School of American Ballet and the American Ballet Company in New York. It was a great break for everyone concerned when he took on the choreography of *On Your Toes*. He made his genius evident in his dance innovations, not only on Broadway, but also in films, ballet, and opera.

"*On Your Toes* was the first of the integrated musical comedies," said George Abbott. "The songs and dances advanced the plot. It fulfilled Dick Rodgers' dream that musical comedies must be written that way."

An electrifying modern ballet, *Slaughter on Tenth Avenue*, was created for it, and Ray Bolger danced the leading role.

Another member of the cast was Tamara Geva, premiere ballerina in Balanchine's company, whom Larry had persuaded to become Bender's client. The dentist-agent had pushed hard for her to be included in the show and Arthur Schwartz remembers what happened:

"Her English was bad. You couldn't understand much of

what she said. All she could do was dance, but they needed someone who could act, too. I think they wanted Vera Zorina, but she was going to Hollywood to do a movie, so finally, in desperation, they gave Miss Geva a chance. It was a key role; the show's success or failure could well be decided on how she scored. In Boston, the first night of the tryout it was 'nervous time' for the producers standing in the back of the theater. But the miracle happened. The audience went wild over her, and as the applause indicating the birth of a new star grew more evident, so did Bender's smugness, pompousness, and unbearableness. 'You see?' he said. 'I always told you she was great, and now I know it!' "

George Gershwin's *Porgy and Bess* was also in Boston, prior to opening in New York. That made for an important week in Boston, with devotees, critics, experts, and movie scouts flocking in to see both shows. Although Gershwin's attempt at opera was recognized as a prestigious forward step, the score of *On Your Toes*, with its revolutionary ballet, *Slaughter on Tenth Avenue* drew such acclaim from the visitors that Dick actually came out ahead, critically, at that time.

The success of *On Your Toes* convinced Dick more than ever that they should write their own shows. They went straight to work on *Babes in Arms*. The vicissitudes of play producing by determined youngsters was an unusual idea in 1937, although destined to be a movie cliché in a matter of months. For this show, they wrote without George Abbot's help. Interestingly, they were able to view it objectively and critically.

Agreeing that the character of their leading lady needed clear exposition, not to mention a socko number, they wrote the words and music to an explanatory song for her in one day. It was called "The Lady Is a Tramp," and vivacious Mitzi Green, former child acress, belted it across the footlights to such effect it rocketed skyward to classic stature.

As usual, Dick wrote his melodies before Larry's lyrics. And as usual, he wrote them to fit particular plot needs. His facility with compositions rarely affected their catchiness and memorability. Larry's lyrics for *Babes in Arms* covered a broad range, from the *déjà vu* of "Where or When?" to the captivating "My Funny Valentine," the martial uplift of "Babes in Arms" and the funny-sad "I Wish I Were in Love Again."

The antics of Dick and Larry at rehearsals were marked by loud discussions, tinged with fun and affection. Naturally, Dick supervised the actions of the orchestra, and Larry continually complained that Dick encouraged louder music in the pit than the music required.

"You want to drown out my words," he would pretend to sob. He felt that even the exit march, without words, was rendered with excessive volume.

Then Dick would pat him on the head, paternally. "Do you expect the audience to go out whistling the lyrics?"

Babes in Arms contained some of their finest songs, although Larry wrote the words at a time of tremendous personal torment. Larry Adler is one of several people who believe the true state of Larry Hart's inner conflict should be brought into the open. "In those days it wasn't an open and acknowledged thing," he told us. "How different it would have been for him now—and how marvelous. You see, he felt permanent guilt because he was homosexual. He was terribly afraid his mother would find out.

"How do I know about him? Well, it's long ago, but I have a feeling he told me he was. I remember sitting in his house once in Beverly Hills, and that is when I believe he told me, because he was in a terribly agitated state. He told me someone had sent something to his mother which he felt was a hint that might make her suspicious, and he just thought his mother would die if she thought her son was homosexual."

Leonard Spigelgass feels there were multiple reasons for Larry's slip and ultimate fall from grace. "It wasn't Hollywood's fault," he says. "He began drinking before that. I think it was entirely due to what he considered his grotesque appearance. He hated the way he looked, and I think that motivated the self-destruction that took over and led to his downfall. He couldn't believe any woman could care for him. I'm sure many of his friends tell you that."

Nanette Guilford must certainly be counted as one of his friends, and she agrees that Larry attached too much importance to his height and appearance, saying forcefully, "Basically, he was *not* homosexual! But the reputation is there, and he was led into things that . . . well, I can't possibly repeat."

After she returned from Europe, she embarked on her acting career. Then Larry's attachment grew stronger than ever.

"He was absolutely adorable," she said, "and to know Larry was to love him. I loved him, but he never believed me. He didn't believe any woman could fall in love with him. My mother, who liked Larry very much, often discussed it. Her uncle was Lew Fields' partner, Joe Weber, who was a very short man. He appeared to be very fat, but he wasn't fat at all: that was padding. My mother said he had no complex at all. All the self-assurance, all the aplomb in the world, it never bothered him that he was short.

"I'll show you how it bothered Larry. He and I were at an opening one night, and he was wearing a top hat, with white tie and tails. We walked over to Broadway to get a

191

cab, and there were some rowdies standing on the street corner, and they started to laugh at him. He never wore a hat again!

"He gave a party with all these great big beautiful men, and believe me, he became the giant in ten minutes, and they were the pygmies. Because that mind was so marvelous!

"At that party, I was standing at a bottom step, and he was about two steps up. Suddenly, he put his hands on my shoulders and said, 'Darling, for once I'm above you.' And, you know, that nearly broke my heart.

"But let me tell you something that is so descriptive of how that mind worked. I was asked to open the *Catholic Hour Radio Station*. I was with the opera then and at the very last moment, the Metropolitan said, 'You cannot sing. You can speak, but you cannot sing.' So I called Larry and said, 'Anything I write will be so pedestrian. Will you write something for me?' He always called me baby, which, of course, at my age now is kind of funny, but he said, 'Of course, baby, what time do you have to be over at the place?' and I said, 'Nine o'clock this evening.'

"So he said, 'I'll be down at seven.' He came down at seven, and I said, 'Where's my speech, where's my speech?' He said, very softly, 'Don't get excited, don't worry. Let me go back to the library, and you'll have it.'

"Ten minutes later, the whole thing! In rhyme! The most brilliant thing! The papers, the next day, they raved. In ten minutes he wrote the whole thing!"

The play she agreed to do for her Broadway debut was called *Caviar*.

"After I signed the contract and rehearsals started," she told us, "I realized that this was a turkey! A very rich man wrote the music; his father was a steel millionaire. The director was impossible, and I said to Larry, 'I can't stand it, this man doesn't know a damn thing of what he's doing and the thing is just . . . .' Well, I wanted to get out of the contract so badly, but I couldn't.

"Anyway, Larry said, 'I'll tell you what we'll do. It's a most unprofessional thing, but do it. Get hold of the cast, have them come to the theater nine o'clock in the morning, and I'll direct them.'

"Well, everybody was tickled pink! Lorenz Hart directing! This was great! So . . . who walks in early that morning but the director! It was a charming moment! We just stood there. There was really nothing to say! I think I stammered something like 'Isnt Larry sweet? He's running us through. He just happened to drop in! Imagine! At nine in the morning!'

"But nothing could help that thing. Every night was a different version. I used to say, 'Tonight *East Lynne!* and tomorrow night *Way Down East!'* When we opened out of town, Larry sent me a big basket of flowers with a card saying, 'Only you can make a swan out of a turkey!'

"But, of course, it's not true. If you don't have the material, I don't care what you are or how good you are or whatever. I did some more musical comedies after that, out on the Coast. You have to forgive me, but I was bored with stage plays. In opera you have a variety of roles. Doing the same thing every night, those who do it as a regular thing take it as a matter of course, but I used to think, 'Oh, my God, the same thing tonight!' To me, it was the variety that I enjoyed.

"I stopped seeing Larry around that time. Another man came into my life, and I got married. It didn't last very long, and later, when I was divorced, I saw Larry again, but only casually."

Everyone with intimate knowledge of Larry's emotions agree that he never lost his warmth and admiration for Nanette Guilford. "She was an elegant woman," Dorothy Hart told an interviewer, "and that inspired him to dress up. He dressed elegantly around her, his clothes were handmade, very expensively. He wore beautiful handmade linen handkerchiefs. He would be very meticulous when he went to take her out—but not necessarily so when he returned."

Of course, Larry wasn't neglecting his work with Dick, and although *Babes in Arms* was having a notable run, they took time to write two songs for a movie, *Dancing Pirate*. It was unique for its time: It was filmed in color. Otherwise, it was an unnotable movie with an unnotable cast and two unnotable songs. It was practical to believe movies would bring their songs to instant attention from worldwide audiences, as compared to the slower thrust of a stage play, but the public didn't take to *Dancing Pirate*, and the songs walked the plank and died in the sea of mediocrity surrounding that film. There was a popular Hollywood expression that "Nobody sets out to make a bad movie," but *Dancing Pirate* cast considerable doubt on that statement.

Then, Dick and Larry went on to their next Broadway show.

It is difficult for people outside the theater to imagine the excitement, the labor, the anticipation, and the intense care necessary to the creation of a musical production. Straight drama and comedy—and there were many on Broadway in 1937—were mainly from the well-known playwrights of the day, fashioned for a small cast of characters in the confines of a few settings. But musical comedies required added dimensions; the performers needed to "have" music, their acting augmented by their ability to sing and dance. The investment required for a musical show far outdistanced the financing of a straight play, the risk factor was high as it will always be in a business which operates beneath a Damocletian sword with the axiom etched on it: "Give the public what it wants."

By this time Dick and Larry were deep into the precarious game of musical comedy; they "had" music, they knew their jobs well and were definite assets to the producer who was putting together a new show. Without doubt, the selection of the right personnel meant much to the successful wooing of the public. Producer Sam H. Harris, an old hand at delivering box-office hits, knew his way with what seemed unerring consistency, and in the summer of 1937 he started to travel the path again. It was to be a political satire called *I'd Rather Be Right*. He arranged for it to open in November of that year, six years after his great hit, *Of Thee I Sing*.

There were strong similarities between the two shows. Both stories dealt with the comic aspects of the presidency of the United States. For *I'd Rather Be Right*, Harris engaged George M. Cohan as the star. Instead of Morrie Ryskind collaborating with George S. Kaufman, authors of *Of Thee I Sing*, Kaufman's writing partner was Moss Hart, one of Broadway's major new comedy writers. With George and Ira Gershwin busy in Hollywood, Harris engaged Dick and Larry. There is an additional requirement to the production of a new show, and that is compatibility, and in the making of *I'd Rather Be Right*, that element was, unfortunately, lacking.

George Ross, of the New York *Times*, managed to pin down Larry for a rare interview:

"We had a three and a half year stretch in Hollywood. Then *Jumbo* and a picture called *Dancing Pirate* and *On Your Toes* and *Babes in Arms*, then Mervyn Le Roy sent for us to write a new score for a talkie, and what I really need is a vacation. Instead, Moss Hart and George S. Kaufman are running the sweatshop for their musical comedy.

"By the way, would you like to hear my definition of an optimist? My definition is Moss Hart and George S. Kaufman. I read in the papers that they already have an opening

195

date for the show and a theater booked, and I heard them arguing at the Sam Harris office if Monday or Wednesday is a better opening night for Boston, and we haven't even written half the score yet!"

Arguments between the participants who created *I'd Rather Be Right* occurred early. Dick and George Kaufman disagreed over the percentages of profits in their respective deals. Instead of the customary arrangements between playwrights and composers, amounting to an equal division, Kaufman and Moss Hart received 8 percent, while Dick and Larry got five. Kaufman refused to consider equalizing it, and Dick resented this.

Dick's irritation increased when Kaufman voiced his permanent distaste for music in the theater. He was directing the play and, in attempting to move it along, gave the songs little time to be heard. In all, Dick and Larry wrote fifteen numbers, three of which were cut by Kaufman. There were no encores.

"Have You Met Miss Jones?" was the hit of the score. It was sung early in the first act and stopped the show. When that happened, Dick, standing close to Kaufman, said loudly, "Now we can have an encore, and maybe somebody will remember a couple of bars!"

Kaufman's angers were as celebrated as his witty remarks. He blew up, but according to Dick, he didn't "come and tell me so; he did it by proxy. He sent Moss Hart. However, during the tryout in Baltimore we had it out face to face on the street in front of Ford's Theater. Kaufman won, in the end. He was bigger, richer, and older."*

*Kaufman knew how Rodgers felt, and as Rodgers grew increasingly successful, it was Kaufman's turn to taste gall. Years later, when Rodgers and Hammerstein had *South Pacific* in Boston, Kaufman could stand it no more. The reviews were glorious, and business was booming. During luncheon at Moss Hart's one Sunday, Kaufman threw down the paper in

The Rodgers-Kaufman unpleasantness did not amount to much more. Although they never worked together again, they saw each other socially. Each went to the other's openings. Dorothy Rodgers thought George was very attractive (which he wasn't)* and very good at parlor games (which he was), and Dick conceded that Kaufman was very good in the theater and very bad on the croquet field.

But the real war that scarred the production of *I'd Rather Be Right* paired off George M. Cohan against Dick and Larry.

Cohan was cast as the President. It was unusual for him to work solo as an actor in a show; he was also a producer (usually in partnership with Sam H. Harris, who was putting on this play) and often the author of the book and the score. He did not like being relegated to actor alone and made life generally unpleasant for those who were performing in the creative areas he believed he could do better.

Cohan, sometimes called the Yankee Doodle Dandy from one of his songs of that title, was a complex individual, whose ambivalent ways almost defy analysis. His revolt against the actors in the big strike has already been told, but he was given to incredible actions offstage.

He never wrote a Jewish character into any of his plays, telling a biographer, "I don't understand them." But once, arriving at a hotel that barred certain guests on religious grounds, he was refused a room. He told the manager, "Because my name is Cohan, you thought I was Jewish, and I thought you were American. We are both wrong!" Then he

_____

disgust. "I see where the Shubert Theater in Boston is locked up on Sunday," he said, "but people are so excited about *South Pacific* they're pushing money under the lobby doors. They don't want anything; they just want to push money under the doors."

*The hell he wasn't.—CLAYTON

197

stalked out of the hotel and gave the story to the press, damning the place for its restrictive practices.

American he was: He loved to wave the flag in his plays, and he wrote magnificent songs exemplifying his love of country, notably "It's a Grand Old Flag" and the great World War I classic "Over There."

Yet his intolerance was paradoxical. Looking back on the actors' strike, to which he contributed so much animosity, he compounded his hostility against the actors. He told reporters, "It would make a swell plot for a musical," and announced his intention of writing it, although he never did. His Americanism had weird limits. Once, while playing baseball, he became annoyed by the presence of a black man on the team and chased him out of the park with a bat in his hands. He dismissed the incident with "He got on my nerves."

He thoroughly disliked the words and music that Dick and Larry wrote for *I'd Rather Be Right*. Doubtless, he believed he could do better in both departments.

He was summoned to hear the score—a presentation by the composer and lyricist. Anyone can visualize how important a meeting of this sort can be, what it means to writers to get some sign of approbation, favorable reactions, praise, perhaps great enthusiasm.

But Cohan just listened, deadpan. When Dick played the last note on the piano and Larry sang the last lyric, Cohan stood up, tipped his hat forward, said, "Don't take any wooden nickels, kids," and strolled out of the theater.

16

"You Goosed My Cook!"*

IN THE late 1930s Dick and Larry became so busy with new productions that their shows were like a jigsaw puzzle. The writing of *On Your Toes* was finished before *Jumbo* but wasn't put onstage until five months afterward. *I Married an Angel* was blocked out and ready for its final touches before *I'd Rather Be Right*, and they were also doing some work on *The Boys from Syracuse*, which was slated to follow *I Married an Angel*.

With all this to do—a time requiring intense concentration—Dick was having problems with his partner. Larry was dropping out of sight when his presence was needed at conferences and rehearsals. He would go out of the city, to nearby Long Island and New Jersey or sometimes as far as Florida. Dick was trying hard to live with this, trying hard to keep his temper under control.

*One of Larry's lines from his dummy lyric of "You Took Advantage of Me."

Producer Dwight Deere Wyman had secured the rights to *I Married an Angel* from MGM. The stage version was on his schedule, and it was to be his third production with Dick and Larry. Being so familiar with the material, they undertook to write the book as well as the score.

The next important ingredient was to get the director so they could move on to polishing, then casting and rehearsals. The one who was hired for *I Married an Angel* was Joshua Logan, a youthful Princetonian who had written and directed some of that university's Triangle Shows.

After an apprenticeship as a stage manager and some Hollywood film direction, Logan was acclaimed for his staging of the Broadway hit *On Borrowed Time*. Producer Wyman suggested him to Dick and Larry, and they accepted him even before the opening night of *On Borrowed Time*.

Logan's recollection of what went on is graphic, and this is how he related it to Fred Nolan of the British Broadcasting Corporation:

"I was sent down to Atlantic City, where Larry was staying at one of the big boardwalk hotels. We had never met. It was a four-hour journey by train, and he was waiting for me at the railway station with a limousine. He must have been very nervous at the prospect of meeting me because he was very talkative, smoking and puffing away at his eternal cigar, rubbing the palms of his hands together in a typical gesture.

"I am going to be almost embarrassingly warm in the terms I use about him because he was most lovable, as cuddly as a honey bear, very small, you know, slightly over five feet, maybe four foot nine; it's hard to tell exactly because he wore elevated shoes.*

*Larry also used "elevators" on his bedroom slippers.

"He was not a beauty, you know; he had a gnomelike face and body but a truly explosive personality.

"We drove to the hotel, and I expected to go right to work on the script. But not at all. He got out a card table and went into a variation of rummy. He explained that the player can do anything he wants, bluff, lie, cheat, anything! Anything, that is, except get caught! He howled with delight over the idea that one could excel at larceny; it delighted him. I think it was because one of the earliest memories of his life was of the chicanery of his father, who was evidently an old crook. He thought anything his father did that was under the table or wrong was hilariously funny. But he had, also, a dear little mother, and his younger brother, Teddy, who was better formed than he—that is, more acceptably formed.

"So we played rummy for hours, and then I thought we would get to work, but no, we had to go to some marvelous place for lobsters . . . and we had a few drinks . . . and more cigars . . . . I couldn't quite take those.

"In short, we wasted about four or five days, and I kept saying when will we get to work, and he would say we have plenty of time for that . . . plenty of time, and then it was Sunday, or whatever day it was we were to return to New York.

"We had two hours before the train, and Larry decided, without any conference with me at all, to write the second act—right then! I said, 'What'll we do, think about it on the train?' and he said, 'No, I'll have it finished before train time, and then we can have some fun on the train.'

"He took a huge pad of paper on this little card table, and as fast as he could write, he would scribble a few lines on each page, and then he would throw the page over his shoulder, one after the other, so fast all I could do was to try

201

to keep the pages in order. I kept waiting for him to run out of steam, but he didn't, he just kept going and going until he had about one hundred pages, but there wasn't one word on any one of them that could be read. It was useless for me to try to get the pages in order because nothing could be read, and that's what we brought back, and I was so embarrassed, because this is what we had to give to Schoolteacher, one of Larry's names for Dick.

"I watched Larry as he 'handed in his papers' to the Principal, who looked very skeptical and then even more so when he looked at the work, and he said, 'This isn't any good, Larry.' Larry said, 'No, it's wonderful. We can put this onstage tomorrow.' Dick said, 'Larry, you *know* this isn't any good. I don't think even *you* could read it.' After a great deal of arguing by Larry—he always argued for his things—protecting his lyrics, protecting himself, saying no, no, it's wonderful. . . . Dick, I've *got* to say, was a wonderful editor for Larry, with great great talent himself, and, as I learned was going to have to write quite a few of Larry's lyrics. I didn't know at that time how much liquor meant to Larry. . . . Oh, it wasn't too bad then; he wasn't in the kind of shape into which he soon grew; we could all see it. But he was delightful, and he was like a small boy who was running away. He was *always* playing hooky—always truant.

"He loved life," said Logan, "but he had a lot of scabrous friends and the most *suspect* of every-kind-of-thing friend he had was Doc Bender. He was acting as Larry's agent, and Larry was trying very hard to get Balanchine to become one of his clients and, I believe, was trying very hard to get Zorina, too. Anyway, Bender was a very puffy-faced man, quite a comic character that everyone suspected as a procurer for Larry, that whatever sex Larry indulged in—and nobody is

202

ever sure of that—Doc Bender found it for him. Larry never talked about his sexual life at all.

"When we got back from Atlantic City, I found we were going into rehearsal. Dick and Larry were taking credit for the book, but there was no book. I was the director and while I had done some writing at Princeton, and helped with a little writing on *Borrowed Time*, I certainly hadn't planned on doing any writing here. I was the director, but I was worried about not having a script. We had the *beautiful* Zorina, and Dennis King as the leading man, then Walter Slezak, and the girl who was to become Larry's favorite performer, Vivienne Segal, in addition to two young people, Audrey Christie, who played the ingenue, and Chuck Walters, who later became a director in pictures. And Balanchine, supposedly the greatest dance genius of his age and a charming man, did the dances. He had a little kind of nervous twitch, but the most attractive, with a charming Russian accent. The really great, glamorous person was Zorina.

"We went into rehearsal, and it seemed to be going all right—we were working on the songs in the first act. Then one night, about four days later, I suddenly realized that I had staged the first act, and people were asking me about the second act, and there wasn't any! So Dick said, 'We'll meet at Larry's apartment tonight and write the second act.' Well, I wasn't used to writing second acts in a night—I'd seen Larry scratching away at it—but I found in Larry's apartment that *I* was writing. I was putting it down with just plain ol' pencil and paper. We had no dictating machines, I couldn't do shorthand, but in a sense, the three of us dictated what should go down. We stayed up all night long, got someone to type part of it for us for the next morning, and by the end of the day I had gone into the second act.

"I kind of learned, as I talked to other people, that that's the way Dick and Larry *always* did their shows. And they'd been writing books for years. The songs always carried somehow. But the thing was they didn't have a score for the second act either. So I knew that we had a sequence where they had to sing something at an all-night party in Budapest, with everybody in the cast waiting up all night to go to the bank and pull out all their money. I can't remember why.

"Larry said, 'You must give everyone a chance to be funny, step out of character for a while.' Larry had a great feeling for how a show should go, developed from knowing so much about the early German musical comedy. He had translated a few of them for the Shuberts. Anyway, that night *I* slept, but they stayed up all night and finished the score of the second act. When they came in with it the next day, I just couldn't believe my eyes or ears, because they had done a song called 'The Roxy Music Hall.' Now the Roxy Music Hall is about as far from Budapest as I could imagine, and I asked, 'How on earth?' and they said, 'We'll do a takeoff on the Music Hall, and everybody in it will take off on his particular part. For instance, Dennis King, who was known for his "And to hell with Burgundy!" will do a song against wine; Audrey Christie and Viv Segal will be the Rockettes—instead of being a great mass of kicking girls, there will be just two of them—and Slezak will do a kind of takeoff on Ted Shawn, and Zorina will do a ballet that is a takeoff on ballet.'

"I asked feebly, 'How do we get into it?' Larry said, 'Oh, they just get to talking about Radio City.'

" 'Oh, no!' I shouted. 'You'd better write it in lyrics. I cannot bear to jump from a Budapest scene into a song about New York and the Rockettes!'

"Immediately Larry ad-libbed a phrase, 'You must come

to New York. It would be such a pity for anyone to go through life without seeing Roxy City,' which Dick promptly put to music. Being a legitimate director, I didn't believe in it, I just couldn't believe it would work. Larry explained, 'You can't sing about Budapest all night, we've got to do something different . . . give them some fun. They'll believe *anything if it's good.'* He was very right.

"This is the way I feel about Larry: There are very few people in the history of our theater who can do any kind of song—*any* kind. He would write specifically for that moment in the show . . . and come through, I would say ninety percent of the time.

"I saw a lot of Larry and Doc Bender. I found that Larry loved to 'put something over' on the censors; he was constantly a naughty boy, but an innocently naughty boy. He never did anyone any real harm in his whole life. He was the constant friend of the underdog, and anyone who was in that category could get a handout from him any time. That was a part of his relationship with Bender—the underdog. I found Larry irresistible.

"Because he had to be a disciplinarian, I think, in a sense, Dick Rodgers got a lot of blame he shouldn't have. Larry must have been impossibly difficult to work with for him. He certainly was difficult for me, and I didn't have the responsibility that Dick did.

"As fond of Larry as I was, I never had much social life with him because he was always out with the, you know, the underworld type of life that he lived. You never knew quite what Larry Hart did; I never saw him at a restaurant, or clubs, any opening night unless it was his own. He had a special after-dark life that was, I think, some kind of escape. He hated anything he considered too ordinary. Respectable, proper, was not only repulsive but stupid and dull. Now, the only thing that happened, he controlled himself pretty well, except on the first dress rehearsal.

"We were at the Shubert Theater and going through the score, you know, with the orchestra. I hadn't realized that Larry had been drinking quite a lot that evening. Rehearsal had gone fairly well, you know, the usual mistakes—lighting, and so forth—and all of a sudden, when Audrey Christie started to sing the Roxy song, she got to the 'it would be such a pity, etc. . . . Now come with me,' and all of a sudden, I heard the most fascinating, terrifying, nervous-sounding sound, and I looked over to my right, and there, like a little windmill, was Larry Hart, screaming and yelling and waving his arms and doing something with his cigar, and talking—it sounded like a foreign language—and he kept repeating a gibberish phrase. I said, 'Larry, Larry, please! What are you trying to say?' and he yelled, 'No now singers in my show!' and I said, 'No *what* kind of singers?' And he repeated, 'No now singers!' and I asked, 'What are now singers?' and someone said . . . he means that Audrey added the word 'now' to the beginning of the chorus. A lot of singers fall into this habit, but we were not to have any 'now' singers.*

"Larry was adamant about his lyrics: you'd better not mess around with them. But he was so upset by this that he went up on the stage, up the little stairway put there temporarily, and sat on the proscenium, as though to protect his lyrics, and I remember we went on with the show, with him sitting there, and there was nothing to do. He was just there, listening very hard, and Walter Slezak leaned over and said to me, 'May I make a suggestion for the decor? I think you ought to have *another* little Larry Hart sitting on the other side of the stage.' "

*With Jerome Kern, it was "well" singers.

206

Vivienne Segal was assuredly Larry's favorite performer, as Josh Logan said. She was such a favorite with Larry that everyone who knew him believed her to be his most serious romantic interest.

But—

"We were never sweethearts," she said when we met in her home in West Los Angeles. "Dick said Larry loved me more than he loved anyone else, and he did ask me to marry him just before he died, but we never had a romance. I knew he wasn't particularly interested in women. I never even kissed Larry! We never could have been married!"

Vivienne recalled her meeting Larry and Dick in California in 1934. She had many years of Broadway stardom behind her. Like many actresses, she had early disappointments; a quarrel with Jerome Kern nearly twenty years before was one of these—but it led eventually to her meeting with Larry.

She was a dancer in the ballet of a musical revue, *Miss 1917*, which had music by Kern and Victor Herbert. But Herbert first heard her sing when he conducted her in a concert. He told her she ought to go into operetta. "You belong on the stage; you're an actress."

"Everybody in the world was in *Miss 1917*," she said. "Bessie McCoy Davis, the widow of Richard Harding Davis, and Irene Castle, two enormous favorites, were among them. But I was producer Charley Dillingham's pet; he looked on me as his baby. I was given a chance to sing, whereupon Kern suggested 'They Wouldn't Believe Me' and Herbert wanted me to sing 'Kiss Me Again.' Dillingham told me I would show off better with 'Kiss Me Again,' and besides, Herbert had coached me in it.

"So comes the dress rehearsal. Herbert is sitting in one aisle; Kern is in the other. I came out, and as I started to sing 'Kiss Me Again,' Kern ran down the aisle and said,

'You're not singing that; you're singing "They Wouldn't Believe Me."' Herbert came down the other aisle, saying, 'No, she's singing "Kiss Me Again."'

"Flo Ziegfeld was also involved with the show. He came down, and so did Dillingham, who asked me, 'What do you want to sing?'

"I said, 'I want to sing "Kiss Me Again."'

"Well, Jerry Kern became my everlasting enemy. But I sang 'Kiss Me Again.' Bessie McCoy Davis, who was returning to the stage after the death of her husband, got the first notices, and I got the second notices. I was very young, and they said I was the only member of the cast who didn't look like a Broadway jade. That annoyed all the chorus girls—I was afraid to come to the theater that night!

"In 1932 Kern's *Music in the Air* was in New York. I was dying to play the part that Natalie Hall played. It was comedy, just the kind of thing I wanted to do. Jerry Kern wouldn't even let me audition for it; he was that vindictive. Then I heard, some time later, they were going to do it on the Coast. So I said to Louis Sher, who was my agent, 'I want to play that part.'

"I was then getting seventeen hundred and fifty dollars a week, and he said they were only going to pay five hundred dollars. I said, 'I don't care what they are going to pay; I want to play that part!' You know, money never meant anything to me. He said, 'That's ridiculous. You take five hundred dollars, and when you want to come back to Broadway—' and I said, 'I don't give a damn. I want to play that part, and I'll take the five hundred dollars. I have to prove to myself that I can do comedy,' I told him. That's my niche. Well, they were very happy to get me for five hundred dollars, and I played it at the Biltmore Theater in Los Angeles.

"Dick and Larry were at MGM, and they came to see the

208

show. They had a party one night, and Larry said to me, 'You're a comedienne!' and I said, 'Thank God someone's found that out!'

"He said, 'I must find the right part for you someday.' I thought it was another one of those promises that you hear so often. When the show closed, I did a lot of radio; I was on Frank Munn's *Album of Familiar Music*. Sometimes I'd run into Larry, and then, every once in a while, I'd say, 'I thought you were going to write a part for me.' One thing I can say for Larry, if he didn't think you were right for a part, you didn't get it. He wouldn't do that for his best friend. No favorites.

"So this went on for at least a year, we were all back in New York, and I bumped into Larry. By that time, I got tired of saying, 'How about that part?' But this time he said, 'You're in my next play!'

"It was *I Married an Angel*. He asked me if I would be interested. Yes. But, as Louis Sher had told me, 'You'll have a hard time getting away from that five hundred dollars a week,' and I didn't get away from it. That's what I got. But I didn't care. I was doing what I wanted to do. It established me as a comedienne.

"It was in that show I got to know Larry. I really don't know if he was drinking more than he should then. I don't think I ever saw him drunk. There used to be a little place on West Forty-fifth Street where we would go and get a most marvelous spaghetti. A gang of us used to go there, and Maria, the wife of the owner, was terribly fond of Larry. But she ran off one day with one of the waiters, and that was the end of the best spaghetti!

"Larry would go in there, and he'd be at the bar, writing lyrics. I never saw him there with any men friends, except Doc Bender. Larry told me to use him as my agent, which I did. He may have been a procurer for Larry—I don't know whether he was or not—I imagine Dick would say that he was.

"I remember once, quite a bit later, I was on the road; it might have been Cleveland, some town in the Middle West. Evidently, Larry said to some guy, 'Let's go out and see Vivienne.' The next thing I know, Larry shows up with this guy who, I'm sure, was a pimp and a procurer! Of *men!*

"This sort of solidified things in my mind. I didn't like this guy immediately, I didn't know why he was with Larry, but I got on the phone and called Bender. I said, 'Get out here right away!' I told him about the guy, and Bender was on the next plane and took Larry back to New York.

"I rather imagine this guy intended to get Larry very drunk and then bring in some floozy off the street—a male floozy. I was sure of this, and I didn't want Larry to get into any scandal, so that's why I called Bender.

"I never saw Larry tied to any man, but then, as I said earlier, I never knew him to be in love with me. Of course, there was that other girl, Nanette Guilford, who had been in grand opera. I heard he had been in love with her. . . .

"It was Larry's size that helped make him feel it was incongruous for him to be involved in romance. I think that's what started him drinking, too. I think he felt that he was so unattractive to women and that he was sort of grotesque. That's the picture he had of himself."

Although everyone who cared for Larry believed him to be seriously in love with Vivienne Segal, it is our view that his admiration for her was an emotion that bordered on love but stopped short of sexual desire. She was easy for him to talk to and be with. She was graceful, ornamental, and she sang his words better than anyone else. He had taught her that she could deal with the most sophisticated words and thoughts so long as she did it with a twinkle in her eye . . . just as he wrote in the song for her. He always said, "She says it and sings it like a lady." That is the way she sang "A Twinkle in Your Eye" to Zorina in *I Married an Angel,* its words imparting sophisticated instructions to the heavenly visitor to earth, from an adorable earthling. Josh Logan said, "Every night the audience ate them up with a spoon."

Larry found in Vivienne Segal the ideal performer; no one ever came along to eclipse her. Many men have been thought to be in love with a woman for less.

Her appearance in *I Married an Angel* restored her popularity and her salary to their earlier proportions. The play was also a triumph for Dick and Larry, as well as for Josh Logan and Zorina. The critics were enamored of the music score, and several picked "At the Roxy Music Hall" as a prime reason for seeing the show. Wolcott Gibbs of *The New Yorker* called it "as memorable as Dick's 'Slaughter on Tenth Avenue" ballet." Ironically, when *I Married an Angel* scored a success on Broadway, the movie studio that feared to make it in 1933 found the courage in 1938 to proceed, even against Catholic disapproval. Somewhat shamefacedly, Metro-Goldwyn-Mayer discovered it had disposed of the rights it needed in order to put it on the screen. The company paid a lot of money to regain a privilege it had once possessed.

There could have been an additional reason why Larry admired Vivienne Segal. She had many of the qualities he found enchanting in Dick's wife. Dorothy Rodgers was regal, charming, and witty. Her intelligence was outstanding; her style and keen professionalism were notable. They were women who stood out in a crowd. They were vivacious and ingratiating; Dorothy also had the boundless energy that Vivienne Segal possessed.

She put some of her restless spirit into business ventures. She opened a workshop that specialized in repairing odds and ends of home furnishings. She advertised "We fix anything," and that drew a telegram from Larry, the inveterate telegram sender, CAN YOU FIX MINE? Dorothy wired back, IF YOU CAN SEND IT WE CAN FIX IT.

Larry loved to tell a story about a temporary lapse in the cool of the usually unflappable Mrs. Rodgers. She made the mistake of confessing it to him, and he spread it gleefully.

Dorothy got into a cab one beautiful, happy, I-love-New-York day that was made even lovelier by the haunting melody playing on the radio. When they pulled up to her destination, she couldn't resist doing something she would rarely, if ever, do. As she paid the cabby, she bragged, "That's my husband's music," to which he replied, in surprise, "Oh, are you Mrs. Irving Berlin?" She looked at him blankly for a moment, said, "Oh, my God!" and fled.

Many noticed a new attitude in Dick toward Larry. Sig Herzig was one. He said, "Dick was snide and critical, but he should thank God for Larry. This was the first time people listened to and *discussed* lyrics."

Josh Logan said Dick and Larry had to change their attitudes many times. It applied to their words and music:

"Dick is very meticulous about his work. One of his great problems was . . . well, it's true of all composers, insisting upon his work being done just as he created it. It's a form of self-protection. His meticulousness also extends to self-protection in many areas.

"Dick was not so generous a person by any means as Larry. Dick always worked hard, I suppose he's as near being a genius in the music world as any man who ever lived, but—

but he's not a generous genius. He's careful and well organized. I doubt if he ever made a big gesture of love, warmth or friendship—certainly not to his friends. There is a barrier in him.

"I've always tried to describe Dick's face when he is at his most brilliant and creative. You ask him his opinion—Shall we put that song there or where? Dick, in a sense, steps into a private Dick Rodgers chamber where he commiserates with himself. When he is in that chamber after you ask him that question, his face is so wincing, so wrinkled, so acerbic, almost disapproving, he looks as though he has a bad case of indigestion. Then he says, 'Great!' or 'Perfect!' or 'Go ahead!' But just before he makes that happy decision, he looks terrifying and unhappy—just the opposite. I don't think he means to show this, I don't think he even knows he does it, but he does go through such a personal decision-making thing that it is actually painful."

Logan's observations made his interviewer, Fred Nolan, suddenly interject, "To think of putting this man with the little, capricious, cigar-smoking, elevated-shoes man, putting those two together and think of it working!"

And working it was. With *I Married an Angel* in New York's Shubert Theater for a run of nearly a year, they began to level on *The Boys from Syracuse.*

Gene Rodman saw Larry at that time:

"I was in Miami, at the Roney Plaza Hotel, when they were writing *The Boys from Syracuse.* Larry had a beach chair right next to mine. He would come down in shorts, a commander's cap, lifts on his sneakers. A Greek god he wasn't.

"He carried a yellow legal pad and scribbled lyrics like mad. Some he didn't like, and so he threw them away. I picked them up and asked if I could have them, and he said

213

yes. He saw no value in them. (I have lost them somehow, like an idiot.)

"One thing I remember vividly. He would sometimes look around and say, 'I love it down here; it's the only place I can relax. New York is crazy—all that night life. Here it is calm and relaxing.' The funny thing was that when he would say that, he would jump around, rubbing his hands together, and change from one beach chair to another—between each sentence! By the time he was through saying how peaceful it was he could be ten chairs away from where he started!

"He had a handsome young masseur with him on the beach, and they went everywhere together all the time he was in Miami."

17

I'd Rather Be Indecisive

THE BOYS FROM SYRACUSE was loosely adapted from Shakespeare's *A Comedy of Errors*. The original story is a variation of a play by Plautus who, some believe, borrowed his plot from Menander, a fourth-century author who wrote contemporary comedies. A lot of geography has been lost along the way, as well as the atmosphere of Ephesus in Turkey (the locale of the action) and Siracusa in Sicily, which is where the principal characters come from.

Despite the comedic nature of the story, Dick wrote a score laced with delicate compositions that breathed more than a little the feeling of Shakespeare's England. One of his finest waltzes, "Falling in Love with Love," was part of it. It was a noticeable thing, however, that he was growing more interested in researching, and from here forward, even beyond Larry Hart, he would seek to inject the color, sensibilities, and impressions connected to those regions in which the stories took place, but in 1938, one year before Hitler's war would shock the world into brutal realities,

215

authentic attention to melodic lines was of little or no importance.

Larry worked on these lyrics with glee. After all, he had not been dubbed "Shakespeare Hart" for nothing. He delighted in the poetry, intrigued with its kinship to his rhyming talents.

Charming, articulate Kay Swift visited with us to tell us:

"Larry Hart was marvelous to me when I was rehearsal accompanist on *Connecticut Yankee.* He taught me something that was invaluable to me for my writing, and that was . . . don't worry if you have a beautiful ballad right after the comic does a routine. You won't get anything on the ballad; it may be the best thing you ever wrote, nobody could get anything. If God wrote the song, it wouldn't get anything. They'll have had a big laugh and they won't be ready to accept anything you write. And it was true, and it happened. It was 'This Can't Be Love,' but it's become a standard since."

George Abbott, a tall, no-nonsense, quadruple threat of the Broadway theater, wrote the book, directed and produced it. He did not act in it, but a very special thespian did.

The Boys from Syracuse finally gave Larry the chance to make good on his long-deferred wish to help Teddy's career. Little brother was given the role of Dromio of Ephesus, while Jimmy Savo, a great mime, an ideal copy of Teddy in physical stature, played the twin, Dromio of Syracuse.

Teddy's unfailing good nature didn't change with maturity. He had none of Larry's mercurial habits; life drifted by him with the same serenity as he drifted through life. Only in looks was a similarity with Larry unmistakable.

Irving Pincus' impression of Teddy is: "He was fifty percent of Larry. For instance"—Pincus laughed—"he wouldn't take a drink, but he would buy you one."

By 1938 their physical resemblance had become more

pronounced than when they were children, and they were often taken for each other. Teddy's new wife, Dorothy, recalled that Larry grew furious with people who thought he was Teddy. The emotions of resentment and affection that Larry harbored for Teddy changed constantly, switching back and forth. The evidence points, however, to affection as his stronger feeling, with only occasional flashes of anger.

Onstage Teddy more than held his own against the highly thought-of talents of Jimmy Savo. *The Boys from Syracuse* gave him the prominence he had so long hoped to attain. That pleased Larry immensely.

Sheldon Leonard, actor-director and a successful television producer, knew Teddy when he was just beginning to make it on Broadway. A cultured, articulate man, Sheldon had a strong physique that lent itself to the popular concept of the gangster, and he played many characters patterned in the manner of Damon Runyonesque racketeers. For fun, he often lapses into their vernacular:

"There's no gainsaying it, if one chooses to say a little gain, Teddy was the most amiable of men, if not the brightest. A bunch of us used to play poker every week. We did not cling to ceremony, some of us would show up and some of us would not, but this particular night we were more than a little surprised when Teddy came in as he was indeed on his honeymoon. He called for a stack of markers and took his regular place at the game. He was shaved and talcumed and had his hair slicked back with some foreign cologne.

"I said to him, 'Theodore, my boy, we are more than delighted to have you here, but why are you not with your bride and besides that, since you are here, why are you wearing the price tag of your lower garment stitched to your belt band?'

217

" 'Sheldon, that shows how very bright you are,' he replied. 'I've been wearing these pants for three days, and I never noticed it.' "

Dick wrote a superlative score for *The Boys from Syracuse*, and Hugh Martin and Ralph Blane were called in to make vocal arrangements of some of the songs.

In a telephone interview with Blane, who has returned to his hometown, Broken Arrow, Oklahoma, he told us how easy it was to succeed with Rodgers and Hart.

"They didn't care what we did as long as we stopped the show!"

The girl who sang two show stoppers, "Sing for Your Supper" and "Falling in Love with Love" was Muriel Angelus, a newcomer to Broadway from England.

"In order to do the play," she said, "I signed a contract, but as I was here on a visitor's permit, I had to go all the way back to London and get a working permit, then return. It was well worth it, as singing and acting were my life. It was marvelous to fall into that setup with Rodgers and Hart doing the music and lyrics and George Abbott directing and Balanchine staging the ballet. Then the young players, Eddie Albert and Burl Ives, who became stars.

"The day I signed the contract, Dick said, 'Let's go out and celebrate,' and he took me to a drugstore on Fifty-sixth Street near Fifth Avenue. It wouldn't have been my choice as a place to celebrate, but I had only been in the States three or four weeks, and I thought it might be the custom. He said, 'You're going to have a Coca-Cola,' and then, while I'm sure it was true, he said humorously, 'Because I own stock in the company.' I had never tasted it before, so had my first Coke with Dick. I hope his stock didn't go down on my account, because I haven't had one since.

"We talked about the show. I told him, 'The only thing I would like to take back to my singing teacher in England is

218

just one song that I'm going to sing. If you only had something for me to take back. . . .'

"Dick said, 'I've got a wonderful waltz that I'm writing for you, but it's not finished yet.' There was a newspaper, and he tore off the top and wrote the first lines of "Falling in Love with Love." Wouldn't it have been marvelous if I had kept that?

"Everybody in the cast was American while I was very British. During the show I was supposed to come on and be displeased with Teddy, and say, 'Well, you can watah plants, cahn't you?'

"Mr. Abbott [no one has ever heard him called anything but *Mr. Abbott*] stopped me at rehearsal and said, 'Muriel, when you say that line, the Union Jacks are flying all over. Try and do it with a little more of an American accent, so you'll sound like the others.' I went back and said to Teddy, 'Wal, yuh can water plants, can't yuh?' Mr. Abbott stopped the rehearsal again and said, 'Go back to the British!'

"During the run of the play Larry always came backstage to see Teddy, whose dressing room was right next to mine. Poor Teddy, so different than Larry and yet so darling. As time passed by he became a very elegant little gentleman. He wore spats and gloves and carried a cane.

"Larry was a demon; he was like Peck's Bad Boy. He was like Puck in *Midsummer Night's Dream*, I could never get to know him, he was here one minute and around the world in forty seconds. But I left the show before it closed, to go to Hollywood and make a film for Paramount. On my last night Larry sent me some orchids. He didn't send me one or two orchids; he sent me a huge box, I haven't the reach to show you the size. I could have opened a shop!"

Larry's extravagances were becoming widely known and viewed with alarm. Most prominent of these, of course, was Dick, who, besides trying to hold the line against his partner's mounting drinking habits, now had to admonish him against excessive financial intemperance, too. But Larry was picking up the check for drinks, meals, travel, plus miscellaneous expenses of friends, acquaintances, and strangers. Bennett Green said, "It was a sin, the way he threw money away."

It was a reckless display of indiscriminate philanthropy. Larry obviously enjoyed it. Doc Bender and the Rocky Twins egged him on. "Larry inherited the habit of squandering money from his Old Man," said Henry Myers. "O.M. would have laughed and called him a miser."

The three big all-night spots for show business personalities were Lindy's, Reuben's, and Dave's Blue Room, big, noisy delicatessen-restaurants. Larry was a familiar figure in all of them into the dawn hours.

Larry was acquring a habit of leaving places without his overcoat. Comedian Milton Berle said that Larry came into Lindy's one night, wearing an overcoat but nothing underneath. "He was drunk and had no recollection where he left his clothes," says Berle.

Frieda was a very worried mother. She was aware of his excessive drinking as he could no longer hide it. He adored her and still was able to keep his sexual entanglements from becoming known to her, at least as far as anyone can tell. The soundproof door that separated her sleeping quarters from his parties attests to his efforts to protect her, not himself.

The drinking problem defied secrecy because it inevitably took over when he went out on the town. However, his final destination was always his home, no matter how harshly the displeasure of Frieda might fall upon his throbbing head. So it is a pleasure to clear up one rather unsavory story that appeared in Ed Sullivan's column, owing to his misunderstanding of an almost-unfailing habit of Larry's. Reaching home, he would hit his room, throw off all his clothes but his socks, curl up in his bed, and sleep it off. Unfortunately, this particular night he mistook the men's room of Dave's Blue Room for his own room, and, following his usual pattern, stripped off his clothes and fell asleep, startling even the sophisticated regulars there. This is what got into the papers, and it is said Frieda's wrath was of magnificent proportions.

Another incident, which happily Larry found amusing, was also a bit expensive. It followed closely upon the Blue Room episode, so he was determined to get home safely. He had a cab take him from Ralph's to the Lambs' Club, where he admonished the driver to wait for him and see that he got home . . . no matter what. The driver was affable, an admirer of Rodgers and Hart, and greedy. The tab of the cab as they drove to Larry's front door in the wee, small hours, was exactly $99.50.

In a taped interview for the BBC, Dorothy Hart recalled that one night she and Teddy were in Reuben's with Larry when Humphrey Bogart came in with his wife, Mayo Methot, who doubled as the star's sparring partner so much that he lovingly called her Sluggy.

"They were drunk and raucous," related Mrs. Hart, "and had been asked to leave the Algonquin Hotel again. They were always being asked to leave the Algonquin. Bogart was funny and charming about trying to find a place to stay. I certainly was willing to offer my place, but Larry nudged me and remained aloof through the whole flamboyant thing. He disapproved. He actually was intolerant of them because they were drunk. He was disgusted. That is typical of heavy drinkers, I've been told. Larry always disapproved of drunkenness when *he* was not drinking."

221

"Larry's drinking was due to the fact that he was a lonesome man," said Bennett Green. "He cared deeply for people; that's why he was hurt so often. He was searching for love, and he didn't know what kind of love he wanted. He had to be around people all the time; he couldn't be by himself. He lavished gifts on people he liked, forced them on them, overly generous, perhaps wanting to buy their love and affection."

A somewhat similar view was taken, coincidentally, by Dorothy Hart when she spoke of Larry's generosity and casual attitude toward money:

"Nothing was too much for people he loved, but he was also given to flamboyant gestures. At a barbershop he would say, 'I'll pay for everyone!' Just faces wrapped in towels, complete strangers! That wasn't generosity; it was just ridiculous. It wasn't as though he tried to buy friends. It was something like 'I'm not as big as you are, but I can pay your bills.' A kind of making up for lack of height, some psychological quirk.

"People touched Larry for money *all* the time. An actor stopped us on the street and asked Larry for five hundred dollars for an abortion for his wife. Larry gave it to him, of course, and a week later I read where this actor had optioned a play. Now you *know* it was with that five hundred. Teddy and I were furious, but Larry thought it was hilarious and very enterprising: The actor had put something over; it was a neat trick."

"Larry loved actors," said Leonard Spigelgass. "He really knew very few writers, which is strange, but he was surrounded by actors. I had just come from the Coast, and I was used to seeing a lot of money around, but you must understand that this was still the Depression—nobody had money in New York then. Noel Coward didn't have money, although he had caught on, but he never made the money Larry made. Nobody had any money, and Larry was loaded."

"You know," said Green, "it didn't mean a thing to Larry if people were broke, if they were paupers, but it did to Dick. Larry wasn't in awe of money; Dick was. Of course, it was difficult to keep up with Larry; you never knew where he was going to be. But you always knew where he stood with you!"

And so. . . .

Although their paths were diverging in vastly contrasting directions, Dick hung on, and he went to work with Larry on another show.

It was Mr. Abbott again who produced and staged *Too Many Girls*. The war had just broken out in Europe. Although the United States would stay out of it for another two years, the holocaust touched people everywhere, and the atmosphere was tense. It was an ideal time for this lighthearted book by George Marion, Jr.

Dick's apprehensions about Larry heightened during the production of this show. Larry simply couldn't be found when needed; Dick had to write some of the lyrics.

Singing and dancing through a small role, programmed merely as Student, was an exuberant red-haired extrovert, Van Johnson, whose fun-loving flair endeared him to Larry.

Johnson didn't stay long in the student role. From there he went to Hollywood, once again enacting the student in the movie version, in which Richard Carlson starred. Then Johnson moved to MGM, where his career continued to rise.

Another spectacular personality made his debut in *Too Many Girls*. Cuban-born Desi Arnaz was beating the bongo in a club called La Conga in New York when he got a call from Dick and Larry. Larry had seen him when he played Miami and remembered him as just the type they needed. Although Arnaz had never appeared onstage and in fact didn't even know the names of Rodgers and Hart when he first heard from them, he scored a solid hit in the show. Like Van Johnson, he went west to reenact his role in the movie version and became an important star.

He followed the route of other Hart discoveries; he took Doc Bender as his agent. He also became a vigorous participant, as did Van Johnson, in Larry's late-night parties.

Another guest told us, "Larry was more of a voyeur. I can remember going to parties and seeing his eyes glittering, watching this orgy going on. When it came to sex, Larry left an awful lot to be desired. I was one of his boys, and I know . . . you'd wake up and find him in the closet. He'd get up out of bed and go sleep in the closet. He had this complex about sleeping with someone. But how he loved those parties!"

Larry never attempted to explain his nocturnal activities; many friendly defenders passed them off as a necessary release from his emotional pressures. He and Dick were preparing another show, but Dick was occupied with a solo effort, a venture into ballet. That was *his* way of escaping the pressures placed on him.

In one of his very few examinations of the songwriting scene, Larry wrote a by-lined article. The New York *Times* headlined it as RUNNING UP A SCORE, with a subhead: "One of the Leading Tunesmiths Talks of Writing Film Song Shows":

"Dick Rodgers and I have been in the music-writing business so long that it has really become a business with us. We get together in the morning and we say, What's the situation, what do we need and how shall we do it? It's like two playwrights writing a play, of course, you realize that a musical show is a little different from a play. You have certain people to take care of who must appear to advantage and songs must be fitted to them. There is a difference also between writing a song for a show and just writing a song. In a show you have to have an evenness in score, each song must balance the others. There's a theme song, a comedy, song, a musical pattern.

"This procedure should be given more attention in pictures, for after seeing *Babes in Arms* on the screen I'm more convinced than ever that the movies are the greatest field for musical comedy in the world. To make them should be easy if there's somebody like Mickey Rooney to cut up in front of the camera. In the naturalness in which he takes to his medium of expression I'd compare him to Zorina on the stage or to the late Marilyn Miller.*

"The camera eye is—or should be—everything in turning out a movie. Dialogue is no good on the screen by itself. Two people sit talking in two chairs. So what? There must be movement. The screen is a visual medium, the camera is the boss and the cameraman is the star. If people don't know that, they're nuts—and a lot of them don't know it yet.

"Dick and I went to Hollywood seven years ago to do *Love Me Tonight* with Maurice Chevalier. The first thing we did was to study pictures, not on the sound set but in the cutting room. Then, with Chevalier and Rouben Mamoulian, we developed for the first time dialogue with a sort of phony little half rhyme, with a little music under it cut to the situation. We also put a portable sound track in an open field with an orchestra. We had a doctor coming to

*By an eerie coincidence, Mickey Rooney would portray Larry in th biographical film of Rodgers and Hart, *Words and Music*, nine years la er.

225

Jeanette MacDonald's room, and the sing-song conversation went something like this:

> Now, my dear, remove your dress.
> My what?
> Your dress.
> Is it necessary?
> Very.

"It isn't rhyme, it isn't anything like it; but it's screen talk and it isn't difficult to write if you know the medium. I'm a great believer in conversational rhythm. I think in terms of a rhythmic dialogue. It's so easy, you can talk naturally. It's like peas rolling off a knife. Take the great screen actors and actresses, Bette Davis, Eddie Robinson, Jimmy Cagney, Spencer Tracy. They all talk in rhythm. And rhythm and movement are the life of the screen.

"It's a sort of kindergarten principle, I suppose, that the story-line of a picture should be graphic from beginning to end. If you have a musical picture, your music must also be directly in the line of your story. It doesn't make any difference why. You turn on a phonograph in the street. They say, how can they do this, where's the cue? But the cue doesn't matter. It's what they sing about that matters. Shaping material to fit the sound track is easy. The technicians can handle that. They're real artists.

"I wouldnt write the same lyric for the stage that I would for films. It's a different medium. In the show *Too Many Girls* at the Imperial Theater I have a blues song called 'The Sweetheart of the Team' which I would never dream of putting on the screen. It's all right for the stage but on the screen you would have to make flashbacks to show it and the subject is too suggestive that way.

"In that first picture of ours Maurice Chevalier was in his

tailor's shop and hummed a song. Different people heard it and passed it on, one to the other till it got to Jeanette Mac-Donald in the castle. That's the picture's movement. And they still don't know it."*

Larry could feel some righteous pessimism about moviemakers, for the best Rodgers and Hart musical films were their early Hollywood ventures. At this time there was one more movie in their future, a very dismal production called *They Met in Argentina* to which Dick and Larry contributed seven songs. The New York *Herald Tribune* said, "Rodgers and Hart's tunes help some [but it is] an American musical at its worst."

Larry was still hopeful, but extremely mistaken in this closing paragraph of his article. He concluded with: "The ideal musical comedy of the pictures will kill the musical comedy of the stage. There will be no chance for musical comedy on the stage. Imagine."

Only three stage musicals lay ahead of them and some of their greatest songs. Time was running out, but not, as Larry predicted, because of the movies.

*This reference is to the brilliant Rouben Mamoulian film, *Love Me Tonight*, which was actually their second film.

18

Lower and Lower

"I MET them early in 1940, at the time of *Higher and Higher*," said Frank Gabrielson, playwright. "By then, the pattern of their lives seemed apparent: Larry acted like a poet who happened to be a lyric writer, and Dick acted like a stockbroker who happened to be a composer."

The idea for *Higher and Higher* originated with Irving Pincus, whose family owned the Alvin Theater in New York. Pincus knew Larry from boyhood, when they went to Brant Lake Camp. They saw each other again when *The Boys from Syracuse* ran at the Alvin. "Larry was always a sweet and lovely guy," said Pincus. "But by the time he was doing *The Boys from Syracuse*, he was sweet, lovely, and screwed-up."

It was then that Pincus suggested the idea that became *Higher and Higher*:

"There was an annual affair in New York called the Butler's Ball. It got space in the newspapers because the maids and butlers who worked for the top families dressed up to go to it at the Waldorf-Astoria Hotel.

"One night, after a performance of *Boys from Syracuse,* Larry and I were sitting around Ruby Foo's Restaurant, and I told him I thought the Butler's Ball would make a good musical and I had some idea of a story about it. He had been drinking brandy and he was so far gone that when he spoke he was incoherent. It must have been three thirty in the morning.

"Next day was Saturday, a matinee day at the theater. I was upstairs in the office when the doorman told me Dick Rodgers wanted to see me. Me? I thought he must have meant my older brother, Norman, who was the important one, but the doorman said, 'No, he wants to see you.'

"I went down, and Dick said, 'We'd like to buy the musical you told Larry last night.' That floored me. I couldn't believe that drunk as he was, Larry could have remembered even seeing me! But he did.

"Then *I* had to remember what I told *him*. I went back upstairs and typed out an outline of my story as best I could. All three of us had Howard Reinheimer as our attorney, and he handled the negotiations. I've since heard that Dick said that Josh Logan brought him the story, but I think Dick is trying to repaint the past."

Josh Logan did work on the adaptation of the idea when, according to Logan, "Dick and Larry didn't find it easy to write." There was an attempted collaboration with Clare Boothe. However, several concepts failed to jell, so finally, Logan went to work on what would be the final version of *Higher and Higher* with Gladys Hurlbut.

All of this consumed months, and the work went on during the entire run of *Too Many Girls,* but it was taking up time, and the fabulous output of Rodgers and Hart musicals was slowing down.

During the run of *Too Many Girls* Larry suffered another traumatic experience because of his height. He had learned to laugh, albeit bitterly, at how the theater usher told him to stand up for the national anthem when he was already standing, but this later happening permanently bruised and wracked his psyche. It had to do with his body, but it scarred his soul.

He had grown exceedingly fond of Desi Arnaz during the run of *Too Many Girls* and loved the company of the outgoing young Cuban. One evening at the Arnaz apartment, which, like Larry's, was a large duplex on Central Park West and also the scene of numerous parties, Larry was telling Desi's mother, Dolores, how much he admired her son. Suddenly she reached out and playfully sat him on her lap as if he were a doll, then held and hugged him, screaming with laughter as he struggled desperately and unavailingly to free himself. Humiliated, unable to pry loose from her grip, he burst into tears.

Commenting on Larry's phobia about his height, Jerome Lawrence said, "I don't think it's just the shortness and the ugliness—it was a built-in unworthiness. It is a concept of love as a slave, too, a little bit, a sickness, in a way, but I think it's a pattern that many people follow, the feeling of unworthiness, partly caused not just by the good-looks-kind-of-thing, but 'everybody's got to make it; everybody's got to be successful.' The ambition drive of the postwar era of the twenties and thirties up to the Depression was so strong. You had to be a success in order to be loved. Actually this prevailed right up to the Flower Children; they were the first to be turned off on ambition. Oh, I'm sure Larry was driven by ambition. But the counter to that is the feeling of 'Do I deserve this?' A kind of guilt feeling, saying, 'I don't deserve this,' and in a way it's a healthy thing. Paul Muni had it . . . the Lunts . . . always trying to be better. You can name many artists who constantly fight their unworthiness, but *Larry Hart articulated it more than almost anybody.* Because of being a songwriter he had to write love songs, and almost all his love songs said, 'I stink. Why would you ever love me? Spring is here, I hear, but for other people, not for me.' He was the poet laureate of masochism.''

Between the productions of *Too Many Girls* and *Higher and Higher* Dick made one of his few incursions into a field other than musical comedy and composed a full-length ballet. For the Ballet Russe de Monte Carlo, it was called *Ghost Town.* The suggestion for it came from influential Gerald Murphy, a wealthy American expatriate who lived many years on the French Riviera, friend and host to other expatriates, notably Zelda and Scott Fitzgerald.

Dick worked on *Ghost Town* with Marc Platt (né Platoff), who staged it for the five performances it was given at New York's Metropolitan Opera House, and Dick conducted the orchestra. A few critics found it charming, but many downgraded it and saw in it a resemblance to musical comedy (without the singing).

Ghost Town was Dick's most ambitious break from the mold of musical comedy creation. But it failed to excite the public attention that was given his *Slaughter on Tenth Avenue,* nor was it lasting in the minds of his admirers. He would write other ballets, but they were always fitted to a musical comedy or operetta plot. Jerome Kern followed an almost identical pattern; his tone poem *Mark Twain* was recorded but rarely played. Breaking away from their accepted posture was not so easily accomplished; Gershwin did it, but his opera, *Porgy and Bess,* received a contemptuous reception from the cirtics when it was first presented,

232

as Dick well knew, and in the two remaining years left to him, Gershwin resumed writing popular songs. Phil Leavitt perceived a virtue in Dick's ability to recognize his own limitations, and this may well be, for he did not wander far from musical comedy again. His lasting place in that sphere could never be dislodged.

But while Dick looked upward, Larry was still sliding down. Gene Rodman said, "I was at the premiere of *Ghost Town*. I saw Larry coming up the aisle and was going to talk to him when I saw tht he was so ossified, plastered, he could hardly navigate. Much as I loved him, I didn't speak to him. He could be impossible when drunk."

In the spring of 1940 *Higher and Higher* was finally ready. All concerned with it expected the sparkling Zorina would dance through the leading role, but after so many delays she was no longer available. A major change had to be effected, and a Hungarian singer, Marta Eggerth, was cast in the role of the maid who masqueraded as a debutante.*

By the use of intense creative imagination, a live seal was woven into the plot line. Frank Gabrielson recalled that two of these bright mammals were employed, respectively named Sharkey I and Sharkey II. Sharkey II was the understudy that, in the manner of many American vice presidents and Broadway understudies, acquired smoldering anger at the continuing good health of his overstudy. Just as the play's romantic characters, portrayed by Jack Haley and Shirley Ross, were pouring out their hearts to each other one night, Sharkey II, apparently overcome with jealousy by the acclaim given Sharkey I, went racing out before the

---

*Masquerade" provided many plot turns in Dick and Larry's musicals; it was the key element in *Ever Green,* and variations occur in *She's My Baby, Present Arms, Spring Is Here,* and *Heads Up!*

footlights, flipping around in a magnificent display of seal histrionics, bowing, honking, and rolling acrobatically from one side of the theater to the other, impervious to the lure of sweet-smelling dead fish and resisting all blandishments of trainers and stagehands to lure him off. Understandably, Dick told friends he learned a lesson: Never get involved with a seal.

Logan says it was due to Dick's patience that *Higher and Higher* worked at all. Dick was always less than enthusiastic about that endeavor, although he wrote some memorable music for it. One song, "It Never Entered My Mind," rates high among his classics. Logan also felt that Larry didn't like writing for that show. He said, "He was terribly hard to reach." Dick had to write some of the lyrics when Larry couldn't be found.

A song called "It's Pretty in the City" was cut out, and Larry was unhappy about it. But he lightheartedly told producer Dwight Wyman, "In spite of the fact that the music was bad, the lyrics worse, the people who were singing it were baffled by its inappropriateness and couldn't put it across and it didn't belong in the show at all, it was a good song."

Taking a "good song" by Rodgers and Hart from the score of a show without placing it in another didn't necessarily end its existence. One of their most beautiful waltzes, "Wait Till You See Her," survived that treatment and "It's Pretty in the City" also has many admirers. It appears in the repertoire of nightclub singers and bistro pianists. It is a common request from piano-bar customers.

After *Higher and Higher* closed, Dick and his wife dropped in on the popular New York nightclub The Blue Angel, where the two-piano team, Edie and Rack, were performing. Dick and Dorothy heard a tune that was pleasant-sounding, even familiar, but they couldn't place it. Rack, who had been rehearsal pianist for *Higher and Higher*, identified it for them. It was "It's Pretty in the City."

Like a classic Greek tragedy, the association of Rodgers and Hart moved to its obligatory denouement. Two new plays and a revival provided background for a climactic situation. On the surface, all would be successful, but the hidden elements were there and it was beneath the surface that the real drama took place. It began with *Pal Joey.*

Dick said, apropos of John O'Hara's Joey Evans, "Larry understood and liked disreputable characters." Sophisticated and quite daring, the O'Hara short stories appeared in *The New Yorker*, adding to the literary reputation of the author. It was his suggestion to Dick that the saga of Joey be transformed into musical comedy. That was when *Too Many Girls* was trying out, but the work on hand didn't prevent Dick and Larry from an enthusiastic assent. Larry related very closely to the unscrupulous antihero and his nightclub background. Besides, there would be an important role in it for Vivienne Segal.

The transition from short stories to musical comedy libretto, handled by O'Hara, took more than a year. George Abbott was to produce and direct it, and a young actor-hoofer from Pittsburgh, Gene Kelly, who had caught Dick's eye when he appeared in Saroyan's *Time of Your Life*, was cast as Joey as soon as the writing of the stage version was begun.

John O'Hara wasn't the type to let his writing interfere with his drinking; like Larry, he frequented the bars and clubs, and it wasn't long before they were doing the circuit together. Gene Kelly told us, "I hung around with Larry and O'Hara mostly because we all loved to drink and because

235

Larry and O'Hara were great company to be with, except . . . O'Hara tended to get belligerent in his cups from time to time, which Larry never did.*

Kelly's recollection of Larry as an amiable drinking companion clashed with Gene Rodman's; "He could be unpleasant when drunk." Many saw him as a split personality. Leonard Spigelgass explained it this way: "I say he was a manic depressive. He was like two men walking around, one so gay and cheerful and then suddenly depressed, and that's manic depression. Of course, we weren't dealing with it in those terms in those days."

(It's regrettable that we can't place a special little disk in the book for readers to hear Leonard Spigelgass' discussion of Larry, but since that is impossible, we're going to write almost everything he said—with his permission—and let you imagine the delicious impertinences, nuances, respect, scathing derision, and humor coloring it.)

"I'm trying to pinpoint when I met him, I know it was at the time of *By Jupiter*. I think I had met him before that, and he ignored me. I'm sure the reason we developed any kind of relationship at all was (a) that I knew all his lyrics, which impressed him, and (b) that we had a kind of intellectual relationship.

"He was spending a lot of time, because of Bender, with a lot of dreary, stupid people, handsome young men, but they were very stupid—tall, slender blond young men always caught his eye. But they were all very stupid, and then I came along into that world, and I had some kind of reputation, even though it was Hollywood, and he thought that was absurd; nonetheless, we could talk. Nobody talked

*Apropos O'Hara's belligerency, I recall walking by him as I went into the Stork Club one night, then realizing and going back. "Sorry, John," I said. "I didn't recognize you." "That's because you got fat," he snapped.—MARX

236

about Hitler. Nobody talked about the world, which was all around us, and that was where we found our first relationship, you see. He didn't have to talk about sex; he could talk about things which he knew; he was a very well-educated man, but no one was asking him about these things.

"Dick was so consistent. I was never comfortable with him. I love Dorothy, and I love Mary, yet there is a kind of thing. You get there at seven; you have dinner at seven thirty; you have the right wines with the right thing. If you should go up to her and say, 'Dorothy, could you please change the place cards because if I have to sit next to this one I will absolutely lose my mind,' she would say, 'Go. Leave the house.'

"I don't know why that makes me think of George M. Cohan, but can you imagine him and Larry Hart? As the world's worst combination? Cole disliked both of them intensely. I think it was because they were competitors. He used to say 'I can always recognize a Rodgers tune, it has a certain holiness about it!'"

"I think in those days, certainly, Jerome Kern disliked all of them, and they all disliked Kern . . . and everybody was right about that! They all laughed at Romberg, who was a laughable man . . . and had bigger hits than any of them. Irving Berlin was beneath their contempt! Now the whole view of Berlin has changed completely. He used to be regarded as just Tin Pan Alley, and now he's kind of *the* songwriter of the twenties and thirties *and* forties, and when Irving did *Annie Get Your Gun*, I suppose he had more song hits per square inch than any composer in the world.

"I knew how much Larry cared for Vivienne Segal, and I knew of Nanette Guilford, but I never met her. Don't forget, homosexuality in that period had two levels: One, it was held in major contempt, and the other was that among his kind it was the most exclusive club in New York. That's terribly important to realize—that it was a club into which you couldn't get . . . I mean, no ordinary certified public accountant could get into the Larry Hart, Cole Porter, George Cukor world. That was *the* world. That was Somerset Maugham. That was Cole Porter. That was Noel Coward. That was *it* if you were in that. And I remember those houses on Fifty-fifth Street, with the butlers and the carryings-on . . . you were king of the golden river! That was it! In spite of the attitude toward homosexuality in those days. On the one hand if you said, 'They were homosexual—oh, my, isn't that terrible!' on the other hand you said, 'My God, the other night I was at dinner with Cole Porter!' Immediate reaction: 'Jesus Christ, what did he have on? What was he wearing? What did he say? *Were* you at that party? Were you at one of those Sunday brunches?' So you had this awful ambivalence. Show folk, show biz people just couldn't make it! Larry was there, of course, at all of them. Oh, sure, he brought Bender along. Bender was a kind of comic. If you wanted Larry, you took Bender.

"My most vivid memories of Larry are those strange nine-course dinners in his house with all the porcelain and miles of silverware on either side. All the servants . . . lots of servants. All elderly. That white, white tablecloth."

At this point, as at many others, Leonard stopped to quote, *in toto*, "Tree in the Park," pointing out, "Now look at all those inner rhymes; now that took absolute genius! He could just spill 'em out. This was a sort of celebration of New York, which of course 'Manhattan' was, and isn't it interesting that later he wrote 'Give It Back to the Indians'?

"You know his apartment was right above Frieda. The door leading into his apartment which I thought for years was a steel door was probably just like one of the sound stage doors. This wasn't to cut her off his life, but he had orchestras ... drums ... people, and he tried always to be considerate of her. But this door (I'm convinced it was a steel door) had to be opened out, so one had to back down three steps to get it open, it sort of opened on top of one. I remember it very well because it frightened me so. I must tell you I was frightened three-quarters of the time just to be in there.

"When Larry gave those parties with butlers, and bartenders, and all the scotch and champagne you could drink, I never remember seeing Dick Rodgers there. Several women would be there—the fag hags as they are called—the ladies who like to be escorted by the homosexuals. And why not?

"People say he was trying to die, those last months were all so dreadful. . . . Was he trying to die, or are we imposing that upon him? I realize there had been the success of *Oklahoma!* with which he had nothing to do, and the death of his mother at about that time, but I can't believe that would have done it. God, how I love his words. There are very few lyricists whose words you can recite as poetry, and look how I can do it with *all* of Larry's songs. He does an incredible kind of iambic pentameter. He was a poet."

Many saw different sides of Larry because he shielded them as best he could from his black periods of loneliness. Naturally gregarious, he kept after them to join him in the clubs, bars, and restaurants, and when they did, he was literally the life of the party.

His devoted friend Irving Eisman remembers that when he first met Larry at the Casa Manana, "he liked to take a drink because it relaxed him," but as time went on, Larry took many more than one.

"One night Larry was, as usual, hosting a big party at Ruby Foo's," says Eisman. "It was rainy out and drunk inside, and after dinner was long over, we waited ages because Larry wanted some change. We all began to get a little im-

239

patient to leave. Larry said he didn't mind being a big tipper, but he'd be damned if he'd leave *all* that change for the waiter. We waited and waited until the captain disclosed that Larry hadn't been given the check yet! That struck us all as excruciatingly funny!"

Lucinda Ballard designed the costumes for *Higher and Higher* and recalls feeling enormous sadness for his obvious loneliness.*

She was sitting out front making notes when Larry came into the theater to ask her across the street for a drink. She demurred, but he was almost pitiful when he said, "Oh, *please* do, I'm so *lonesome*." Unable to resist this, over they went. While they were having their drinks, an insurance man from whom Larry had bought a policy came into the bar. He was almost ecstatic when he saw Larry because he had been trying for days to reach him. Larry had been trying just that many days to avoid him. The problem was a simple one: Larry had never indicated whom he wanted as a beneficiary. However, he found this easily solved right there in the bar. Tearfully he said, "Make it out to Lucinda, my friend. My *only* friend!"

According to Miss Ballard, "Doc Bender came in right then and raised holy hell!"

As opposed to the small-boy antics of Larry, Dick was gaining fast on maturity. He could see no sense in time-wasting attendance at dissolute parties; he was out of step with overindulgence and so dedicated to whatever work he had at hand that he couldn't help being irritated by Larry's disregard for convention. He had become a conservative

---

*Now Mrs. Howard Dietz, Lucinda is a Southern belle with whom you immediately associate her ancestor Jefferson Davis. If you don't she sets you right. She was also the designer of a *Show Boat* revival who put me, with my red hair and whimpering all the way, into a gorgeous pink outfit that landed me on the cover of *Life*.—CLAYTON

family man who enjoyed the comforts of home. By sober judgment (which, of course, was the only fitting description for one who looks with distaste at intemperance), he was entitled to that irritation. It was at this point that he stressed that his partner was uncontrollable and usually "unfindable."

Dick listed three articles of his faith to an interviewer and not only lived by them but accurately predicted the course of the musical theater in which he toiled so diligently.

1. Respect for the American audience and its capacity to enjoy the best.

2. Firm reliance on theater craftsmanship.

3. Joy in musical comedy and faith that out of it will come a new form of musical theater more serious in its intent and more lasting in its nature than that to which we have been accustomed.

Pal Joey was far more serious in its intent than musical comedy audiences had been accustomed.

Larry was excited about *Pal Joey* from the start. The basic premise of "the rotten guy" appealed to his delight in knavery, and he found great fun in the mixing of double entendres into his lyrics. "He often awakened me in the middle of the night," Josh Logan said, "to read a new sly rhyme he had just invented. The thought of 'putting something over' on the censors was delicious to him. 'Watch them trying to figure this one out: "Lost my heart, but what of it, He is cold, I agree. He can laugh, but I love it, Although the laugh's on me," and then how *he* would laugh! Larry counted a lot on sophisticated appreciation of *Pal Joey*."

Dick's music was brilliant, too. *Pal Joey* was a show they both loved working on.

Larry was also inspired by the presence of Vivienne Segal in the cast, and she, too, was stimulated by the chance to

241

play the offbeat role of a wealthy married woman who falls for an arrogant, insolent youth.

"Not only did the show free Broadway musicals from their naïve sugar-and-spice formulas," she says, "but it rescued me once and for all from a hapless life as a wide-eyed ingenue. A girl can't be eighteen forever, and yet there I was year after year, show after show, always the sweet young thing—the sweet young bore. Pure saccharine! I used to hate those parts, just hate them. . . .

"John O'Hara could write; he didn't pull his punches. It was quite a shock. A lot of people accepted it, but they accepted it in silence. They were afraid to laugh. They said to themselves, 'Oh, my God, I'm not supposed to know what this is all about.' Today everybody laughs out loud. We have all grown up."

The name of the woman character Miss Segal portrayed was Vera Simpson, and she feels that not only Larry but O'Hara, too, anticipated she would play the role because "John gave her the same initials as mine."

Investing Vera Simpson with dignity, charm, and wit, the actress sized up this high society lady in pursuit of low life. "Yes, she buys her fun; her money does help. But she knows what she is."

Dick and Larry gave Vera four songs to sing out of a memorable score, of which "Bewitched, Bothered and Bewildered" would step forth into an all-time hit.

"None of us really knew what we had in 'Bewitched,'" said Miss Segal. "It was in the wrong spot during rehearsals; I was singing it early in the show. I got them to move it back, but even then it created no sensation at our Philadelphia tryout. No one yelled for encores, so Larry wrote no extra verses for me to sing."

It is Irving Eisman's belief that Larry wasn't impressed

with "Bewitched." He told him that his favorite song was the sweet-flowing "I Could Write a Book," which Joey sings to the innocent ingenue who doesn't know that he has never even read one.

The original cast of *Pal Joey* could boast many names that few had heard in 1940. As time went on, some grew familiar and some grew famous. June Havoc, sister of stripper Gypsy Rose Lee, played the descriptively named Gladys Bumps. Robert Mulligan and Stanley Donen became ultra-successful film directors; Van Johnson, a star. Jerome Whyte played the part of a stagehand but graduated into Dick's longtime production manager. Jean Casto, too, would add to her laurels in Dick's musicals, but in *Pal Joey* she nearly ended her career forever during the Philadelphia tryout.

In a letter to Clayton (with whom she appeared in *Carousel*) she wrote about it from her home in Florida:

"I had on a lounging robe which I had been warned was highly inflammable, sober as a judge, sitting in my hotel room writing Christmas cards and smoking, as is my wont. I lit a Stork Club match, the head of which flew off and landed on the robe which went swoooosh, flames everywhere. I yelled blue murder, and Gene Kelly and another player, Cliff Dunstan, who were on the same floor, came rushing in and snuffed out the flames by landing on me full force, burning themselves but damn near killing me. However, I prefer to think they saved my life, and I was really lucky to have only my hands and one arm burned badly. To hear Larry Hart tell it, you'd think I was a stretcher case and practically Joan of Arc to go on opening night in New York."

On Christmas night, 1940, *Pal Joey* came to New York, where the inhabitants, more sophisticated than those of

243

Philadelphia, found it an extremely welcome offering. Richard Watts, in the *Herald Tribune*, called it brilliant, sardonic, and strikingly original. He noted that it contained "one of Rodgers' most winning scores and the spiritual kinship between Lorenz Hart and John O'Hara is something to be applauded."

Not surprisingly, the usually scornful *New Yorker* was comparatively ecstatic, for the original stories about Joey had run in that magazine. Wolcott Gibbs said, "Musical comedy took a long step toward maturity. I am not optimistic by nature but it seems to me just possible that the idea of equipping a song-and-dance production with a few living, three-dimensional figures, talking and behaving like human beings, may no longer strike the boys in the business as merely fantastic. Mr. Rodgers and Mr. Hart have written some of their best songs."

An unusual note crept into the critique of *Time* magazine, for after characterizing the show as "a bang-up musicomedy, a profane hymn to the gaudy goddess of metropolitan night life," the reviewer went afield from the accepted boundaries of such reflections to add, "*Cigar-chewing Hart, the pint-sized genius with a two-quart capacity,* abets the spirit of the occasion." (Author's italics)

John Lardner, in *Newsweek*, called it "Rodgers' best score. . . . Hart is in there punching too. I think he is running in a private little sweepstakes with Cole Porter to see which can be the wickedest little rascal in the lyric-writing dodge."

Unlike its reception in Philadelphia, "Bewitched, Bothered and Bewildered" did arouse yells for encores.

"Suddenly, on opening night it happened," said Vivienne Segal. "They wanted more, more. I remembered a couplet Larry had written but thrown out because he didn't like it:

244

Dumb again, numb again,
Like Fanny Brice singing "Mon Homme" again,
Bewitched, bothered and bewildered, am I!

"I sang it. Our director, Mr. Abbott, asked me afterward, 'How on earth did you ever remember it?' I told him I was so damn mad Larry didn't write any encores for me, I had to remember something. The couplet stayed in, and Larry wrote more of them, including:

Vexed again, perplexed again,
Thank God I can be oversexed again.*

But in all the critical acclaim, there was one blue note, and as is often the case, it gave so much pain that the hurt couldn't be erased by praise from others. Brooks Atkinson, critic of the New York *Times*, wrote, "There are scabrous lyrics to one of Rodgers' most haunting tunes, 'Bewitched.' Although it is expertly done, can you draw sweet water from a foul well?"

No one ever wrote a worse criticism of Larry's lyrics. Gene Kelly saw him actually weeping over it. But thinking back on this years afterward, he wondered if Larry hadn't read into it a critique of his personal life.†

---

*Screen playwright William Bowers, who worked on the movie version of *Higher and Higher*, had fun with a parody:
    I'm wild again, with child again,
    You might even say I'm defiled again,
    Betrayed, bothered and be-pregnant am I.

†Twelve years later, the same Brooks Atkinson reviewed the revival of *Pal Joey*. "No one is likely to be impervious to the liveliness and versatility of the score and the easy perfection of the lyrics." But his well-eaten words appeared much too late for Larry to know.

245

During the year and a half that followed *Pal Joey*, the public had no new reminder of the existence of Rodgers and Hart except an innocuous little score for an innocuous little movie, *They Met in Argentina*.

But there would be movement, uncertainties, and rumors, and some outspoken talk. In 1941 the *Times* declared that "the well-known team of Rodgers and Hart is reported to be breaking up," and while it was denied a few days later, there were many who knew the story had a foundation in fact.

It was always difficult, along Broadway, to keep whispers from being loudly heard.

19

"I Didn't Care What Time It Was"

DICK INVITED Leonore and Ira Gershwin to dinner at his New York apartment.

"I had just written the words for Kurt Weill's music of *Lady in the Dark*," said Ira, "and I remember that night that Dick seemed to always steer the conversation around to the troubles he was having with Larry Hart. Later Lee and I agreed that he seemed to be hinting that he would welcome some signal from me that I wanted to work with him."

It might have been a happy alliance. Ira was a sober and cerebral individual. His sharp, highly acclaimed lyrics fitted perfectly to the sharp, highly acclaimed music of his brother, George. They worked together twenty years, until George died in 1937. But in the four years that followed, Ira was gradually retiring.

247

The feeling that Dick wanted him was borne out when he received a phone call from Max Dreyfus, who asked if he enjoyed the evening he spent with Dick and would he care to consider an association on some upcoming show? "By that time I had decided to do very little lyric writing anymore," said Ira, and so informed Dreyfus.

Dick was definitely looking. He visited Oscar Hammerstein at his Doylestown, Pennsylvania, farm and came right out with the purpose of his call, that he might break up with Larry.

Through the years since the Columbia Varsity Shows, theirs had been an ongoing friendship. It was difficult *not* to be friendly with Oscar Hammerstein, one of the most genuine and compassionate of all human beings then circulating through the haunts and byways of the Broadway musical theaters.

Working with various composers, including Romberg and Kern, he turned out many shows and beautiful songs. But there had been a downward slide in Hammerstein's career. Nevertheless, he didn't want to see the now-historic combination of Rodgers and Hart split.

Thoughtful as ever and sympathetic to Dick's plight, he would go only so far as to say he would come to the rescue if desperately needed.

That was not the case at this time. Dick and Larry simply couldn't decide what they would do next. The possibility of a "divorce" wasn't being mentioned, but they did no work together for many months, and the year 1941 went by without a single new Rodgers and Hart offering on Broadway, an unwelcome first of its kind.

A year of inactivity was too much, and Dick's impatience reasserted itself. He decided to make a musical out of a comedy of ancient Greece, *The Warrior's Husband*, a straight play that had been around for a decade. He went to

248

work on it with Larry, but with greater misgivings than ever because his partner was indulging in long drinking bouts and given to even longer disappearances.

On one of these extended periods of intoxication Larry got so sick that he had to be carried into Doctors' Hospital and confined there. During the drying-out period, Irving Eisman stayed close to him.

There was a rule at the hospital that nurses worked only one complete shift on an alcoholism case, and much was Eisman's delight when the girl assigned to see Larry back to his apartment was, in his words, "a stunner." Never impervious to feminine attraction, Eisman accompanied both of them to Larry's home.

"I was making great lines," he said, "and had just about persuaded her that she should go to dinner with me after she went off duty when Larry woke up. Naturally, he wanted a drink first thing, but Nursie insisted a Coke would be just right for him.

"He refused to drink it. 'Oh, no no no!' he insisted. 'I'm on to your tricks, Miss Nightingale, and you're not going to get a sedative down me, no matter how cute you are.' He knew exactly what she was up to," reflected Eisman, "and he knew what *I* was up to also! I said, 'Come on, Larry, please,' and he said, 'No, my boy, *you* drink it. You look thirsty.' I thought I would humor him, and one sip wouldn't hurt me. The next thing I knew it was morning and I never saw that girl again. Larry loved telling that story to everyone."

Despite the royalties rolling in and high payments from the protective American Society of Composers, Artists and Publishers, Larry's massive extravagances cut deeply into his finances. Dick suggested he turn over the handling of his income to William Kron, an astute money manager who was seeing to Dick's interests, as well of those of Kern,

Edna Ferber, and similar affluent members of New York's creative community.

Larry, sometimes deriding but always aware of his partner's business acumen, agreed. Irving Eisman spoke of Larry's deep respect for Kron and assessed him personally as "an honest, solid citizen who, after Doc Bender, exerted the greatest influence in Larry's life, a kind of balance for good against Bender's evil."

Work on *The Warrior's Husband* moved ahead in spite of Larry's transgressions. But in February, 1942, when they were supposed to finish the adaptation, Larry disappeared. He had gone to see his favorite actress-star, Vivienne Segal, in Chicago, where she was on tour with *Pal Joey*. He simply took off, telling no one his destination. But he returned to the distracted composer in a few days.

At this same time Dick took his first step toward producing when he partnered with Dwight Wyman and Richard Kollmar in presenting the new version of *The Warrior's Husband*, now called *By Jupiter*. Producing was a long-wished-for desire, an important part of the grand design of his life.

Then Larry again landed in Doctors' Hospital, this time taken to it by Dick, who found him passed out in his apartment. On this occasion Dick rented a room for himself at the hospital, moved in a piano, and worked with him on songs while he dried out.

Like an elastic band, Larry was soon back in shape, his old sprightly self again, the cherubic enthusiast at rehearsals.

Johnny Green was musical director of *By Jupiter*. Upset by what he believed a rotten rendition of a song, he went running up on the stage, shouting, "No, no, *no!*" Larry, quiet for a change, sitting next to director Logan, said, "Ahhhh, the Green is corn!"

250

Inside the company, it was well known that a married-to-others couple was having a flaming romance, and in honor of that love affair, Larry parodied his lyric, "I've a terrible tongue and a pecker for two and Everything I've Got Belongs to You!"

But just as Larry could snap back to sobriety, he could go the other way. That path led to another brief stay in the hospital. Talented Constance Moore, one of the stars of *By Jupiter*, remembers that a new song was needed for the end of the first act, so Dick and Margot Hopkins, the rehearsal accompanist, got a melody together which they took to Larry's bedside. They whistled it and wouldn't leave until they got his lyric. It was titled, ironically, "Now That I've Got My Strength."

Stories of Larry's hospital incarcerations circulated so much that some believed that he was constantly locked in a room to get him to work. Dorothy Hart was one who denied it vehemently, asking, "How could he be locked up for twenty-three years? Ridiculous! He would have used all his ingenuity to try to get out."

When *By Jupiter* went to try out in Philadelphia, Dick, recalling that Oscar Hammerstein said he would come to the rescue if desperately needed, drove back to Doylestown. He told his friend that Larry was in worse shape and he was afraid he wouldn't be able to do what was needed to fix up the show. He wanted Oscar to help out.

But since Larry was in Philadelphia, available and on the scene again, Oscar refused, saying no, he couldn't do it. If Larry *really* reached the point where he simply couldn't work at all, couldn't finish work he had started on the show, then he would certainly come do the job. But—without credit.

Josh Logan had been aware of Dick's concern about Larry on *Pal Joey*. Dick told him then that he had gone to see Oscar Hammerstein once more and repeated, "I'm going to have to try to go on without Larry. Our last show has been hell!"

Dick told Logan, "I had it out with Larry after Oscar turned me down. I begged him again to go get psychiatric help, but he refused, of course. That word is like a red flag to him!"

Logan was extremely sympathetic to Dick—and to Larry's condition, too. He himself had recovered from a highly publicized nervous breakdown. "I thought no one would ever hire me for the theatre again, but Dick Rodgers, bless him, called me as soon as I returned to New York, to do *By Jupiter*. I can never forget that."

Later he analyzed the song "Nobody's Heart Belongs to Me" as "the last beautiful ballad Larry ever wrote in his life . . . and the most poignant. It's the thing I remember the most about *By Jupiter*," he said.

Connie Moore Maschio, now a Beverly Hills society matron who makes occasional returns to the stage, treasures a memory of the show, an incident on opening night in New York:

"We'd all been so involved with the heavy rehearsal schedule and playing, *and* many, many changes, not to mention the uncertainties caused by our mercurial lyricist I hadn't really thought about the big opening night until that afternoon in my dressing room at the Shubert Theater. It hit me. I thought, 'My God, this is it, this is what I've been waiting for.' I looked into my mirror and started to say, 'This is it,' again, dramatically, and I had no voice. It wasn't there. It was gone. Completely panicked, of course, I sent for Dick. 'Find someone to take my place, Richard,' I croaked. 'My voice is gone.' Dick didn't seem unduly alarmed, which infuriated me. He sat down casually and said, 'It's probably a little disease that's going around now.

Ray Bolger has a touch of it, but it seems to have hit him in his legs which have turned to a combination of cement and rubber. Johnny Green was telling me that he thinks he has bursitis in his shoulder. I've even had it strike my fingers when I've had to play an audition. It always seems to hit us in our vulnerable spots, yours is your voice. Relax, love, you're going to be wonderful.' He patted me on my shoulder, started out the door, and then turned to say, 'I wonder what happens to prostitutes!''

By Jupiter settled down to a year's run at New York's Shubert, starting early in June, 1942.

Three weeks after the premiere the New York *Times* carried this item: "The Theatre Guild announces that Richard Rodgers will write the music, Lorenz Hart the lyrics and Oscar Hammerstein II the book for its adaptation of the play, *Green Grow the Lilacs*, by Lynn Riggs. The authors will commence work shortly."

It brought a flurry of denials, some branding the entire announcement as untrue.

However, there was some truth in it. The heads of the guild—Theresa Helburn and Armina and Lawrence Langner—had considered doing that play in musical form many times through the eleven years since their original production.

When it appeared from the denials that the idea might be up for grabs, Kern and Hammerstein went to the guild to express their interest. They learned that it had indeed been submitted to Rodgers and Hart for consideration but there was no word from them, and the guild said no decision could be made about any other team until they gave their answer.

There were reasons for the delay, of course. Dick's enormous enthusiasm for it was up against a roadblock with Larry, who was positive that *Green Grow the Lilacs* would not make a musical. It had always been crucial to their partnership that they mutually agree on their work ahead; reaching that agreement was more difficult than it had ever been, however, because Larry was in and out of hospitals, not only from drinking, but also from recurring bronchial ailments.

During one of these confinements, he called Nanette Guilford and asked her to come see him.

"We had little in common any longer," she said, "but of course I went. I think Larry was having his second or third bout with pneumonia. Dick called him while I was there. Larry picked up the phone. He was lying in bed and I heard him say, 'No, Dick! No, no, no! no!' And this kept on. He said, 'I don't see it. I just don't see it,' and finally he hung up the phone and said, 'Dick wants me to do this ridiculous thing and I asked, 'What's that?' and he said, 'Green Grow the Lilacs,' and I said, 'Well, it wasn't a successful play, but it *was* charming, and if he has that feeling and it's such a strong feeling, why don't you do it?' And I kind of thought, too, it would take him away from a lot of the other things, but he said, 'No, baby, I don't see it. I *just* don't see it!' And that was it. I just happened to be there that very day."

When Larry left the hospital, he closed the subject with finality. He took off on a trip to Mexico.

When Dick learned from the guild that Kern and Hammerstein were interested, that, naturally, interested him. At least, half of it did, the lyric-writing half. He spoke to Josh Logan first, for that director was the guild's choice for staging the play, if and when it reached the status of production.

"I couldn't accept any assignment because I was going overseas in the Army's Special Services," he said, "but Dick spoke to me about Oscar, and I fell apart with approval. How I longed to do it with them."

How to get Oscar to write the show called for delicate negotiations. Although they did work apart at times, the team of Kern and Hammerstein had a very affectionate place in the hearts of the public and had authored many notable successes.

But Oscar's enthusiasm for *Green Grow the Lilacs* was so great, matching Dick's, that when Kern heard this, he stepped aside.

The team of Rodgers and Hart was no more.

For the first time in twenty-three years Larry Hart was on the open market, with no ties to Richard Rodgers. He was back from Mexico, where he said he had gone to improve his health, but it was evident he had not succeeded. He was pale and drawn; the black circles under his eyes had actually grown darker. However, he retained his usual surplus of energy and went shopping for something to do.

He was not without opportunities. The phone in the apartment kept ringing, and Frieda kept track of his calls. The entire entertainment world knew his ability, and many who lived in that world showed interest in using it. Larry decided he would dramatize *The Snark Was a Boojum*, a long poem, for producer Alex Yokel. He and Paul Gallico made an effort to whip that far-out fantasy into a stage presentation, but it proved unworkable and was abandoned.

Larry teamed with Emmerich Kalman, composer of many famous European operettas, all known to Larry from his translating days. Kalman had managed to flee Hitler's persecution; he was living in New York with his wife and two children. His daughter, Yvonne, told us, "My father was delighted by his partnership with Mr. Hart, and they held meetings at our apartment at 417 Park Avenue, working on a show they called *Miss Underground*. It was a miserable experience for my father because Mr. Hart often came in drunk, and I guess that's why it was never produced."

Dick and Oscar, of course, had the Theater Guild to produce their book and music of *Green Grow the Lilacs*. Many great talents were lined up, Rouben Manoulian as director, Lemuel Ayres as scenic designer, and Agnes DeMille was preparing history-making dance styles calculated to tumble the ballet world upside down. However, a serious hitch had developed; the guild didn't have the money to put it on.

History repeated itself. As he did with *Dearest Enemy*, Dick auditioned fifty times, but with Oscar beside the piano to serenade the prospective angels. Obviously, many would-be investors harbored doubts whether Rodgers and Hammerstein were able to function on the same high plane as Rodgers and Hart; they walked away in droves. Their first collaboration might have expired before a curtain was raised, but last-minute money was supplied by volatile movie tycoon Harry Cohn and quiet, scholarly playwright S. N. Behrman. Its title changed to *Away We Go!*, the curtain did rise at last, in New Haven, early in March, 1943.

Larry was there for that first night, seated next to Billy Rose. As Rose told Henry Myers: "Every once in a while he would lean over to me and whisper, 'It's a flop, isn't it?' and I'd answer, 'Sure, it's a flop,' knowing all the time it was the most sensational kind of success. But what could I do?"

When it bowed into the St. James Theater, New York, Larry was there again. It had a different title.

Josh Logan said, "The sad thing was opening night of *Oklahoma!* Larry sat in a box, applauding, howling with laughter, and yelling bravos. O, my God, it must have been painful. He had taken his mother and had to sit there with her, this sensitive, sensitive man, seeing a revolutionary development in the theater, brought about by his partner but without his participation. Larry didn't go to the party afterwards—that would have been too painful—but he told

256

them, 'You guys have a show that will run longer than *Abie's Irish Rose.*'"*

Frieda died a week later on Easter Sunday, snapping Larry's last fragile hold on the accepted standards of orderly behavior.

Henry Myers, who loved him dearly, said, "The loss of his mother wrecked him. He became—let's use the right word, which he always liked to do—a drunk.

"'Became' is the right word, too. That is, he *came to be* one and from then on was never anything else."

Myers also said, "His mother must have kept him right side up—because they *were* each other. Mirrors."

After she was gone, he did not speak of her. He did not speak of her at all. He took off on a flight path to self-destruction.

---

*Oklahoma ran 2,212 performances, including 44 special matinees for the armed forces. Anne Nichols' ethnic comedy, *Abie's Irish Rose*, ran 2,327.

20

Bewitched, Bothered, and Bedeviled

SUDDENLY, IT was all Rodgers and Hammerstein. People didn't divide into critical camps immediately over "Which do you like better, Rodgers and Hart or Rodgers and Hammerstein?" The theater world loved Dick and Oscar together, those who said they were meant for each other and those who said it would never last. They gave beaming, almost fatuous approval.*

The incredible success of *Oklahoma!* was glorious fulfillment to Dick . . . almost. There was no way he could forget or walk away from his former partner. Implanted in his memory, indelibly, was Larry working his way through opening night crowds to hug him and say, "I've never had a better evening in my life. This show will be around twenty years from now!"

*Jerome Kern called the score of *Oklahoma!* "condescending music!"

He meant it, of course. Dick knew that. He also knew that Larry was aware that Broadway's newest and greatest hit was the fruition of all that he and Dick had worked toward—and had not reached together. *Oklahoma!* was an R and H show, but now the initials stood for Rodgers and Hammerstein.

Meanwhile, Larry was still getting offers. There was talk of his taking Oscar's place with Kern, but that composer was living in Hollywood, and Larry still preferred Manhattan. Arthur Freed, MGM's most important maker of film musicals, considered him for *Royal Wedding*. That, too, meant a Hollywood sojourn. Larry was indecisive, and Freed switched to a bright new writer of lyrics, Alan Jay Lerner.

Irving Eisman went to Atlantic City with Larry, who had been drinking steadily. Walking past a baroque boardwalk hotel, he suddenly clutched Eisman's arm and said, "It's finally happened! I'm having the DTs! I see pink elephants!" Eisman looked and saw the same elephants. They were decoratively etched into the pink stucco front of the building.

Larry's circle of friends was diminishing as so many men were being called into the service. The war effort was at its height, and Larry was very much alone, sitting morosely in the Broadway bars. He spent considerable time with Teddy and his wife. Her explanation of this unrewarding period is that Larry was tired of working. "He'd been at it for more than twenty years," she told the BBC, "and Dick and Larry had no more to offer each other."

But Dick didn't see it that way; he saw that he *must* try again with Larry, and this was the time it could be done. Oscar was fulfilling one of *his* dreams, to update *Carmen* into an all-black version. He would be involved with *Carmen Jones* for a year.

All who knew him were saddened and worried by Larry's now-shocking deterioration. Herb Fields was among them, and he went to Dick at this significant point to say, "We've got to do something, we've built too much together, we've gone through too much together to let him go without one last try."

Dick, who had borne the brunt of Larry's peccadilloes more than anyone, agreed that they had an obligation. Their love and respect for his talent demanded that they do something that would intrigue Larry. "What do you think can possibly bring him back?" asked Herb.

They remembered, then, how enthusiastic Larry had been about *Connecticut Yankee*. Laughing, Herb pointed out that Larry had thrown in the idea to protect himself from attacks on his laziness, that he dredged it up in a defense against their accusations of indecision. It had proved to be a memorable show, when they had done it sixteen years before. If Larry loved it then, by just relating it to "the good old days," he ought to love it even more now.

They knew it was important to make him feel a large cushion of familiarity, without any intimidation. He mustn't be allowed to suspect conspiracy; he had to know he was needed. It was then that Dick thought of extra ammunition they could use—Vivienne Segal. She was another friend who would surely want to participate, this time in the part of Queen Morgan LeFay. It would require writing just enough new material to excite Larry.

Preliminary talks were held, the proposal was put to Larry, and he went along with it. It seemed to have an immediate and beneficial effect; he began to act like his old self and even to see old friends again.

Herb and Larry always had an easygoing, teasing camaraderie when Larry wasn't drinking and this was reestablished with ease, as if they had never lost touch with each

261

other for a day. Like Larry, Herb had never married, although he had a sort of obsession about maintaining a reputation for virility. He "kept" a stunning lady at all times, visiting her seldom but providing her with tangible evidence of his affection: flying that most convincing of all flags—about half an acre of mink coat.

Larry loved this and assured Herb that it proved he was the classiest of gents. Preparing the revival of *Connecticut Yankee* was a romp, an exercise that was invigorated by the renewal of their friendship, with regrets relegated to the past and nothing but fun ahead. It was part of their enjoyment that they could interrupt work to digress into matters pertaining entirely to themselves. One or the other needed only to quote a phrase that meant something outrageous to them, the muttering of the first part of which was a guarantee of breaking up even the most serious of conferences. It was: "Just because you're paranoid doesn't mean they're not out to get you."

Dick didn't mind their silliness. He took advantage of their mood and had no trouble persuading Larry to go to his country place—Connecticut, appropriately—to work on the rewriting there. Larry climbed on the wagon and, to Dick's delight, stayed there comfortably. He wrote the words to six new songs, replacements for four that were sung in the original. All had merit, and one of them, a solo for Vivienne, "To Keep My Love Alive," he truly considered his best, an opinion shared by Dick.

But then his part of it was done, and his own private devils stirred again: he was facing a new trial by fire, the critics, as well as the overwhelming and constant reminders of success of *Oklahoma!* These were all driving him back to the anesthesia of drinking.

They went to Philadelphia, worried about Larry. Teddy was appearing in *One Touch of Venus* on Broadway, so Dorothy Hart accompanied Larry and they shared a suite. She noticed that he started losing overcoats again, a strong indication that he had been out drinking even when there were no other telltale signs. She was frightened it would bother him to read RICHARD RODGERS PRESENTS on the Forrest Theater marquee while one had to look harder to find "Lyrics by Lorenz Hart, Book by Herbert Fields." In fact, it infuriated Herb, but Larry just laughed. Dorothy said, "He didn't really care at this point. He was so considerate of me. *Carmen Jones* was opening at the same time, and Larry called Oscar Hammerstein to see that I had special seats."

It didn't matter, really, what any of them did for Larry. Opening night in Philadelphia he started on a drinking cycle that was his last one. It brought on another bronchial attack, which kept him in a hospital until the show moved to New York.

In Larry's mind these severe respiratory seizures that were landing him in the hospital so often were viciously crimping his drinking, and he didn't want that to continue. Winter in New York was imminent, and so, finally, he decided he was willing to face the rigorous agony of California's milder climate—he accepted a new offer from Arthur Freed, this time to write the lyrics for a movie on the producer's future schedule, *Ziegfeld Follies*. Contracts were being drawn.

But that was not to be.

Wednesday, November 17, 1943, presaged Larry's death. It is keenly etched into the memories of many of the people we talked to. Differently but keenly. The variance isn't all that great, and the blame, which is probably not the right word, has been placed on several shoulders.

That was the night the curtain was rising on the revival of *Connecticut Yankee* at the Martin Beck Theater, New York.

It was a stormy night and bitterly cold. Helen Ford's evening started with Larry calling to beg her to join him at Delmonico's for dinner, then on to the opening.

"I hadn't been seeing any of the group for some time," she said, but although she realized Larry was drinking, she accepted anyway, "as I wanted to see the show and really did love him!"

When she entered the step-down dining room at Delmonico's, Larry stood up—barely—saying to a young couple at an adjoining table, but in a voice that carried through the whole room, "Here comes the most beautiful singer in America!"

"Now I've mentioned before that I love a good entrance," said Helen, "but this was *mortifying,* and it didn't get any better. There was no food ordered, only drinks. We finally persuaded Larry it was time to go to the theater, but when we got there, there were no tickets for him at the box office. Imagine the embarrassment! He was one of the writers, and he couldn't get in!

"I saw Dorothy Hart, and as I was talking to her about it, Larry disappeared. We went backstage to see if we could find him. He wasn't there, but Dick was, and when we asked him if he had seen him, he said 'Is Larry *here?* Oh, my God!' He had left orders for him not to be allowed in the theater.

"I hurried back to the lobby, looked around for Larry, Dorothy, *anybody!* Finally, I said to myself, 'Oh, the hell with it,' and went home, where I promptly came down with a terrible cold."

Others continued the search, and for a time it was a series of comedic moves. Two men whom Dick had set to watch out for him in case he got obstreperous missed him when he checked his coat downstairs. Dorothy Hart lost him

264

when he went to the men's room. Certain he must be in the theater, they all converged on the lobby, crowded with arriving first nighters. But no Larry.

A doorman saw them looking and signaled "He's in the bar across the street." They dashed across just as Larry strolled back unseen through the side entrance.

The curtain was up when Dorothy and the two men came back and saw him standing quietly in the back of the theater. He remained so until Vivienne Segal started to sing "To Keep My Love Alive." Then he began his familiar pacing, at first nervously and then frenetically and finally joining in with her singing, louder and louder.

There were annoyed murmurings of *shhhhhhhh* from his immediate audience. The theater manager, who also had instructions from Dick, moved in and asked Larry to leave. When he refused, the manager and the two men grabbed him and then removed him, protesting and struggling, to the outer lobby just as the audience broke for intermission and spilled into it. The laughter and titillation and the enjoyment of "To Keep My Love Alive" with its marvelous lyrical twists dwindled into silence. Too many people were treated to the sight of Larry Hart, fighting mad, being bodily removed from the theater. His coat, of course, stayed in the checkroom.

Jack Harrison and Billy Friedberg, a press agent cousin of Larry's, saw what was happening and left the theater raging over the ousting of Larry.

Dorothy Hart managed to get him into a taxicab and sent him to her apartment, then went to meet her husband after his show. When she and Teddy got home, Larry was asleep on the sofa, sweating profusely, and they assumed it was the liquor.

At 4 A.M., Dorothy got up to check on him, and he was

gone. She called downstairs to their doorman, who said he'd ordered a cab to take him to Delmonico's, where he was living. Two days later he had himself taken to Doctors' Hospital.

During the next four days word spread that this time he was really very ill. Friends and relatives took up a vigil. Dorothy and Teddy Hart, Dorothy and Dick Rodgers were in regular attendance. Willy Kron and Doc Bender were others. Some, like Irving Eisman, detained by army service, had to be content with word about his condition from telephoned reports.

Helen Ford, still plagued by the cold she caught on opening night, prevailed on husband George to go to the hospital for news. He was not even permitted on the floor where Larry was confined. He wandered up and down other corridors and finally found a sympathetic nurse who told him enough that he took this grim message back to Helen: "I think he's going to do a die of it, girl."

George Ford's words were prophetic. At 9:30 P.M., on November 22, 1943, a practice air-raid alert sounded over Manhattan, and the lights in Doctors' Hospital went off. When they came back on, the gossamer spirit of Lorenz Milton Hart was free.

His last words were: "What have I lived for?"

Curtain Call

"OPPOSITES ARE necessary, one to the other, both day and night, the Universe being half light and half dark, and neither can prevail, yet both together in their mixture do create an order."

Dualistic philosophies live now; they date back to the ancients of China, centuries before Bernard de Treves wrote those lines in 1490, and the story of two such opposites is what attracted us to write this book.

We did not leap at it with the feeling we knew them so well that outside opinions were unnecessary. Perception is fine, but authenticity is better. We tried not to inject overly personal judgment of our own, but biographers are forced by the nature of their task to observe and explain. It was incumbent on us, we felt, to have a point of view. We hope that ours intrudes no more than the sound of grace notes in a symphony for horns and brass.

We believe that every biographer has a duty to learn everything he can about his subject. It is *not* his duty to tell everything he learns; that is a fine line that he alone must decide to cross.

Why did we bring Larry's homosexuality out into the open? It would have been so easy not to. But after all the research we did, it would have been impossible not to.

Hostile labels were put upon alcoholism and homosexuality in Larry's lifetime. There was little professional or social help. Had he lived in these what we call enlightened times, *would* his life have been so different? How can that be answered, because even with his inner struggles his incredible talent emerged. He functioned, and he triumphed.

Perhaps he couldn't have written with anyone else—but he *did* have Richard Rodgers, and they *did* stay together twenty-four years and gave the world a fund of imperishable songs, and they had a hell of a lot of fun.

In his notes Marx wrote, "Dick has always been the stronger of the two in my consciousness, probably because we were boys together. But beyond that, too, we corresponded, I with jokes and gossip from Hollywood and he from New York. Underlying the humor in his letters was a tough and determined soul and, of course, an impatient one. He was always impatient to get to the melodies he had to write and knew he must write and did.

"But Larry is vivid to me, too. How could he be anything else? It was a pleasure to be around him. Today one mentions him mainly in connection with Dick, for he wrote almost exclusively with Dick, and nobody even tries to remember any others. Rodgers and Hart, in music, are identical twins. I would leave a theater humming the melodies, but then the words would assert themselves and what, at first, were just notes strung together, catchy in their way, finally assumed a complete identity."

"Early in our preparation of this book," Jan Clayton wrote, "I found it difficult to get acquainted with Larry

Hart, thirty-two years after his death. So, I attempted a bit of a writing exercise which I mailed to Dick.

" 'Getting to know Larry Hart,' to mix my lyricists briefly, has been an incredible experience, as interview after interview began to sketch the outline of this man who was a *most* shadowy legend to me. One adjective continued to pop up instantly at the mention of his name from men *and* women . . . adorable. A strange word for a man, no? It would often lead to 'pixie' and 'enchanting' . . . a lot of 'enchantings,' but great fun, witty, a marvelous conversationalist . . . loved to help people.' "

"Richard Rodgers is very real to me, of course," continued Clayton. "Our interviews have shown, certainly, that he does have detractors, but I was exposed to him at the second great upsurge of his career, his new professional marriage to Oscar Hammerstein when they did *Carousel,* following *Oklahoma!* Dick is a fantastic workman . . . stern, you bet, but fair, courteous and exuding the confidence I absorbed like a new sponge.

"He was never give to extravagant compliments. Like Mary Martin, I never heard him use the word "marvelous." "Adequate," yes, or in glowing moments "very adequate," but these came to mean more than the biggest compliment.'

"His scoldings could be gentle, too—pointed but gentle. I breathed a couple of extra breaths singing 'If I Loved You' one night, forgetting that Dick could be out front at any given performance—and he was. Backstage, I waited for him to show up in the dressing room and thought to head him off, so the moment he appeared I spoke right out.

" 'I know, I know. I breathed between words. Never again, I promise.'

" 'Between words I don't mind,' said Dick. 'But between *syllables?*'

269

"The reminder was never forgotten, but the point is that all the artists who worked with Dick were conscious of his desire and demand for the best that could be given. He watched his shows carefully, even through long runs, and the security this gave to the entire cast is of an incredibly important value.

"When I think how Dick got better and more work out of us during every rehearsal, followed up by tender loving care the weeks of playing, I also think of what incredible patience he must have had and how sorely tried he must have been *constantly* by Larry, who also had other adjectives tacked onto him: tardy, elusive, irresponsible.

"Here is Dick's reply to my letter:

Dear Jan,
    It may be because of the fact that people tend to enjoy the negative rather than the positive that you've not been able to discover enough about Larry. For instance, someone might have remembered that he was immovably loyal, that he had a tremendous appreciation of other people's work and that he was more than "pixie" and "witty." He had an enviable and unquenchable sense of humor. He was free with his money but always in the sense of helping someone. These are just a few of the qualities that might have been mentioned.

Love,
Dick

"Strangely, though, it was those very adjectives that helped me see Larry Hart finally and clearly—they reminded me of a character by Richard Strauss I met in a music appreciation class. His name was *Tyl Eulenspiegel*."

Dan Sullivan, theater critic of the Los Angeles *Times* and

warm aficionado of lyrics by Larry Hart, also delved into his life a bit. He came to this conclusion: "Hart was a man who needed a home to come home to and wasn't able to find one himself like most men. When it disappeared with his mother's death, he lost his moorings and gave in to the worst in himself, which eventually killed him against his conscious will but in obedience, perhaps, to his deepest will."

Josh Logan, one of the most thoughtful of all who worked with Dick and Larry, voiced this tribute: "Musical comedies weren't that good when Rodgers and Hart came along. They, in a sense, invented it, started it. I don't know of anyone who hit the public's sensitivity and memory and risibility the way they did in their very first show.

"I do think that Larry Hart is one of the great milestone genius lyricists of the musical comedy. There's no question he was the most sensitive, the most touching, the most, I don't know, Chaplinesque—like Chaplin in that he could get laughs and make you cry at the very same time. He has a color, a tone, a sort of bitter beauty that no one else ever had or ever will have and I think he must be saluted—must be honored. He must be remembered, and he must be kept alive somehow because he's something we all need, especially in our profession as well as in our hearts. I believe that Larry Hart and the spirit of Larry Hart will prevail, but not if we don't remember and if we don't keep him in our minds."

Lyricist Fred Ebb saluted with this memorable line: "Larry Hart made us all a little braver!"

Larry's funeral had some of the bittersweet qualities of his life; it attracted all kinds, but notably the men who shared his childhood and the women who loved him.

Henry Myers said that Larry's words kept coming back to him: "Bad luck sticks to me like a disease," and, "I'll show the bastards I can write lyrics."

"You sure did, Larry," thought Henry. "But to do it, you gave up everything else!"

Doc Bender, weeping, walked away by himself, knowing Larry's friends, men and women alike, no longer would even acknowledge he existed.

Dick's father, "Doctor Bill," standing beside Nanette Guilford, pointed melodramatically at Bender and said, "There goes the murderer!"

Acknowledgments

WE ARE immensely grateful to the wonderful people who took time to contribute their impressions and memories of Rodgers and Hart. Among those who merit special thanks are Henry Myers, Phillip Leavitt, Dan Sullivan, and Fred Nolan. Also Larry Adler, Muriel Angelus, Herbert Baker, Joyce Barbour, Richard "Dickie" Bird, Ralph Blane, Ben Bodne, Gwen Bolger, Ray Bolger, Leighton Brill, Samson de Brier, Richard Carlson, Jean Casto, Edward Chodorov, Harold Conway, Dorothy Dickson, Howard Dietz, Lucinda Ballard Dietz, Irving Eisman, John Fearnley, Helen Ford, Frank Gabrielson, Lee and Ira Gershwin, Bennet Green, Nanette Guilford, William Hammerstein, Dorothy Hart, Sig Herzig, Al Hirschfeld, Gene Kelly, Frank Kenton, Jerome Lawrence, Sheldon Leonard, June Levant, Josh Logan, Dr. Edward Lyons, Rouben Mamoulian, Armina Marshall, Jessie Matthews, Edith Meiser, Mabel Mercer, Howard Miller, Constance Moore, Sandy Mosley, Ken Murray, Richard

273

Oliver, Milton Pascal, Peggy Phillips, Irving Pincus, Jack Reed, Frances Richard, Gene Rodman, Morrie Ryskind, Mel Shauer, Arthur Schwartz, Vivienne Segal, Anne Seymour, Marty Shwartz, Al Simon, Ann Southern, Leonard Spigelgass, Sandy Sturges, Kay Swift, Dr. Jokichi Takamine, Jay Velie, Robert M. W. Vogel and Alice Weaver. Finally no acknowledgments in this book would be complete without our sincere thanks to our editor, William Targ.

Index

275

"Atlantic Blues," 87
Away We Go!, 256
Ayres, Lemuel, 256

Babes in Arms, 189–90, 194, 225
"Bad in Every Man, The," 173
Badger, Clarence, 142
Baker, Belle, 102–3
Baker, Herbert, 102–3
Baker, Josephine, 114
Balanchine, George, 187, 188, 202, 203, 218
Ballard, Lucinda, 240
Ballet Russe de Monte Carlo, 188, 232
Band Wagon, The, 22
Bankhead, Tallulah, 171
Barbour, Joyce, 124–26
"Barney Google," 32
Baruch, Bernard, 178, 182
Behrman, S. N., 157, 256
Belasco, David, 62, 79
Belle Héleǹe, La, 34
Bells Are Ringing, 116 n.
Benchley, Robert, 60, 74
Bender, Milton G. "Doc," 39–40, 42, 91, 94, 95, 98–99, 116, 137, 167–68, 187–89, 202–3, 205, 210, 220, 224, 236, 238, 240, 250, 266, 272
Bennett, Robert Russell, 133–34

Bergin, Louie, 137
Berkeley, Busby, 124
Berle, Milton, 220
Berlin, Irving, 102–3, 132–34, 237
Bessie, Alvah, 72 n.
Betsy, 102–3, 135
"Bewitched, Bothered and Bewildered," 242–45
Bird, Richard, 125–26
Black Oxen, 108
Blane, Ralph, 218
Blond Beast, The, 61–62, 65
"Blue Moon," 173, 174
"Blue Pyjama Song, The," 22
"Blue Room," 103
"Blue Skies," 103
Bogart, Humphrey, 221
Bolger, Ray, 122, 188
Bolton, Guy, 30, 82, 84, 123, 135
Boom Boom, 151
Boothe, Clare, 230
Bowers, William, 245 n.
Boys from Syracuse, The, 199, 213, 215–18, 229–30
Brackett, Charles, 128–29
Braun, Eric, 111–12
Brent, Romney, 69, 72 n.
Broun, Heywood, 49, 60, 139
Brown, Teddy, 108
Buckner, Emory R., 98

277

282

284

285

286

Wynn, Milton, 62

Yokel, Alex, 255
"You Are Too Beautiful,"
158
"You Took Advantage of
Me," 124
You'd Be Surprised, 39, 42
You'll Never Know, 50
Youmans, Vincent, 133
Young, Stark, 60

"You're What I Need,"
123–24
"Yours Sincerely," 132

Ziegfeld, Florenz, 101–3,
135–36, 142, 144, 208
Ziegfeld Follies, 263
Zorina, Vera, 189, 202–4,
211, 225, 233
Zukor, Adolph, 158